RESEARCH AND PRACTICE I

Wayne Journell

Making Classroom Discussions Work

Methods for Quality Dialogue in the Social Studies

EDITED BY

Jane C. Lo

Foreword by Diana E. Hess

TEACHERS COLLEGE PRESS

TEACHERS COLLEGE | COLUMBIA UNIVERSITY
NEW YORK AND LONDON

Published by Teachers College Press®, 1234 Amsterdam Avenue, New York, NY 10027

Front cover image by softulka / Adobe Stock.

Library of Congress Cataloging-in-Publication Data is available at loc.gov

ISBN 978-0-8077-6664-4 (paper)
ISBN 978-0-8077-6665-1 (hardcover)
ISBN 978-0-8077-8087-9 (ebook)

Printed on acid-free paper
Manufactured in the United States of America

Contents

Foreword

For decades the field of social studies has been wrestling with how to solve the *problem of discussion*. In brief, the problem is that while there is plenty of evidence to support the importance of infusing social studies lessons, units, and courses with high-quality discussions, it is also the case that such discussions are more rare in social studies (and in other subjects) than is desirable. What accounts for this discrepancy? Might teachers just not value discussion? Or might some teachers conflate other forms of classroom talk (such as recitation) with discussion, and therefore mistakenly believe they create discussion-rich classrooms? Or could it be that discussions are just too hard to pull off, so teachers either shy away from them altogether or try unsuccessfully and then give up? Or, even though they do value discussion, might many teachers lack the professional training and experience needed to develop the skills and a broad enough repertoire of various types of discussions required for consistent success in teaching discussion skills and conducting discussions?

In fact, few teachers dismiss classroom discussion as unimportant. Certainly, a small number either think that other pedagogical strategies, such as lecture, should be the coin of the realm and/or that their students lack the knowledge or skills for good discussion. But discussion and democratic norms are so tightly connected that it is hard to imagine how schools could play the key role we need them to in democratic education while eschewing discussion. As Jane Mansbridge put it: "Democracy involves public discussion of common problems, not just a silent counting of individual hands" (p. 122). Thus, to be *against discussion* is akin to opposing democracy, so devaluing classroom discussion is probably not the main reason for its paucity.

Confusion about what discussion is, and the tendency to conflate it with other kinds of classroom talk, probably play a larger role. Recitation, and lecture with occasional questions to students, both involve classroom talk. Observational evidence suggests that when teachers report high levels of discussion, they often mean these other forms of talk (Hess & McAvoy, 2015). Unless teachers themselves had a rare education in which discussion was pervasive rather than occasional, they likely need to develop a conception of discussion that marks it out from other classroom talk.

Another key explanation for discussion being both lauded and rare in social studies education is probably just how difficult it is for the instructor to pull it off. Planning for and executing high-quality discussions in social studies classes involves complex and demanding intellectual and emotional work. Teachers need to figure out what is, and what is not, discussable *by their students* and must prepare both themselves and their students for the discussion. They need to know a range of discussion models and be able to select which model is most appropriate for achieving their specific learning goals. They need to know how to teach students the skills they need to participate in discussion and how to assess what their students are learning from discussion. Given just how difficult all these components are, it is not surprising that some teachers don't jump on the discussion bandwagon. Instead, they ask, "Why bother?"

You, the reader, are probably not asking "Why bother?" Instead, you sought out this book because you are teaching social studies or teaching people how to teach social studies; believe that it is important for students in social studies classes to learn from high-quality discussions; and want to improve your own discussion teaching practice. You may have encountered great success with some forms of classroom discussion and want to learn others. You may recognize that some students in your classes are fully engaged in discussions whereas others are not, and you want that to change. You might be interested in teaching your students how to discuss really challenging questions and issues, especially about race, and you don't know how to do that (yet). You may wonder whether your own definition of discussion is discussion and want to learn more about what makes discussion uniquely different from other forms of classroom talk.

Several good books have been written about classroom discussion in the past. But to my knowledge, this is the first book that comprehensively focuses on classroom discussions in social studies in a way that is foundational, thoroughly rooted in practice, intensely practical, and forward thinking.

Foundationally, the first part of the book grounds us in a definition of quality discussion that is both ambitious and clear:

> We define quality discussions as content-specific, educative group conversations (between teachers and students or students and students) that provide participants with (1) different points of view, (2) a chance to reflect on their own opinions and varying perspectives, and (3) an opportunity to develop their understanding and co-construct knowledge of the subject at hand (Bridges, 1979, Larson & Parker, 2006). The goal of quality discussion is to allow students to voice different, evidence-based assertions so that all students who are engaged in the discussion might learn something new through the co-construction of knowledge. (p. 3)

The rest of Part I provides an outstanding, detailed, and well-structured primer that acquaints readers with the basics of discussion in social studies, introduces them to detailed information on how to have discussions of current and controversial issues, and then makes a case for why young children should be taught how to participate in discussions. All three of the chapters that make up Part I are engaging and up-to-date and mix theory and practice in a way that honors both.

Part II delves deeply into several well-known and research-warranted discussion techniques, such as Socratic seminars, structured academic controversy, the differences between deliberation and debate, and document-based discussions in history classes. These uniformly excellent chapters provide rich and detailed examples of what different kinds of discussions look like in classrooms, what teachers need to do to be accomplished at them, and importantly, how the type of discussion produces different kinds of learning for students.

The chapters that comprise Part III focus on how to create discussions that are equitable—in terms of who participates in them, what forms they take (such as online compared to in-person), and ensuring that the actual content of the discussions is designed to build a more equitable and just society. By dealing authentically and forthrightly with the many ways in which contemporary society unfortunately works to reinforce and harden various forms of inequality and injustice, these chapters provide a clear vision for how discussion in social studies can work to create equality and justice.

Theoretically, empirically, and practically, *Making Classroom Discussions Work: Methods for Quality Dialogue in the Social Studies* is a powerful and important book. I commend Professor Lo for bringing together such a rich collection of chapters written by some of our field's best thinkers. If you care about the importance of high-quality discussions in social studies and also want to become a better discussion teacher, I strongly encourage you to read this book.

—Diana E. Hess
Dean
Karen A. Falk Distinguished Chair in Education
University of Wisconsin–Madison School of Education

REFERENCES

Hess, D. E., & McAvoy, P. (2015). *The political classroom: Evidence and ethics in democratic education*. Routledge.

Mansbridge, J. (1991). Democracy, deliberation, and the experience of women. In B. Murchland (Ed.), *Higher education and the practice of democratic politics: A political education reader* (pp. 122–135). Kettering Foundation.

Acknowledgments

The authors and editor would like to thank the teachers, students, and communities who have participated in the various projects outlined in this book. This collection of studies and lessons would not be possible without them. The editor would like to thank each contributing author for their dedication and work on making discussions more manageable for teachers and equitable for all students. Finally, we want to express our gratitude to internal and external reviewers, as well as myriad funding agencies, for their contributions to this work. Please see footnotes in each chapter for detailed acknowledgements of specific chapters.

Making Classroom Discussions Work

Introduction

Jane C. Lo

Imagine a classroom where students' hands are hoisted high in the air, with a few students so eager to be called on that they spill out of their seats. The teacher eventually motions to a willing participant in the back, who blurts out an answer as groans of annoyance echo throughout the room. But the exasperation fades and hands go up in the air again as the teacher poses another question, all the while feeling a sense of pride and satisfaction that her students not only know the material but are eager to participate.

This episode of student engagement is a far cry from traditional portraits of a social studies lesson, where the teacher lectures as pupils studiously take notes. If an administrator walks into the room described, she might be satisfied to see student engagement and congratulate the teacher for sharing airtime with her students. If someone asked the teacher what they did in class that day, she might even say they had a good discussion where her students were eager to share their thoughts. However, the episode seems to be missing key attributes of actual discussions; features like teachers asking students to elaborate or students providing differing perspectives and responding to one another are not evident in the scene.

In an era where meaningful conversations are stifled because of a fear that discussing current events can lead to antagonism and altercations in the classroom, conducting quality discussions in social studies can be complicated. This is where this book can help. This is a book about facilitating discussions in the classroom—not just any discussions, but high-quality discussions that can help leverage productive dialogue for student learning and democratic engagement. Despite the challenges, this book argues that discussions are necessary and should not be avoided. More than that, each chapter presents real classroom examples and lessons learned from researchers and teachers on how to conduct quality discussions that are equitable, powerful, and engaging. To begin, this introductory chapter highlights a brief history of discussion as a pedagogical technique—what it is as well as what it is not—and previews the subsequent chapters. I hope this book guides teachers toward a better understanding of high-quality discussions, why they are necessary, and how to facilitate them equitably in the classroom.

1

A BRIEF HISTORY OF DISCUSSION IN THE SOCIAL STUDIES

People often associate discussion with classroom engagement and student talk—and for good reason: An obvious benefit of conducting discussion in the classroom is increased student engagement (e.g., Del Favero et al., 2007; Kawashima-Ginsberg, 2013; Walsh & Sattes, 2015). Similarly, students' participation in classroom talk is an important indicator of productive disciplinary engagement (Engle, 2012). However, as the chapters in this volume will attest, true quality discussion goes beyond student engagement in the classroom. Discussion, as a pedagogical technique, also requires students to engage in knowledge construction, complex thinking, and genuine inquiry (Kavanagh et al., 2019). Specific to the social studies, quality classroom discussions should also help students engage with democratic deliberative practices (e.g., Larson & Parker, 1996; Parker & Hess, 2001).

Discussion has a long history in the social studies. Beginning with Oliver, Newmann, and Shaver's Harvard social studies project in the 1960s, discussion has been established as an instructional strategy that can help students address complex societal issues and develop rational decisionmaking skills (Bohan & Feinberg, 2008). The Harvard project eventually led to a series of publications known as the Public Issues Series that supported the use of discussion in the classroom, with the subsequent establishment of the National Issues Forum (Oliver & Feldmann, 1983). In both of these projects, discussion—framed as students talking about particularly complex texts or issues—is seen as a way for students to engage in knowledge construction by considering multiple perspectives. This constructivist view of social studies also paved the way for inquiry-focused instruction and other student-centered forms of instruction (Bohan & Feinberg, 2008).

Since then, social studies scholars and researchers have taken up the discussion banner, in support of its capacity to help students engage in problem-solving, rational argumentation, and democratic deliberation (e.g., Beck, 2005; Henning, 2007; Hess, 2009; Larson, 2000; Parker & Hess, 2001). The idea of using discussions as a strategy in the social studies is so ubiquitous, and its benefits so illustrious, that discussion has been listed by reputative social studies organizations as a best practice of civic learning (e.g., National Council for the Social Studies [NCSS], 2013; Campaign for the Civic Mission of Schools, 2011). But even with this reputation, quality discussions in the classroom are rare and notoriously difficult to pull off (e.g., Alvermann et al., 1990; Bain, 2006; Cazden, 2001; Larson, 1997). They are especially difficult to facilitate equitably in the classroom (e.g., Crocco et al., 2018), and even if teachers know discussions are an important strategy to use in their classrooms, they may not necessarily know how to implement or facilitate them. But before jumping into how teachers can facilitate quality and equitable discussions in the classroom, let us clarify what counts as discussion.

WHAT IS (AND IS NOT) DISCUSSION

Research shows that teachers often report conducting discussions in the classroom when they are actually engaging in some other form of student talk (e.g., Alvermann et al., 1990). Teachers might mistake recitation or call and response (where teachers ask a question and elicit responses from students) as discussion, because students are talking and are engaging in a tête-à-tête (Larson, 1997). Similarly, teachers might count asking an open-ended question and calling on a few students for answers as facilitating discussions in their classrooms because it feels like they are having a conversation. But a true discussion requires more than just hearing multiple voices in a room. While conversations can help decrease the amount of teacher talk in the classroom and increase the level of student talk and engagement, not all conversations can be considered discussions, and some discussions are more effective in helping students engage in complex thinking than others (Murphy et al., 2009).

In this volume, we define quality discussions as content-specific, educative group conversations (between teachers and students or students and students) that present participants with (1) different points of view, (2) a chance to reflect on their own opinions and varying perspectives, and (3) an opportunity to develop their understanding and co-construct knowledge of the subject at hand (Bridges, 1979; Larson & Parker, 1996). The goal of quality discussion is to allow students to voice different, evidence-based assertions so that all students engaged in the discussion might learn something new through the co-construction of knowledge. Applying this stringent definition to discussion may cause teachers to rethink their willingness to incorporate quality discussions as an instructional technique; however, rest assured that the chapters in this volume will alleviate those trepidations and help guide teachers forward with examples and suggestions.

ORGANIZATION OF THE BOOK

The book is arranged into three major parts: (1) Making Discussions Work in the Classroom, (2) Well-Known Discussion Techniques in the Social Studies, and (3) Expanding Toward More Equitable Discussions. Each chapter presents at least one quality discussion practice and includes practical applications for teachers to adopt/adapt in the classroom. Part I focuses on the basics of discussion as an instructional technique and may be especially useful for teachers who are attempting to conduct discussions for the first time, or for educators and administrators who hope to support teachers in facilitating discussions. Part II outlines well-known discussion techniques in the social studies and provides teachers with lesson ideas on what can be done in their own classrooms. Since research shows there is a disparity in *who* has access to quality discussions (e.g., Kahne & Middaugh, 2008) and a main goal of social studies is to help create a more just society (NCSS, 2013), Part III of the book focuses on how discussions can be both more equitably distributed and help students engage in justice-oriented dialogue.

Part I opens with Larson's chapter on guiding principles for facilitating quality discussions in social studies lessons. Besides providing a more in-depth look on what counts as discussion in the social studies, Larson's chapter explores five main approaches that can help guide classroom discussions. This foundational chapter will help teachers with varying experiences consider how discussions can be used in their classrooms. However, since leading discussions might be new or uncomfortable for some teachers, Kawashima-Ginsberg, Daneels, and Hayat's chapter presents structural and school-level supports that can help teachers with diverse backgrounds engage more effectively with discussion techniques. This chapter will help teachers reflect on their own practice as well as support anyone conducting professional development for teachers on the facilitation of discussing controversial issues. Part I ends with Beck's chapter on facilitating discussions with younger students. Often, discussion is seen as a secondary-level instructional technique, where students are "old enough" to provide perspectives and opinions. Beck's chapter debunks this myth and shows how young students can successfully engage in meaningful discussions. The chapter provides strategies for elementary teachers to implement foundational interdisciplinary discussion practices and techniques in their classrooms.

Part II extends teachers' understanding of quality discussion by presenting examples of several well-known discussion practices used in the social studies and tips for implementing these strategies. Part II opens with chapters on Socratic seminars by Kohlmeier and structured academic controversy by Parker; these chapters showcase two well-known discussion strategies used often in government and civics courses. Kohlmeier presents the intricacies and importance of Socratic seminars through reporting on students' experiences conducting a seminar on the Pledge of Allegiance. Her study shows that the seminar prompted students to think deeply and differently about something that many of them had mindlessly recited for years. At the same time, Parker's chapter provides a description of the procedure as well as the potential uses of structured academic controversies (SAC) in social studies classrooms. SAC is a deliberative model that has been in the social studies for decades (Johnson & Johnson, 1985; Parker, 2010), and Parker's chapter highlights its uses and possibilities for a new era.

The third chapter of Part II explores the use of deliberation and debate in social studies classrooms. Even though some teachers use debate and deliberation interchangeably, McAvoy and Lowery's study shows how these strategies differ in their utility and effectiveness on student outcomes. This chapter helps teachers understand the difference between debate and deliberation, as well as when and how to use these techniques. Reisman follows this chapter on debate and deliberation by positing that teachers can and should engage in quality historical discussions. Teachers often view history as a subject matter that is set in stone, but Reisman presents a whole class document-based format that provides a way for teachers to conduct generative productive discussion around history content.

In the final chapter of Part II, Estrada, Monte-Sano, Jennings, and Kabat showcase how sensemaking and argumentation in discussions help engage *all* students, from diverse backgrounds and experiences, in substantive inquiries. Specifically, they present the implications for enabling all students to participate in inquiry, with particular attention to students learning English or needing support for reading complex sources, because all students deserve and can participate in quality discussions.

Part III of the book has two major goals: (1) to help teachers envision how discussions can be more equitably distributed and facilitated in their classrooms, and (2) to elucidate how quality discussions can help students support a more just and equitable society. By leveraging young people's voices and experiences, the strategies outlined in these chapters help teachers see the importance of committing to high-quality discussions in their classrooms.

First, Hodgin's chapter describes how teachers can help students talk about politics online as discussions expand into the digital era. Specifically, the chapter provides ideas and strategies to support teachers' facilitation of productive contentious discussions in digital formats and spaces. Next, Bennett, Milner, and Best's chapter presents a powerful rationale for the need to implement race-centered discourses in the social studies. As current events suggest, our inability to productively engage with our system's racist past hinders our ability to move forward as a society. Bennett, Milner, and Best argue that schools and social studies classrooms have a responsibility to help students grapple with and discuss racism. By presenting techniques around racial dialogue, this chapter shows teachers how they can use quality discussion to advance racial justice. By extension, Stickney, Cordova, and Hipolito-Delgado present how teachers can leverage transformative student voices in the classroom to help elevate student agency through discussions. They showcase how teachers can intentionally build trust and share power with students of color before, during, and after classroom discussions.

Finally, Mirra and Garcia's chapter builds on previous chapters and touches on how young people's lived experiences can fuel powerful quality discussions that lead to productive community and civic engagement. An important aspect of equitable and quality discussions is the leveraging of student voice. In this chapter, teachers will see how quality discussion can help students use their voices and opinions to not only construct new knowledge but to gain authorship and authority. As chapters in Part III of the book suggest, empowering young students through facilitated and authentic discussions can help them engage with and tackle relevant societal issues. The book then closes with final thoughts and conclusions about making discussions work in the classroom that are drawn from the 12 featured chapters.

* * *

For the past 2 decades, the field of social studies education has seen an increase in research on the use of discussions in the classroom as an essential instructional technique. The goal of this book is to provide a collection of these well-known, evidence-based, equitable discussion techniques, so that preservice and practicing teachers can (1) read across the uses of discussion practices in one volume, (2) study research-based, classroom examples of these methods, and (3) learn how to better conduct equitable productive discussions in social studies classrooms. Ultimately, I hope the book opens a world of possibilities to all teachers, from those learning about discussion for the first time to those looking to expand their proficiency. This book shows that, whether conducted in person or online, about historical events or current controversial issues, quality discussions are a staple in the social studies for a reason. And even though quality discussions will take time and effort to accomplish, the chapters in this volume will guide readers on that journey and show them why the rewards are well worth the effort.

REFERENCES

Alvermann, D. E., O'Brien, D. G., & Dillon, D. R. (1990). What teachers do when they say they're having discussions of content area reading assignments: A qualitative analysis. *Reading Research Quarterly, 25*(4), 296–322. https://doi.org/10.2307/747693

Bain, R. B. (2006). Rounding up the unusual suspects: Facing the authority hidden in the history classroom. *Teachers College Record, 108*(10), 2080–2114.

Beck, T. A. (2005). Tools of deliberation: Exploring the complexity of learning to lead elementary civics discussions. *Theory & Research in Social Education, 33*(1), 103–119. https://doi.org/10.1080/00933104.2005.10473273

Bohan, C., & Feinberg, J. R. (2008). The authors of the Harvard social studies project: A retrospective analysis of Donald Oliver, Fred Newmann, and James Shaver. *Social Studies Research and Practice, 3*(2), 54–67.

Bridges, D. (1979). *Education, democracy and discussion.* Delmar Pub.

Campaign for the Civic Mission of Schools. (2011). *Guardians of democracy: The civic mission of schools.* The Leonore Anneberg Institute for Civics of the Annenberg Public Policy Center at the University of Pennsylvania and the Campaign for the Civic Mission of Schools. http://www.civicmissionofschools.org/the-campaign/guardian-of-democracy-report

Cazden, C. (2001). *Classroom discourse: The language of teaching and learning* (2nd ed.). Heinemann.

Crocco, M., Segall, A., Halvorsen, A.-L., & Jacobsen, R. (2018). Deliberating public policy issues with adolescents: Classroom dynamics and sociocultural considerations. *Democracy and Education, 26*(1). https://democracyeducationjournal.org/home/vol26/iss1/3

Del Favero, L., Boscolo, P., Vidotto, G., & Vicentini, M. (2007). Classroom discussion and individual problem-solving in the teaching of history: Do different instructional approaches affect interest in different ways? *Learning and Instruction, 17*(6), 635–657. https://doi.org/10.1016/j.learninstruc.2007.09.012

Engle, R. A. (2012). The productive disciplinary engagement framework: Origins, key concepts, and developments. In D. Y. Dai (Ed.), *Design research on learning and thinking in educational settings: Enhancing intellectual growth and functioning* (pp. 161–200). Routledge.

Henning, J. (2007). *The art of discussion-based teaching: Opening up conversation in the classroom.* Routledge.

Hess, D. E. (2009). *Controversy in the classroom: The democratic power of discussion.* Routledge.

Johnson, D. W., & Johnson, R. (1985). Classroom conflict: Controversy versus debate in learning groups. *American Educational Research Journal, 22*(2), 237–256. https://doi.org/10.3102/00028312022002237

Kahne, J., & Middaugh, E. (2008). High quality civic education: What is it and who gets it? *Social Education, 72*(1), 34–39.

Kavanagh, S. S., Monte-Sano, C., Reisman, A., Fogo, B., McGrew, S., & Cipparone, P. (2019). Teaching content in practice: Investigating rehearsals of social studies discussions. *Teaching and Teacher Education, 86,* 102863. https://doi.org/10.1016/j.tate.2019.06.017

Kawashima-Ginsberg, K. (2013). *Discussion, debate, and simulations boost students' civic knowledge, but gaps remain.* https://circle.tufts.edu/latest-research/discussion-debate-and-simulations-boost-students-civic-knowledge

Larson, B. E. (1997). Social studies teachers' conceptions of discussion: A grounded theory study. *Theory & Research in Social Education, 25*(2), 113–136. https://doi.org/10.1080/00933104.1997.10505798

Larson, B. E. (2000). Classroom discussion: A method of instruction and a curriculum outcome. *Teaching and Teacher Education, 16*(5), 661–677. https://doi.org/10.1016/S0742-051X(00)00013-5

Larson, B. E., & Parker, W. C. (1996). What is classroom discussion? A look at teachers' conceptions. *Journal of Curriculum & Supervision, 11*(2), 110–126.

Murphy, P. K., Wilkinson, I. A. G., Soter, A. O., Hennessey, M. N., & Alexander, J. F. (2009). Examining the effects of classroom discussion on students' comprehension of text: A meta-analysis. *Journal of Educational Psychology, 101*(3), 740–764. https://doi.org/10.1037/a0015576

National Council for the Social Studies. (2013). *College, career, and civic life (C3) framework for social studies state standards: Guidance for enhancing the rigor of K-12 civics, economics, geography, and history.* Author.

Oliver, L. P., & Feldmann, A. (1983). *The art of citizenship: Public issue forums.* Charles F. Kettering Foundation.

Parker, W. C. (2010). Listening to strangers: Classroom discussion in democratic education. *Teachers College Record, 112*(11), 2815–2832.

Parker, W. C., & Hess, D. (2001). Teaching with and for discussion. *Teaching and Teacher Education, 17*(3), 273–289. https://doi.org/10.1016/S0742-051X(00)00057-3

Walsh, J. A., & Sattes, B. D. (2015). *Questioning for classroom discussion: Purposeful speaking, engaged listening, deep thinking.* ASCD.

Part I

ENGAGING IN CLASSROOM DISCUSSIONS

CHAPTER 1

Guiding Principles for Using Classroom Discussion

Bruce E. Larson

Classroom discussion can be used to help students understand the topic being discussed and learn how to engage and talk with others. When these purposes are met, it becomes intentionally planned talk, which can help students engage deeply with complex ideas in the classroom. The purpose of this chapter is to examine guiding principles that underlie strategies and procedures for engaging students in various forms of classroom talk. When teachers plan a classroom discussion, they often have content and skill learning targets in mind. Content learning is tied to the topic of the discussion and the information and ideas that drive the interactions. Skill learning is tied to the interactions and terms of engagement with one another as students think and talk their way to new insights and understandings. Said more simply, content is the topic of the talk and skills are how to talk *with* others. One hope for discussion is that students talk with one another and with the teacher at a level that allows for deep understanding of the content, of different points of view, of the dispositions required to talk with others, and of the nuanced requirements needed for civil discourse. Educators have known this for years. Over three decades ago, Gall (1985) promoted classroom discussion in the social studies as an effective way to promote higher level thinking, develop student attitudes, and advance student capability for moral reasoning. In short, discussion provides opportunities for student thoughtfulness about a chosen topic or issue. Classroom discussion is at its simplest a structured activity in which the process of conversing encourages students to pool ideas and information and illuminate alternative perspectives.

Discussions are not a natural interaction in classrooms, just as civil, well-reasoned conversations are not a given in the broader public life. Students need to listen and respond to classmates, contribute from different perspectives or understandings, and consider their knowledge, understanding, and/or judgment on the matter under discussion. Discussion is not merely a time for talking but a structured activity. When not structured, teachers are left hoping that an entire classroom of students will somehow engage with a topic. But what usually occurs is a small number of students participate; four to seven students engage in the talk while 20 students watch and listen. However, as participation and talk increases, assessments are more easily used to determine learning.

Rather than providing step-by-step procedures for specific discussion strategies, which will be covered in later chapters, this chapter suggests five sets of guiding principles for facilitating student learning during classroom discussions. First, cooperative learning provides direction for student grouping during discussions and for developing needed discussion skills. Second, critical and "higher order" thinking provides principles for evaluating student engagement and the type of thinking students employ before and during a discussion. Third, the inquiry design model from the National Council for the Social Studies (NCSS) offers principles for informing students and gaining new knowledge. Fourth, assessment principles help us examine discussion and student learning by learning about both the discussion topic as well as the interactive and social skills required to engage with others. Fifth, principles help teachers guide discussions with students who are emergent bilingual or multilingual learners. Each of these principles will be examined in more detail later on in the chapter, but first, let us briefly consider the crucial role of classroom discussion in a democracy.

POTENTIAL IN A CLASSROOM AND IN A DEMOCRACY

In social studies classrooms, discussions of historic and current issues hold the potential for developing civil discourse skill, critical thinking, and engaging with others who hold a disparate point of view. Skills and dispositions such as these are needed in democracies as individuals engage in civil, critical discourse to make policies about important public issues (Barber, 1989; Parker, 1996). The social studies classroom can become a space for students of different ethnicity, gender, social status, and ability to learn how to engage one another in discussions about issues of common concern. And then in the process of discussing, content is contextualized, personalized, and learned.

To achieve academic and skill-based learning targets, discussion requires students and teacher to talk back and forth with deep understanding about the topic and heightened awareness of others. These are interpersonal skills that must be practiced: Establishing group norms such as rephrasing what other people say, supporting claims with evidence, critiquing ideas and not individuals, and seeking to improve the group's shared understanding of the problem or issue all enable the discussion. Thought of this way, classroom discussion is a structured activity that encourages students to collaborate and explore hypotheses, pool ideas and information, and then illuminate alternative perspectives. The College, Career, and Civic Life (C3) framework of the NCSS (2013) offers a direct tie to classroom discussions in a democracy, and states the following on their website:

> Abundant research bears out the sad reality that fewer and fewer young people, particularly students of color and students in poverty, are receiving a high-quality social studies education, despite the central role of social studies in preparing students for the responsibilities of citizenship. Active and responsible citizens are able to identify and analyze public problems, deliberate with other people about how to define and address issues, take constructive action together, reflect on their actions, create and sustain groups, and influence institutions both large and small. They vote, serve on juries when called, follow the news and current events, and participate in voluntary groups and efforts. (NCSS, 2020)

Classroom discussions hold potential for students to practice these important democratic skills. Each of the five sets of guiding principles addressed can assist the development of individuals who discuss important democratic issues and topics: cooperative learning, critical thinking, inquiry, assessment, and emergent bilingual/multilingual learners.

PRINCIPLES FROM COOPERATIVE LEARNING

Structured classroom discussions often use small groupings of students to allow for more time to talk and to diminish student concerns about speaking to the whole class. Cooperative learning theories posit that as students work together in groups, they help each other learn content and skills. Thinking of classroom discussion as a cooperative group learning activity creates opportunities for students to complete tasks that help them learn individually and that help group members learn as well. In short, discussions that use cooperative learning groups can maximize student learning of the topic and social skills needed to engage with each other.

Educational researchers consistently find that cooperative learning has positive effects on student achievement because the process of interacting with others promotes learning. Students often learn more and learn more quickly in cooperative groups when compared to students working alone, or not working in cooperative groups (Johnson et al., 1994). Cooperative learning groups typically range from three to seven students, with the ideal number being four or five (Cohen & Lotan, 2014). Student achievement is highest when the cooperative learning activity requires group goals and tasks, students' interdependence on each other, and group collaboration to attain higher levels of achievement (Slavin, 1989–90). Most research studies conclude that group goals, positive interdependence, and individual accountability decrease competition among students and motivate them to help each other learn and enhance their own learning. What is missing in this research, however, is the explicit tie to classroom discussion. Some cooperative learning activities such as structured academic controversy (Johnson & Johnson, 1988) or jigsaw 2 (Aronson et al., 1978) require students to talk in ways that could be considered classroom discussions. Discussion strategies that require a move from large class interactions to small groups would benefit from using cooperative learning strategies.

Consider the following example of one approach for holding students individually accountable. A civics teacher places students in groups of four and assigns them the task of analyzing current city policies about an 11:00 P.M. curfew for minors in the central business area. The teacher then specifies that each student in the group needs to analyze one of four different perspectives: business owners, children under 18, crime rates in the city, and civil rights advocates. Each student needs to compose a report comparing their analysis with the other group members' analyses. This activity will allow for individual writing time in addition to group talking time. During the talking/discussion, group members look for similarities and differences from their own analysis, and they seek clarification about topics of points that are unclear. The group of four will create a slide deck on the "curfew for minors in our community" that addresses each of the four areas. The group is interdependent during the discussions, but each member is assessed on their individual work. Classroom discussions take place in the groups of four as they deliberate about the four areas and develop a policy. At any point, a group could discuss the topic amongst the four members, or with one or two other groups. By keeping them focused on how they talk with each other, the teacher can also assist students in learning discussion skills. This is a type of "informed action" (NCSS, 2013) that will translate into democratic skills needed to explore public issues of concern. Keeping the size of the groups small encourages students to work together and to more actively participate.

Findings from 164 research studies on cooperative learning specify that placing students in groups (as opposed to having students select their own groups), assigning a task where they must work together, and teaching specific social skills has a positive effect on student achievement (Johnson et al., 2000). For example, placing students in heterogeneous cooperative learning groups at least one time a week had a significantly positive effect on learning (Marzano et al., 2001). Similarly, students spend more time "on task," are more motivated to complete assignments, and are more capable of transferring their learning to other contexts during cooperative group activities (Johnson & Johnson, 1999; Kohn, 1994). Cooperative learning research findings suggest a positive impact on social interactions among students because students learn how to interact with one another. One of the most consistent findings is that "when students of different racial or ethnic backgrounds work together toward a common goal, they gain in liking and respect for one another" (Slavin, 1989–90, p. 53). When taken in the context of classroom discussions, it becomes apparent that cooperative learning can be used as a planning strategy for classroom discussions.

Cohen (1994; Cohen & Lotan, 2014) examined how student "status" leads to different behaviors in groups, and leads to different treatment by peers; she notes:

> A status characteristic is an agreed upon social ranking where everyone feels it is better to have a high rank than a low rank. Examples of status characteristics are race, social class, sex, reading ability, and attractiveness . . . high status individuals are expected to be more competent than low status individuals across a wide range of tasks that are viewed as important. When a teacher assigns a task to a group of students, some of whom are higher and some lower on any of the status characteristics described above, these general expectations come into play . . . those who are higher status come to hold a high rank in the status order that emerges in the group interaction. Those who hold lower status come to hold a low rank on that status order. (Cohen, 1994, p. 33)

Even if no one formally assigns status to students, it is one aspect of a diverse society that perpetuates the status quo and the current power structure in that society. High-status students are expected to be better (and they come to expect it of themselves), and low-status students are not expected to make important contributions to the group (and they begin to believe they have little to offer). If left to their own, most student groups will reiterate the existing status of students. Even when groups are changed, students' status often follows them to the next setting (Cohen & Lotan, 2014). However, teachers can assist students in overcoming the barriers of status and marginalization by taking actions such as assigning students to groups and structuring tasks to require interdependence. Students will need opportunities to practice necessary interactions of dividing the workload, listening, and paraphrasing ideas. Each of these actions and skills can be learning targets during a classroom discussion. When a discussion is planned as a strategy for developing these interactive skills, cooperative learning provides useful principles for grouping students and engaging them with each other. Moreover, students increase friendships with groupmates after working together in cooperative learning groups or teams, and over time students increase their abilities to listen to others, consider ideas from all members of a group, assign tasks equally, and have a greater sense of concern for the success of all members in the group. These are also critical skills for participants of a democracy. The research clearly suggests that cooperative learning promotes learning of skills and content. The idea that cooperative learning promotes more opportunities for informed discussion and prosocial behavior among students is another benefit of using cooperative learning strategies when planning a discussion.

The educational merits of classroom discussions and especially of discussing controversial issues does assume that students are willing and able to think and engage in these discussions. For example, some students may consider controversial issues to be too difficult to think about because they are closely tied to emotions and past experiences, a particular point of view is deeply rooted in their system of beliefs, or even that such discussions/issues are "taboo." In this case, students will not likely participate in class activities that center around controversial public issues. Similarly, the milieu or social climate of the classroom must allow for students to sense that the space is psychologically safe. To some extent, participants are taking risks and engaging their ego as they interact publicly about a topic. If students have concerns such as a belief they will be mocked or critiqued for their comments, that classmates will ignore their comments, or that comments will be used against them outside of the classroom, then participation in the discussions will be hindered. The classroom must be considered to be a safe space for thinking together. This is one very specific example of how classroom discussions differ from debate or other forms of talk that have an emphasis on "winning" or convincing others about one specific point of view. When classroom discussion instead has the purpose of improving all participants' insights, and the emphasis is on increasing understanding of the issue or topic, then the group disposition during the discussion changes drastically. Couple with this group norms of criticizing ideas and not people, and seeking to understand and not refute a comment, and a more genuine learning environment that will allow for honest and safe talk begins to emerge. More about this is discussed later in this chapter when assessment principles are explored.

PRINCIPLES FROM CRITICAL THINKING AND HIGHER ORDER THINKING

Cognitive psychologist Benjamin Bloom's (1956) famous taxonomy is widely used by teachers and often taught in teacher preparation programs. In 2001, it was revised by Anderson and Krathwohl, and the following updated version recasts, using new insights from 21st-century cognitive science, the original six categories that go from simple thinking to more challenging and complex thinking:

- Remembering: Can the student recall the details around the topic being discussed? This level is crucial because students who do not possess basic knowledge cannot carry out meaningful analyses of language issues or exercise any disciplined creativity. This is the "starting point."
- Understanding: Can the student explain ideas or concepts? It is one thing, for example, to be able to "remember" different regions of

the world, but to be able to explain how these regions influence international relations requires understanding.

- Applying: Can the student use the information in a new way? The issue at this level is whether students can use skills, concepts, and information in new situations. For example, in history, one needs to know how to remember events in time sequence to understand concepts and to apply these ideas appropriately during the classroom discussion.

- Analyzing: Can the student distinguish between the whole entity and the parts that comprise it? For example, when preparing for and discussing propaganda and nationalism, students will analyze persuasive techniques and identify appeals made to status, power, group affiliation, and gender.

- Evaluating: Can the student justify a stand or decision? Thinking at this level is divergent, and differences of opinion are to be expected. Students make judgments and determine "best options" based on their evaluations of all information and factors. A classroom discussion about a policy issue that includes students' individual opinions or judgments is an example of evaluating.

- Creating: Can the student create a new product or point of view? At this level, students might seek out people who represent a range of arguments for and against a controversial issue. Or, having taught your students the mechanics of letter writing, you ask them to create/write a letter following a classroom discussion using the fundamentals they have learned (Larson, 2017).

Bloom's original taxonomy and this revision were devised to allow teachers to assess student learning of course content. The use of discussion for helping students think deeply and critically as they talk with classmates about the topic is strongly supported by this taxonomy and helps determine the structure and format of a classroom discussion and the accompanying assessments of student achievement. It is difficult to engage students in discussion about a topic at the first two levels of the revised taxonomy (remembering, and understanding). Comparatively, classroom discussion at the last three levels can push students to have deeper understanding. For example, if a learning goal for a discussion is to critique a U.S. immigration policy or create a stimulus package to help a lagging economy, then the taxonomy can provide a purpose for the discussion as well as successful criteria for student learning.

Implied in this is the role of critical thinking, which is described by Paul and Elder (2007) as "the art of analyzing and evaluating thinking with a view to improving it" (p. 4). Critical thinking intends to have outcomes such as raising vital questions and problems, gathering and assessing relevant information, forming well-reasoned conclusions and solutions, thinking open-mindedly, recognizing assumptions, and communicating effectively with others in figuring out solutions to complex problems. Case (2013) refers to critical thinking and its ties to Bloom's Taxonomy by stating that

> all rigorous thinking is evaluative (critical) thinking, [and] it is important to establish expectations for reasoned judgments where students know to assess or judge the merits of available options in light of relevant factors or criteria. For example, 'Explaining' should not be seen as a mechanical task, but rather as one that requires thoughtful choices about what to say and how to say it, and informed by the purpose, audience, and content to be explained. A similar point can be made about any intellectual task at any level in the taxonomy. (p. 200)

Discussion in the classroom carries the potential to elevate student talk to analyzing, evaluating, or creating on Bloom's revised taxonomy, which promotes thinking that is critical and rigorous. This level of thinking, however, needs to be planned for by the teacher and students. This taxonomy and an emphasis on critical thinking can provide a scaffold for the teacher when posing questions or discussion prompts to students. Thinking about student responses and interactions with each other and what level of thinking is taking place can be assisted when considering higher level and critical thinking.

PRINCIPLES FROM THE INQUIRY DESIGN MODEL

The C3 framework from the NCSS supports the use of an inquiry arc that "calls upon students to use the disciplines of civics, economics, geography, and history as they (1) develop questions and plan investigations; (2) apply disciplinary concepts and tools; (3) gather, evaluate, and use evidence; and (4) work collaboratively to communicate conclusions and take informed action" (Herczog, 2013, p. 331). At the heart of this framework is a goal for students to develop knowledge and skills needed to engage in inquiries about social issues. Inquiries meet many of the higher level thinking principles addressed in the previous section and are often best done in cooperative student groups. The nexus of inquiry to discussion is in points 3 and 4 (gather, evaluate, and use evidence; work collaboratively to communicate conclusions and take informed action). Inadequate student preparation inhibits well-informed classroom discussions.

While techniques abound for informing students, the process advocated by the inquiry design model emphasizes key tools such as gathering, evaluating, and using data. Each of these will allow for small group discussions to communicate conclusions and take informed action (Herczog, 2013). New insights, developed while following the inquiry model, can be talked about among students. Said another way:

> The general focus of the C3 Framework's Inquiry Arc—investigating compelling questions, building knowledge, constructing arguments, and taking a stand—are the same building blocks for a good discussion. . . . Because the students are consulting common materials to build understanding, they are engaged in a puzzle and not merely trying to win an argument. (McAvoy et al., 2020, p. 290)

Discussion becomes the place where the newly informed students "go public" with their ideas and insights. The discussions are informed and intended to develop deeper understanding of the content. Rather than helping students write reports or develop presentations, students work on their skills in supporting verbal opinions with facts and listening for understanding of a different perspective. Consider, for example, ending an inquiry on the history of voting rights and voter suppression with a discussion about whether ID cards should be required to vote. This discussion would be more informed because students could evaluate the issue within the larger historical context of restrictions on voting rights. In addition, it would offer students an opportunity to listen to how others reason about an issue that affects their lives and the larger community.

As mentioned, groups larger than seven discourage many students from participating. If students are in a group with seven or less classmates, greater participation by all students occurs (Cohen & Lotan, 2014). Integrating inquiry and discussion to promote critical thinking requires having students in smaller groups that are intentionally formed by the teacher. Once in the small groups, the teacher (and students) monitors the discussions to be sure everyone understands the task, all are aware of any time limits, and all are engaged in discussing the topic. Encouraging students to talk with their groupmates about the topics develops their own understanding of the topics. The teacher's primary tasks during group discussions are to be sure students understand the question or problem about which they are inquiring and discussing (e.g., by asking a question such as "What are the strongest points on your side of the issue") and that they are discussing this with their partners.

PRINCIPLES FROM ASSESSMENT OF STUDENT LEARNING

Classroom discussions depend on student talking, be that with the whole class, a small group, or a partner. During whole class discussions, a teacher can easily step in and correct errors, challenge student comments, instruct students to respect classmates, or even help the class to remember a learning target such as understanding the topic better. However, as mentioned, whole class discussions often result in many students not participating because they are not prone to talk, or because they rely on the more verbal students to carry the conversations. This is problematic for a couple of reasons. First, students who do not engage in a class activity are not able to meet learning targets that assess student skills in their talk. Students who avoid talking during the whole class discussion may not be learning from the talk. Second, students may feel inhibited from talking to the whole class because of their gender, race, or status in the classroom. Parker (2001) states this second problem this way: "Discussion may appear open and democratic while masking domination" (p. 111). Moving students into groups encourages more participation, and usually is more engaging for a larger number of students. However, smaller groups may inhibit a teacher's ability to assess student learning. Instead of monitoring one discussion, teachers need to oversee seven or eight groups. Discussions, therefore, require assessment strategies that are unique for the type of talk taking place and that are planned and told to students before a discussion begins. A set of guidelines for student behavior is helpful to ensure the behavior is conducive to learning. For example, the following expected behaviors during a discussion can allow opportunities for self-assessment by each student (Barber, 1989; Larson, 1997; Parker, 1996):

- Am I listening to what other people are saying or did I miss an important point?
- Am I clearly making claims and supporting claims with facts?
- Am I critiquing ideas and not individuals (keeping a high respect for human dignity)?
- Are we developing a shared understanding of the problem or issue?

Assessing classroom discussions creates unique challenges, because the different purposes require different assessments. The two purposes that are emphasized in this chapter are as follows:

1. Discussion is used as an instructional strategy, where the purpose is to have students engage in verbal interactions to help them learn more about the topics being discussed.
2. Skill in discussing becomes the desired outcome of using this strategy, where the discussants become more capable in their verbal interactions with others.

The first purpose is to increase understanding of content. Assessments might include a report, presentation, or written response, because these will provide valid data to determine student learning—for example, writing a dialectic essay where the student provides an opinion and then uses different arguments and counterarguments to prove the strength of the opinion after a small group discussion such as a structured academic controversy. The second purpose is to increase skill—the ability to engage in a discussion. To assess this purpose, the process and engagement during the discussions are examined. For example, students might be assessed on their skill in explaining their ideas and thoughts, or on their ability to build off a classmate's comment. Usually, these two combine and teachers assess students' knowledge and skill.

Meanwhile, formative assessments of discussions help students listen and respond to each other appropriately. Most teachers believe that discussion skills need to be taught, and students left to their own will not engage in fruitful discussions (Larson, 1996, 2017). The self-reflective questions listed require skill and practice. These need to be practiced and assessed by peers and by the teacher. To help promote these discussion skills, teachers might consider assessing students on the following during classroom discussions (Larson, 2017; Parker, 1995):

- Describes issue clearly
- Elaborates with relevant examples
- Asks thoughtful questions re: issue
- Restates arguments/then counters
- Gives relevant support
- Notes gaps in logic

At the same time, written assignments, or other appropriate tasks after the discussion, could be used to assess students' understanding of the discussion topic:

- Summarizes others' ideas
- Develops on thesis
- Gives arguments to support thesis
- Examples strengthen argument
- Organizes main points to build argument
- Strong closing

In addition, self-assessment by students of their participation allows teachers to compare observations with students' perceptions. This not only provides instructive feedback, but it also is an evaluation-level thinking task on Bloom's taxonomy. The following set of four categories requires the teacher and students to decide before the discussion what a score of "0," "1," or "2" might be for each. For example, a "0" might be "not observed," and a "2" might be "integrated into the discussion." This allows students' self-assessment, an effective type of formative assessment (Hattie, 2012).

- Building on other students ideas (0, 1, 2)
- Using information from the text (0, 1, 2)

- Using information from the handout/readings (0, 1, 2)
- Integrating new ideas/outside information (0, 1, 2)

Formative assessments are very important to help students learn the skills needed to engage in discussion. Formative assessments of student under-standing also occur during the pair-share segments of discussions and as the students talk about the compelling points of the issue.

However, students who are unenthusiastic about talking pose a chal-lenge to assessing student learning during classroom discussions. A stu-dent who is "shy," or who feels the classroom is not a safe space, may not feel comfortable speaking and will require opportunities to talk in smaller groups. Gender has been shown to influence talking in classrooms. Some studies suggest that girls may talk less frequently than boys, especially if the conversations are perceived as combative (Sadker & Zittleman, 2012). Culture is also an influence on student talk. Some cultures promote talking out loud, while others view excessive talking as disrespectful. This type of nuance helps differentiate the form and use of discussion assessments.

PRINCIPLES FROM EMERGENT BILINGUAL (MULTILINGUAL) STUDENTS

The number of secondary-level (grades 6–12) students who are emergent bilingual or multilingual is growing rapidly in the United States. Students learning English as an additional language begin by learning social language; they learn what they use in everyday conversations. However, it takes longer to negotiate more formal academic language or the language of schooling. It may take a child at least 5 years to reach academic proficiency in the new language (Baker & Hornberger, 2001). School talk is different in its form and function than typical talk. For example, children rarely use terms such as "synthesize," "discuss," or "democracy" outside of school. As a result, emergent bilingual students may appear to have a solid command of English, when in reality they have command of conversational English and not academic English. The catch is this: Unknowing teachers may assume that because they hear a student speak English during class that the student is equally proficient in academic language, the language of teaching and learning (Franquiz & Salinas, 2013).

The research on teaching emergent bilingual (multilingual) learners sug-gests that many of the techniques are helpful for all students, despite their language proficiency (Zwiers, 2014). Therefore, if a middle school social studies classroom has students with a range of English proficiency levels, then a teacher's efforts to purposefully modify or add techniques that aid language development will purportedly benefit all students (Thornton & Cruz, 2008). The opposite may not be the case, however: Effective strategies for monolingual English speakers will not have positive effects on emergent bilingual students. Theories suggest that emergent bilingual students must be taught with intentional strategies that may not come from research based on students who have English as their first language. The following comment provides a clear summary of this:

> Many assume that reading intervention programs designed for low-literacy native English speakers would also be appropriate for [emergent bilingual students] who do not read English well. However, while [emergent bilinguals] at the secondary level typically do have limited English vocabularies and reduced reading fluency and comprehension in English, they usually do not have the more basic decoding difficulties displayed by many 'struggling' readers. Interventions aimed at improving decoding skills may therefore be inappropriate for many [emergent bilingual students]. (Harper & deJong, 2004, p. 157)

Effectively teaching emergent bilingual and multilingual students in reading and speaking requires a new approach altogether.

As teachers consider planning and facilitating social studies discussions with students who do and do not speak English as their primary language, the existing research is lacking about how to engage them. In other words, emergent bilingual students may not engage in discussions for a variety of reasons, but little has been done to determine ideas for increasing their participation (California Department of Education, 2010). In addition, most of the research has been done in English language arts classrooms, and more is needed in social studies classrooms. A later chapter in this volume will specifically address this gap.

At its simplest, providing discussion time in class between English-only students and emergent multilingual students is one aid to language and content learning. Age peers are likely to speak in a way that is more comprehensible for the emergent multilingual student, and the emergent multilingual student may feel more comfortable with a partner or peers in a small group because it is less "public" than interacting with the whole class. Pair discussion, small group discussion, and large group discussion can be successfully used but should be sequenced to provide the scaffolding an emergent language learner needs to actively participate. Additionally, providing the words and language patterns to carry out those roles, in the form of sentence starters or sentence stems, helps all students practice academic vocabulary and academic language patterns orally. For example, providing a list of "formal" language either for the discussion or for a follow-up assessment provides mini-scripts that will support language learning and discussion skills. The following supporting sentences provide some examples:

- I see what you mean, but I think . . .
- You've got a point, but I've found that . . .
- Could you explain that some more?

- I believe _____ because _____.
- Can you give me an example of that?
- I agree with you because _____.
- I can see where you are coming from, but have you ever thought about _____?

Supports such as these might provide very basic assistance for engaging in classroom talk. Researching strategies for engaging emergent bilingual (multilingual) students in social studies classroom discussions is an area that teachers and teacher educators could examine in the future. Teachers will benefit because classrooms continue to become increasingly more language diverse. Teacher educators will benefit as they prepare teachers to consider how classroom discussion can benefit all students to learn content and improve their discussion skills.

CONCLUSION ON GUIDING PRINCIPLES

Discussion strategies vary greatly, often due to the topic, student discussion skill, and the expected outcome or learning target. Teachers may plan for an entire classroom of students to engage with a topic but realize that a small number of students actually talk. Discussions that allow students to talk back and forth at a high level of insight do not happen naturally in the classroom. One unique aspect of classroom discussion is the need for students (and the teacher) to practice the skills needed for discussions. This practice not only involves learning how to express ideas and opinions, but also how to listen and build on others' ideas. Establishing group norms such as rephrasing what other people are saying, supporting claims with evidence, critiquing ideas and not individuals, and seeking to improve the group's shared understanding of the problem or issue are all ideas for enabling the talk. Classroom discussions that follow many of the tenets affiliated with cooperative learning seem to hold promise for enhancing student learning.

Helping students think critically and in more complex ways through classroom discussion is informed by recent thinking about Bloom's revised taxonomy and the NCSS inquiry design model. Planning discussions that allow students to inquire about problems and ideas at a high cognitive level could allow for more-informed discussions. Thus, cooperative learning provides ideas for placing students in discussion groups and learning the skills needed to work and talk together, while current thinking related to critical thinking and inquiry are useful when planning how students will think about and learn the information they will discuss. Thought of this way, classroom discussion links to several strategies to form a structured activity that encourages students to collaborate and explore hypotheses, pool ideas and information, and then illuminate alternative perspectives. Formative and self-assessments of student learning will then be tied to the type of discussion in which the students engage and will greatly inform future discussions. The link of classroom discussion to civic participation is an oft-touted reason for its use. How to ensure that students are learning civic skills, and that all students in a heterogenous classroom are engaging with the content, should continue to be areas of emphasis when teaching with or considering the practice and effectiveness of discussions in social studies classrooms.

REFERENCES

Anderson, L. W., & Krathwohl, D. R. (2001). *A taxonomy for learning, teaching, and assessing: A revision of Bloom's taxonomy of educational objectives.* Longman.

Aronson, E., Blaney, N., Stephen, C., Sikes, J., & Snapp, M. (1978). *The jigsaw classroom.* SAGE.

Baker, C., & Hornberger, N. H. (2001). (Eds.). *An introductory reader to the writings of Jim Cummins.* Multilingual Matters.

Barber, B. (1989). Public talk and civic action: Education for participation in a strong democracy. *Social Education, 53*(6), 355–356, 370.

Bloom, B. S. (1956). *Taxonomy of educational objectives, Handbook I: The cognitive domain.* David McKay Co Inc.

California Department of Education. (2010). *Improving education for English learners: Research-based approaches.* CDE Press.

Case, R. (2013). The unfortunate consequences of Bloom's taxonomy. *Social Education, 77*(4), 196–200.

Cohen, E. G. (1994). *Designing groupwork: Strategies for the heterogeneous classroom.* Teachers College Press.

Cohen, E. G., & Lotan, R. A. (2014). *Designing groupwork: Strategies for the heterogeneous classroom* (3rd ed.). Teachers College Press.

Franquiz, M., & Salinas, C. (2013). Knowing English is not enough! Cultivating academic literacies among high school newcomers. *High School Journal, 96*(4), 339–357.

Gall, M. D. (1985). Discussion methods of teaching. In T. Husen & T. N. Postlethwaite (Eds.), *International encyclopedia of education* (Vol. 3, pp. 1423–1427). Pergamon.

Harper, C., & deJong, E. (2004). Misconceptions about teaching English-language learners. *Journal of Adolescent and Adult Literacy, 48*(2), 152–162.

Hattie, J. (2012). *Visible learning for teachers: Maximizing impact on learning.* Routledge.

Herczog, M. (2013). The links between the C3 framework and the NCSS National Curriculum Standards for Social Studies, *Social Education, 77*(6), 331–333.

Johnson, D. W., & Johnson, R. T. (1988). Critical thinking through structured controversy. *Educational Leadership, 45*(8), 58–64.

Johnson, D. W., & Johnson, R. T. (1999). *Learning together and alone: Cooperative, competitive, and individualistic learning.* Allyn & Bacon.

Johnson, D. W., Johnson, R., & Holubec, E. (1998). *Cooperation in the classroom.* Allyn and Bacon.

Johnson, D. W., Johnson, R. T., & Stanne, M. B. (2000, May). *Cooperative learning methods: A meta-analysis.* Cooperative Learning Center, University of Minnesota. http://clcrc.com/pages/cl=methods.html

Kohn, A. (1993). *Punished by rewards: The trouble with gold stars, incentive plans, A's, praise, and other bribes.* Houghton Mifflin.

Larson, B. E. (1997). Social studies teachers' conceptions of discussion: A grounded theory study. *Theory and Research in Social Education, 25*(2), 113–136.

Larson, B. E. (2017). *Instructional strategies for middle and high school social studies: Methods, assessment, and classroom management* (2nd ed.). Routledge.

Marzano, R. J., Pickering, D. J., & Pollock, J. E. (2001). *Classroom instruction that works: Research-based strategies for increasing student achievement.* Association for Supervision and Curriculum Development.

McAvoy, P., Lowery, A., Wafa, N., & Byrd, C. (2020). Dining with democracy: Discussion as informed action. *Social Education, 84*(5), 289–293.

National Council for the Social Studies. (2013). *Social studies for the next generation: Purposes, practices, and implications of the College, Career, and Civic Life (C3) framework for Social Studies State Standards.* Author.

National Council for the Social Studies. (2020, January 4). *Why do we need the C3 framework?* https://www.socialstudies.org/standards/c3

Parker, W. C. (1995). Connecting with the community and the world of work. *Educational Leadership, 52*(8), 84–85.

Parker, W. C. (1996). Curriculum for democracy. In R. Soder (Ed.), *Democracy, education and schooling* (pp. 182–210) Jossey-Bass.

Parker, W. C. (2001). Classroom discussion: Models for leading seminars and deliberations. *Social Education, 65*(2), 111–115.

Paul, R., & Elder, L. (2007). *The miniature guide to critical thinking concepts and tools.* Foundation for Critical Thinking Press.

Sadker, D., & Zittleman, K. R. (2012). *Teachers, schools, and society: A brief introduction to education* (3rd ed.). McGraw-Hill.

Slavin, R. E. (1989, December–1990, January). Research on cooperative learning: Consensus and controversy. *Educational Leadership, 47*(4), 52–54.

Thornton, S., & Cruz, B. C. (2008). *Teaching social studies to English language learners.* Routledge.

Zwiers, J. (2014). *Building academic language: Meeting Common Core standards across disciplines* (2nd ed.). Jossey-Bass.

CHAPTER 2

Preparing Teachers for Current and Controversial Issue Discussion[1]

Kei Kawashima-Ginsberg, Mary Ellen Daneels, and Noorya Hayat

Young people, including those who are not of voting age, seem to be more politically energized than generations of the past. Today's teens and young adults who are collectively called "Zoomers" voted in record numbers as they came of age in 2018 and showed no sign of stopping in the 2020 presidential election, in which youth turnout figures increased by 11 percentage points (Center for Information & Research on Civic Learning and Engagement [CIRCLE], 2021). Zoomers are also more likely to pay attention to news, create social media content to share their political views, and participate in movements and protests than the Millennials when they were in their early 20s (CIRCLE, 2020a). Today, teachers across grades and subjects are likely to find their students talking about political issues at school and wanting to share their opinions about current events with others—whether formally structured (or not) as a discussion in the classroom.

Are engaged (and maybe enraged) students enough for a successful current and controversial issue discussion? We define "successful current and controversial issue discussions" (CCID)[2] as those that advance students' comprehension of key concepts and content, deepen their understanding of the topic at hand, validate and leverage students' diverse identities and lived experiences, and promote classroom's democratic culture. However, successful discussions rarely just happen. Although it is important that students are interested and engaged with the topic at hand, they still have to learn how to discuss productively and reflectively. As Justice Sandra Day O'Connor, a longtime advocate of civic education and the founder of iCivics[3] once famously stated, "The practice of democracy is not passed down through our gene pool. It must be taught and learned anew by each generation of citizens" (Livini, 2018). Teachers have the challenge of modeling, simulating, and doing ideal discourse among active and effective participants of a constitutional democracy for students.

In the era of political polarization, the teaching of civics, especially using CCID, can be daunting for both students and educators alike. Often educators are tasked with facilitating and teaching ideal versions of CCID rather than mimicking existing discussions between some pundits and government officials (Kawashima-Ginsberg, 2013). This requires teachers to be highly self-aware and observant of students' behaviors, even while negative examples of discourse abound in the media and society.

Yet, students need to practice various democratic processes throughout their education because the United States, as a government, relies on people to participate, engage in discourse, make decisions about civic and political matters, and change laws and systems when needed. We have worked with numerous educators who took on this challenge even as our political climate became increasingly polarized during a global pandemic that exposed disparities previously invisible to many. Based on what we saw and found through our partnership, we are thoroughly convinced that educators can and often do shift how they teach if they understand why changes benefit students when best practices are used and training is conducted with the unique challenges of teaching civics in today's classrooms.

In this chapter, we argue that CCID is an essential part of social studies classrooms at any grade. We will briefly summarize elements of best practice in professional learning based on review of research and lessons learned from a large-scale, network-based effort called "#CivicsIsBack" to train teachers across the state of Illinois following the passage of a state law and changes in the social studies standard around 2016 that required teachers to begin using CCID.[4] This effort, then led by the McCormick Foundation and involving numerous local and statewide partners, supported well over 10,000 teachers who learned and adopted CCID and other evidence-based, interactive instructional strategies even as the political climate worsened and American people's trust in institutions declined in the following years (Pew Research Center, 2019). Through our long-term partnership, we came to believe that all educators can learn to value classroom discussion of controversial issues, embrace diversity of student voice, build a safe and inclusive learning environment, and respond to students' need to explore issues that they care about.

HOW TEACHERS LEARN TO TEACH—RESEARCH ON PROFESSIONAL DEVELOPMENT

The topic of professional development (PD) in civics sometimes elicits similar responses students give when asked about their civics course experience: boring, irrelevant, and stable. Professional development for teachers as a field has evolved and goes well beyond workshops, conferences, and institutes and encompasses a broad community and social interaction among learners who attain dispositions, as well as knowledge and skills, needed to achieve desired growth (Desimone, 2009; Stein et al., 1999). A large-scale review of professional development research (Desimone, 2009) identifies five essential factors for improving teacher knowledge, skills, disposition, and practice: (1) content focus, (2) active learning, (3) coherence (e.g., among state standards, PD content, and consistency with teachers' existing knowledge and beliefs), (4) duration (span of time and total hours), and (5) collective participation. As you will read later, the work we have been involved in through Illinois's teacher training effort is consistent with these factors.

Additionally, teaching civics to today's students who are diverse on multiple dimensions requires teachers' own understanding of their identity, beliefs, and implicit biases that drive their choice of topics for deliberation, which can be used to develop and support an inclusive civics classroom that helps all students achieve excellence (Educating for American Democracy, 2021). Studies found that an emphasis on critical self-reflection in a training for history education teachers promoted more informed pedagogic practice (Barr et al., 2015), and one of the most powerful forms of professional development is teachers' own self-reflection and learning from everyday interactions with students and fellow educators (Desimone, 2009; Putnam & Borko, 2000).

DISCUSSIONS AND PRODUCTIVE DISAGREEMENTS PROMOTE FUTURE CIVIC ENGAGEMENT

Benefits of well-facilitated CCID has been well documented. For instance, it facilitates content learning by (1) allowing students to digest, reflect on, and communicate about the content (Hess, 2009); (2) deepening students' skills to hold civil dialogue with others who may disagree at times (Hess & McAvoy, 2014); (3) developing students' confidence about discussing issues that they learned about outside of class (Lawrence et al., 2016; Levy et al., 2018); and when done well, we argue, can strengthen a classroom community by (4) facilitating students' knowledge about each other and creating a shared experience of learning through disagreements (Educating for American Democracy, 2021). More can be done to understand how and why discussions work, + but results from the NAEP exam indicate students who recall having current issue discussions are more likely to achieve strong civic knowledge than those who do not (Kawashima-Ginsberg, 2013), while issue-based discussions can build students' efficacy about discussing current events in real life (Lawrence et al., 2016). This can in turn promote young people's participation in other civics activities such as voting, protest/activism, issue advocacy, and running for office, because the more young people interact with peers who are also civically engaged, the more they are likely to vote and engage in other civic activities (CIRCLE, 2013). In fact, young adults who recall engaging in meaningful controversial issue discussions later recall their social studies classes as positive and show more interest in political affairs (Hess & McAvoy, 2014).

BUILDING TEACHER DISPOSITION AS A KEY TO SUCCESS

Facilitating CCID seems intimidating at first. Community and parent reactions to CCID are one of the contributing factors. Some teachers said
that they feared or experienced community backlash (i.e., criticism from
parents and others that having balanced issue discussions in a classroom
forces particular ideologies on students), and these sentiments have been
verified by a national survey (Commission on Youth Civic Knowledge and
Voting, 2013). So how did teachers we worked with overcome their fear
through training?

First, teachers, even experienced ones, came to CCID training with
some ambivalence. In this section, Mary Ellen shares two examples from her
training sessions that illustrate teachers' mixed sentiments at the beginning
of training. These activities "break the ice" by showing that not everyone is
ready to jump into CCID, and the second example allows teachers to talk
about and/or reflect on their feelings. These are also examples of how teachers can learn by engaging in the same activities that they can use in their own
classrooms with their students.

The first example (Figure 2.1) is a word cloud[5] a group of teachers
made in response to a prompt, "What does a classroom where students
are engaged in civil and productive current and controversial issue discussions look, feel, and sound like?" given at the beginning of a CCID
training session. A quick review suggests that teachers see value in
student-to-student dialogue but are realistic about the challenges such
conversations can pose. Educators could enter more than one word in
the word cloud, and it is possible, if not likely, that many educators hold
mixed emotions and opinions; CCID holds both opportunities and challenges for them.[6]

When asked to engage in a four-corner reflection (as shown in Figure 2.2)
where teachers chose an image that best represented how they felt about

**Figure 2.1. A Word Cloud Generated from Responses to a Prompt, "What Does a
Classroom Where Students Are Engaged in Civil and Productive Current and
Controversial Issue Discussions Look, Feel, and Sound Like?" (Used at the
Beginning of a Training Session).**

Figure 2.2. A Picture Shown to Educators During a Four-Corner Reflection Activity

Four-Corner Reflection

facilitating classroom discussions, teachers, like the students they serve, put themselves in a wide range of starting places.

- Teachers who identified with image A most often described feeling trepidation and hesitation in engaging students in current and controversial issue discussions because of lack of training, control, administrative support, or poor past experiences.
- Image B was chosen by educators most familiar with using current and controversial issue discussions in the classroom to represent the sense of exhilaration and accomplishment both educators and students felt when such conversations went well.
- Image C was often chosen by teachers because of the "risk" involved in such conversations, but also the "thrill and excitement" in the classroom when such dialogue occurred.
- Image D was the image most often chosen by educators giving voice to the notion that this work was a "journey" rather than a "destination," and it required a collective effort.

The combination of the word cloud activity and four-corner reflection is a powerful tool to use in professional development to build rapport and mutual empathy for each other's diverse experiences and perceptions of CCID. Having educators start the conversation about using current and controversial issue discussions in the classroom by engaging their voice demonstrates how they can safely engage students' voices to reflect on the past, recalibrate practices to build norms, and engage in a collective renewal of goals throughout the process.

WHAT PROMOTES SKILLS FOR FACILITATING CCID?

While many teachers were unsure in the beginning, our findings speak to the effectiveness of these sessions. More than half (55%) of the teachers surveyed said they were "very" comfortable with facilitating CCID, while

18% still saw CCID as "very challenging." Eighty-two percent of educators who had received PD through this initiative saw that their students became more engaged in their classroom instruction. Students benefited too. Students who had taken a civics course after the mandates reported more positive civic attitudes and engagement (e.g., experiencing a classroom climate that promotes critical thinking and deeper learning), more interactions with current events, and feeling a deeper connection and commitment to making a difference in their communities than students who were yet to take such courses (Hayat & Kawashima-Ginsberg, 2020). Through the iterative evaluation process, our team was able to document how teachers learned to facilitate CCID through observations and structured interviews (Daneels et al., 2019; Hayat & Kawashima-Ginsberg, 2020). In the remainder of this chapter, we describe factors that related to an increase in efficacy and skills.

1. Start With the "Why" and Build Teacher Efficacy

An important reason teachers hesitated to use CCID was fear of "losing control" in their classroom when engaging with current and controversial topics. We observed that many teachers started with a belief that students didn't have enough skills to engage in CCID, and their classrooms would be chaotic. Understanding that many teachers start with this mindset, Mary Ellen designed PD modules to help teachers understand *why* incorporating CCID into the classroom in a thoughtful and strategic manner would help engage students and develop their voice while deepening knowledge of the topic and relevant systems and processes. This was so important that the new online PD course on CCID (through an initiative called Guardians of Democracy) begins with a module on "why" CCID is critically important to each teacher by incorporating self-reflection exercises that help them identify their own motivations and a discussion board where teachers can share their anxiety and sense of urgency and hope with other teachers. These align with a key ingredient of best PD practices—collective participation—where teachers learn with and from one another (Desimone, 2009). We found this teacher-centered approach to communicating the mandate to be effective. For instance, teachers began the online CCID course by taking the Discussion Inventory (Hess, 2009), then later revisited their responses in a reflection activity alone and with peer teachers, which seemed to be highly engaging. Reflecting on their past beliefs about CCID and how they changed by the end of the course helped teachers develop deeper understanding of "how they learn," which is a core principle of deeper learning (Hewlett Foundation, 2013).

2. Connecting the (Seemingly Random) Dots

As is the case with any educational reform, teachers in Illinois could easily feel overwhelmed by all the "new" instructional approaches they had to adopt when a new mandate was passed. Lack of time is often the number one barrier teachers face when implementing a new instructional approach (Tichnor-Wagner et al., 2021). About 70% of social studies teachers are involved in extracurricular student activities, and 61% have extra duties outside of teaching such as coaching and tend to teach more courses than teachers in other disciplines (Hansen et al., 2018). The trainers in Illinois took the time to help teachers turn what looked like a cacophony of mandates from all directions[7] into a harmony of connected ideas that, together, made up "good pedagogy" by making explicit connection to other mandates and requirements while teaching about CCID (Hayat & Kawashima-Ginsberg, 2020).

3. Showing, Not Just Telling, What Good Pedagogy Feels Like

A key ingredient of successful PD initiative in Illinois, we think, can be summarized simply as "show not tell" (Daneels et al., 2019). In other words, teachers learned the new instructional strategies by experiencing what it felt, sounded, and looked like to be a student engaging in CCID. Seeing is believing in these training sessions. Even experienced teachers had "aha!" moments as they participated in CCID, which helped them synthesize the way to facilitate discussions. As you saw in Figure 2.2, teachers start out having mixed feelings about CCID because they also have varied experiences with controversial issue discussions. Over the course of their training, they began to gain a holistic understanding of an effective discussion and when and how to use different types of discussion as they engage in, for example, a Socratic seminar and then in philosopher's chair and compare the main purpose and outcome of each.

The "show not tell" principle didn't just apply to the technical aspect of conducting CCID. Climate for discussion was just as essential as content and strategies. Students come to the classroom with diverse lived experiences (Cohen et al., 2018), especially when it comes to contentious issues. Hence, teachers must strive to create a climate where students feel they are worthy and their voice, even if it's different from others, still matters while maintaining their commitment to creating a safe climate by identifying and intervening in statements that harm individuals or marginalized groups. Mary Ellen modeled this climate and also made an explicit connection between how teachers were feeling as learners and built an inclusive and safe climate to conducting effective CCID. First understanding the importance of climate and then seeing specific strategies teachers can use to support a conducive climate for CCID, such as pair-share, a discussion forum with specific prompts, and journaling, have enabled teachers to gain a comprehensive understanding of what it means to facilitate CCID while respecting and supporting students. Teachers reported using these strategies with their own students with overwhelmingly positive results.

4. Helping Teachers Build a Support Team for CCID

As mentioned earlier, we need to teach civics that serve all students now more than ever. Yet, teachers are also likely to face great challenges outside of the classroom. It was known anecdotally from early on that support from school and district administrators was very important for teachers to start using the instructional strategies named in the law, especially CCID (Kawashima-Ginsberg & Junco, 2018). Although concerted efforts were made to inform administrators from the start, teachers reported significant challenges in gaining administrator support largely because administrators did not understand what the law (and the new standards) required after the first year. In response, an "Administrator Academy" was developed to provide training to administrators who could support their teachers. The objectives of the academy, as communicated to the administrators in verbatim here, were to

- learn the benefits of civic learning across the curriculum;
- understand the ancillary attributes of civic learning, including the development of 21st Century skills, improved school climate, reduced drop-out rates, and improved community connections;
- analyze the new IL Social Studies standards and civics requirements for implementation in schools with emphasis on connections to literacy (CCSS/ELA) standards, Social Emotional Learning competencies, Culturally Sustainable Pedagogy, as well as Charlotte Danielson's Framework for Effective Teaching;
- examine the requirements for civics in both middle school and high school including issues related to certification, course components and assessment;
- audit their district social studies curriculum per the new standards & civics course requirements and develop a plan for revisions and professional development.

As you might notice, the learning objectives for the Administrator Academy touched on many aspects of the job that had no apparent connection to civics at a first glance. But the objectives, like the teacher training, made clear connections between the civics law and other initiatives (such as literacy skills, Danielson standards, and inquiry-based learning). PD research finds that PD is more effective when educators do not have to figure out why doing something benefits them by helping them do their job better (Desimone & Garet, 2015). Mary Ellen would say civics was not something being "added to their plate," but it was "the plate" on which they could carry other mandates. This was a particularly effective strategy with administrators, who, once they understood these connections, became more supportive of the civics mandate over time, according to the teachers (Hayat & Kawashima-Ginsberg, 2020).

Gaining administrator buy-in did not just help the civics teachers. In many cases, administrators encouraged teachers outside social studies disciplines to attend workshops devoted to CCID and other topics like inquiry-based learning, performance assessments, and media literacy as they realized "good pedagogy is good pedagogy." The knowledge, skills, and dispositions gained from civic inquiry have connections to other disciplines. As one high school math teacher explained at the conclusion of completing the online CCID course with teachers from various disciplines:

> When I think about engaging students in current and controversial issue discussions in the classroom, I used to think that this did not fit into my curriculum and it was other courses' responsibility to facilitate controversial discussions because of the content that was taught in those courses, but now I think it is every teachers' responsibility to engage students in current and controversial issue discussions—and this certainly doesn't leave out mathematics. There are so many controversial topics surrounding mathematics, computer science, and the STEM field. For students to see themselves as mathematicians, they must be engaging in these conversations.

Based on the early findings, the team recognized that implementing CCID in an extremely polarized era, in a state that is as ideologically diverse as the whole country, meant that training needs to be more than just about classroom instruction. This strategy propelled the pace of implementation in our view.

5. Designing for Everyone and Creating Universal Access

It is easier to only work with so-called "good teachers" who are motivated to become even better teachers. In fact, that is how some teachers, concentrated in affluent suburban schools, provide excellent civics instructions to their students. There are notable exceptions like Chicago,[8] but inequality in civic participation is in part attributable to the fact that not all teachers can access high-quality training and so few systemic efforts to remedy this challenge exist.

The implementation design in Illinois centered accessibility in critical ways. First, it removed physical and financial barriers to PD almost entirely by having the Illinois civics team travel to different regions of the state so that teachers didn't have to travel far and no district had to pay a fee. Second, Mary Ellen broke down complex ideas (the ones that we said would be overwhelming earlier) into bite-size pieces, often saying, "How do you eat an elephant? Well, one bite at a time!" to make overwhelmed teachers at ease. This idea later became the core design of the Guardians of Democracy courses (three levels, each with five modules touching on one idea at a time), which is a series of online courses that results in pedagogical micro-credentials. This included breaking down information in tables and worksheets to make teachers' learning and thinking visible and showing examples in person and in video clips. In the online CCID course, teachers begin with a Bronze badge where they have an orientation to the course (Why CCID is important?) and learn about the types of CCID (e.g., structured academic controversies and philosophical chair) and when they should use each type. The aim is to build knowledge and confidence, enough for most teachers to want to try at least one CCID session in their classroom. In our Illinois in-person PD evaluation, we saw that teachers would often replicate exactly what they did in the PD session with their own students, which is a great way to build competency.

That said, teachers in Illinois represented diverse geographical locations and different political climates. While commitment to building an inclusive and supportive classroom and facilitating productive discussions are universal, the way something is framed or which topics are likely to engage students and teachers vary quite widely within the state. An important component of the Illinois model was the use of regional mentors to represent the diverse ideological, socioeconomic, and geographic regions of the state to serve as "point people" in their respective areas. These regional mentors "spoke the language" of their respective regions and helped connect the larger #CivicsIsback initiative with the stakeholders in their respective communities (Hayat & Kawashima-Ginsberg, 2020). In one community, the important institutional partner might be a regional office of education, and in another it could be the local university. The regional mentors also worked with the McCormick Foundation team to curate examples of best practice and content that would resonate in each region. For example, while a service learning project that engages students in a walk to the polls for early voting may work in urban areas, it would not be feasible in rural areas with larger geographic voting precincts. The regional mentors helped iterate examples of best practice so that it "worked for their teachers."

TEACHING FOR EQUITY STARTS WITH TEACHERS

We write this chapter in the immediate aftermath of the U.S. Capitol insurrection by white supremacist mobs on January 6, 2021, and talks of impeachment dominate the news. In addition, young people from diverse backgrounds are leading protests and policy advocacy everywhere in response to our society's biggest challenges such as repeated murder of Black and Brown people by police. Alongside climate change, mental health crises,[9] and the COVID-19 pandemic, it is true that CCID at times like this can feel "dangerous," and many teachers may feel unsure about whether or how to facilitate such discussions. But these are especially the times students need teachers to show up and try, even if discussions are not going to be "perfect" or comfortable. Teachers need ways to help students who are looking for support and answers, or at least wanting to process what happened outside the classroom. An important part of facilitating current and controversial issue discussions is building a community to lay a groundwork for rigorous and inclusive discussions even through civil disagreements.

In the pilot version of the online CCID course, many teachers, including those who had been teaching for several years, admitted being scared and apprehensive of incorporating current and controversial issue discussion in their classroom. Some of their concerns included potential backlash from the community, perceived loss of control of their classroom, and students being harmed by the dialogue. But most of the teachers were scared of being wrong in this space; of saying the wrong thing or being perceived in the wrong way by students and their parents. Even though race and racial disparities have been at the center of American politics and tragedies almost daily, CCID that involves race and racism is always hard, especially when social studies teacher's (most of whom are white [84%], Hanson et al., 2018) backgrounds are different from most of their students (predominantly Black and Brown students). Moreover, most curricula and media narratives also center whiteness, and teachers, regardless of their own race and ethnic background, still have to tackle challenging issues like racism through CCID to build students' knowledge and voice on these matters.

If educators give up CCID because it is uncomfortable or scary, they could potentially expand the disparities students have at household levels. Research, including ours, shows that families vary in the amount and quality of current issue discussions at home and the degree to which disagreements are allowed (Commission on Youth Voting and Civic Knowledge, 2012). Not surprisingly, "CCID at home" happens more in affluent families who often have college-educated parents. The pandemic has affected communities of color disproportionately (CIRCLE, 2020b), possibly leaving many households without a capacity and energy to talk about these important issues in a way that grows young people's knowledge and ability to think critically. Therefore, we argue that using CCID must be part of every social studies classroom instruction but also that use of CCID without a firm commitment to equity, first and foremost, can be harmful.

Imagine a teacher who uses the U.S. Capitol insurrection and its aftermath as an opportunity to teach about freedom of speech. The teacher could plausibly develop a good essential question to explore and use one of the CCID techniques correctly and make sure that many students have a chance to speak up after the teacher clearly communicates norms for civil discourse. These are in fact part of facilitating an effective discussion. But what if the teacher fails to acknowledge the fact that the numerous individuals who broke through the barriers to enter the U.S. Capitol belonged to self-identified white supremacist groups, waved the Confederate flag, and put up a noose in front of the capital? And what if most of the students in the room are Black? How do we expect these students to stay engaged and not be made to feel invisible or enraged by this teacher?

Professional development to support equitable civic education starts with allowing the teachers to be vulnerable in a safe space (either online or in person) and learn through trial and error. This also helps teachers understand how to create such an environment and support their students. An urban educator of color who took the same CCID course wrote the following in this reflection that speaks to the importance of how facilitating these discussions with his students evolved in the course:

> When I think about engaging students in current and controversial issue discussions in the classroom, I used to think that parents would disagree with that idea, but now I think that it is truly important for students to get exposure to these conversations. Moreover, students of color especially need to learn the ways in which they are oppressed and to develop the language and knowledge to be able to fight against it. Having these discussions will empower students to do so.

Teaching for equity is a journey, and when teachers are feeling vulnerable, or lost, they need a community where they can go. PD can sometimes evolve into that community. It starts with sharing ideas and views across differences. On the online course discussion board for the Guardians of Democracy course, the opportunity to learn about the varying challenges to implementing CCID was an important component to learning.

Self-reflection is an important part of deepening teacher commitment toward equity. Offering social support and ongoing opportunities to connect with peers who are going through a similar process appears to be very important in a teacher's ability to reflect and persist. Teaching for equity is a journey, and when teachers are feeling vulnerable, or lost, they need a community they can go to. PD can sometimes evolve into that community that supports teachers to share views across differences. Many teachers who have participated in the CCID micro-credentials course have continued their support and collaboration through Facebook, Twitter, and text chains with one another and the course facilitator. IllinoisCivics.org serves as a hub of ongoing professional development opportunities and blogs to respond to teachable moments and a place to crowdsource resources around CCID and other proven practices of civic education.

In response to the violence on January 6, 2021, teachers struggled to make sense of the events in real time, while wanting to help their students process. In the midst of this chaos, communities of educators and civic learning providers, including alumni of the Illinois PD initiatives, met in this moment and showed support for one another by sharing resources and being there for one another through an emergency social studies Twitter chat (#sschat) that night. The tweet in Figure 2.3 is one such example where

Figure 2.3. Twitter Post by Mary Ellen Daneels

Mary Ellen Daneels
@IL_CivicsHub

This is NOT the time to have a debate. Dialogue to process current and evolving events are different from current and controversial discussions. It is time to be present, listen, question, and have students do the same. Policy debates come LATER. #sschat

7:23 PM · Jan 6, 2021 · Twitter Web App

she emphasized the importance of taking time to pause, reflect, and choose the right strategy for dialogue (Daneels, 2021a).

Leveraging technology is a key ingredient to ongoing efforts to support educators across a diverse state. Oftentimes, social studies teachers, especially in rural and small districts, are the only social studies teachers in their district and have had limited, if any, interaction with other social studies teachers. Peer-to-peer interactions, including reflections and feedback, not only validate their challenges but also help them see how others like them "in the trenches" have mitigated these challenges. Creating an exclusively online course for CCID has significant advantages, though some may think it cannot match the "real" experience of watching someone "do it live." One advantage is that it can connect teachers from very different places in meaningful ways, as discussed. Importantly, it allows teachers living under circumstances that normally prevent them from participating in in-person training to take part and learn because the course is designed to be asynchronous and has a built-in support system that teachers can use during the course and a resource bank they can come back to any time. In addition, it has created a place where teachers no longer have to feel judged for feeling lost and struggling to figure out how to support and teach students. Teachers need spaces to reflect on their own implicit biases and lived experiences.

CONCLUSION

This work is often uncomfortable; that is why it is important to engage and have teachers *experience* the strategies and resources and reflect and recalibrate their practices *before* they can safely engage students in discussion of these essential questions facing our republic. We hope that you will revisit this book often to review the specific discussion techniques and research about discussion.

We would like to close our chapter with a reminder that learning to incorporate effective discussions in the classroom while making sure that these discussions are serving students across diverse backgrounds equitably is a journey, but one that need not be taken alone (exemplified by Mary

Figure 2.4. Twitter Post by Mary Ellen Daneels on the Day of U.S. Capitol Insurrection.

Mary Ellen Daneels
@IL_CivicsHub   ...

BTW- ALL Ts are civic teachers tomorrow. The way we engage Ss voice, the space we make for Ss lived experiences, the norms we employ, the choices we make in content send messages about power, justice & representation. Be an ambassador #sschat friends and help colleagues.

7:33 PM · Jan 6, 2021 · Twitter Web App

Ellen's Tweet seen in Figure 2.4, Daneels, 2021b). As you embark on your equity-centered civic educator journey, I hope you will use our chapter to remember what you should look for and create in your training and hear one fellow teacher's voice speaking to the power of teachers coming together to be present and support CCID in the classroom, even in, especially in, troubling times (Daneels, 2021b).

NOTES

1. Data collection, analysis, and report writing were sponsored by the Robert R. McCormick Foundation. Portions of the findings presented in this chapter are in a report published through the primary author's organization website at circle.tufts .edu. Authors have no conflicts of interest to disclose. All data and quotes derive from research projects, which have been reviewed and approved by Tufts University's institutional review board.

2. We use the term *current and controversial issue discussion*, or CCID, in reference to the high school version of Illinois's civics law. The middle school version of the law mandates "current and societal issues discussion."

3. iCivics is a nonprofit organization that provides free digital civic learning games and lesson support materials.

4. For a list of partners, see https://www.illinoiscivics.org/2019/partners.

5. A word cloud is a technique to quickly visualize participants' opinions and feelings in a live setting. Figure 2.1 depicts a word cloud from one of the real training sessions, where the most common responses appear larger than less frequent responses.

6. Words like *vulnerable*, *tense*, and *challenging* may have held positive connotations for some educators and negative ones for others, depending on how they see the role of emotions in learning. Learning scientists, based on empirical research, put a strong emphasis on the value of evoking emotional reaction and engagement in learning and retaining information. The more emotionally engaged students are in the topic at hand, the more they retain. The emotional valence can include a degree of anxiety, but not to an extent or nature where students feel as though they are in danger (e.g., when they feel that they are personally attacked or they feel

victim to prejudice or bias), which depletes their cognitive processing capacity. See Immordino-Yang et al. (2018).

7. For instance, Illinois had a socioemotional learning requirement, culturally responsive teaching requirements, new LGBTQ history mandates, and inquiry-based learning standards in addition to the civics mandate.

8. The Chicago Public School district has invested in establishing a whole department on civic engagement and continues to innovate deep collective learning, not only among social studies teachers but among principals, and provides consistent in-house training and support for teachers. The district also developed and uses its own course called "Participate."

9. For instance, see https://www.stuvoice.org/start-with-students.

REFERENCES

Barr, D. J., Boulay, B., Selman, R. L., McCormick, R., Lowenstein, E., Gamse, B., Fine, M., & Leonard, M. B. (2015). A randomized controlled trial of professional development for interdisciplinary civic education: Impacts on humanities teachers and their students. *Teachers College Record*, *117*(2), 1–52.

Center for Information & Research on Civic Learning and Engagement. (2013). *All together now: Collaboration and innovation for youth engagement.* (The Report of the Commission on Youth Voting and Civic Knolwedge). Center for Information and Research on Civic Learning and Engagement. http://www.civicyouth.org/wp-content/uploads/2013/09/CIRCLE-youthvoting-individual Pages.pdf

Center for Information & Research on Civic Learning and Engagement. (2020a, June 30). *Poll: Young people believe they can lead change in unprecedented election cycle.* https://circle.tufts.edu/latest-research/poll-young-people-believe-they -can-lead-change-unprecedented-election-cycle

Center for Information & Research on Civic Learning and Engagement. (2020b, November 2020). *The impact of COVID-19 on young voters.* https://circle.tufts.edu/latest-research/election-week-2020#the-impact-of-covid-19 -on-young-voters

Center for Information & Research on Civic Learning and Engagement. (2021). *Half of youth voted in 2020, An 11-point increase from 2016.* https://circle .tufts.edu/latest-research/half-youth-voted-2020-11-point-increase-2016

Cohen, C., Kahne, J., & Marshall, J. (2018). *Let's go there: Making a case for race, ethnicity, and a lived civics approach to civic education* (GenForward). University of Chicago. https://static1.squarespace.com/static/5e20c70a7802d9509b9aeff2 /t/5e66cd4feddd0f57bb759f21/1583795568756/LetsGoThere_Paper_V17 .pdf

Commission on Youth Voting and Civic Knowledge. (2013). *All together now: Collaboration and innovation for youth engagement: The report of the Commission on Youth Voting and Civic Knowledge.* https://www.civicyouth.org /about-circle/commission-on-youth-voting-civic-knowledge/

Daneels, M. E. [@daneels_m]. (2021a, January 6). *This is NOT the time to have a debate. Dialogue to process current and evolving events are different from current* [tweet]. Twitter. https://twitter.com/daneels_m/status/1346975610690809859

Daneels, M. E. [@daneels_m]. (2021b, January 6). *BTW—ALL Ts are civic teachers tomorrow. The way we engage Ss voice, the space we make for Ss* [tweet]. Twitter. https://twitter.com/daneels_m/status/1346978228330778624

Daneels, M. E., Kawashima-Ginsberg, K., & Healy, S. (2019). From paper to practice: Lessons from the #CivicsIsBack campaign. *Success in High-Need Schools Journal, 15*(1), 58–69.

Desimone, L. M. (2009). Improving impact studies of teachers' professional development: Toward better conceptualizations and measures. *Educational Researcher, 38*(3), 181–199. https://doi.org/10.3102/0013189X08331140

Desimone, L. M., & Garet, M. S. (2015). Best practices in teachers' professional development in the United States. *Psychology, Society, & Education, 7*(3), 252–263.

Educating for American Democracy. (2021). *Home page.* www.educatingforamerican democracy.org

Guardians of Democracy Teachers. (n.d.). *Home page.* https://guardiansofdemocracy teachers.org

Hansen, M., Levesque, E., Valant, J., & Quintero, D. (2018). *The 2018 Brown Center report on American education: How well are American students learning?* Brown Center on Education Policy at Brookings. https://www.brookings .edu/wp-content/uploads/2018/06/2018-Brown-Center-Report-on-American Education_FINAL1.pdf

Hayat, N., & Kawashima-Ginsberg, K. (2020). *Building for better democracy together: Final report on the Illinois #CivicsIsBack civic education initiative.* Center for Information and Research and Civic Learning and Engagement. https:// circle.tufts.edu/sites/default/files/2020-12/illinois_ciivcs_report_full_0.pdf

Hess, D. E. (2009). *Controversy in the classroom: The democratic power of discussion.* Routledge. https://doi.org/10.4324/9780203878880

Hess, D. E., & McAvoy, P. (2014). *The political classroom: Evidence and ethics in democratic education.* Routledge. https://doi.org/10.4324/9781315738871

Hewlett Foundation. (2013). *Deeper learning defined.* https://hewlett.org/wp -content/uploads/2016/08/Deeper_Learning_Defined__April_2013.pdf

Illinois Civics Hub. (n.d.). *Partners.* https://www.illinoiscivics.org/2019/partners

Immordino-Yang, M. H., Darling-Hammond, L., & Krone, C. (2018). *The brain basis for integrated social, emotional, and academic development: How emotions and social relationships drive learning.* The Aspen Institute. https://www.aspeninstitute .org/wp-content/uploads/2018/09/Aspen_research_FINAL_web.pdf

Kawashima-Ginsberg, K. (2013). *Do discussion, debate, and simulations boost NAEP civics performance?* Center for Information & Research on Civic Learning and Engagement. https://circle.tufts.edu/sites/default/files/2020-01/discussion _debate_naep_2013.pdf

Kawashima-Ginsberg, K., & Junco, R. (2018). Teaching controversial issues in a time of polarization. *Social Education, 82*(6), 323–329.

Lawrence, J. F., Francis, D., Paré-Blagoev, E. J., & Snow, C. E. (2016). The poor get richer: Heterogeneity in the efficacy of a school-level intervention for academic language. *Journal of Research on Educational Effectiveness, 10*(4), 767–793. http://dx.doi.org/10.1080/19345747.2016.1237596

Levy, B. L. M., Dacus, L. C. & Smirnov, N. (2018, April 13–17). A mixed methods comparison of two civic education models: Legislative semester and A.P. government courses [Paper presentation]. American Educational Research Association Annual Meeting, New York, NY.

Livini, E. (2018, October 23). *Sandra Day O'Connor's farewell letter is a plea for country before party.* https://qz.com/1434224/sandra-day-oconnors-farewell-letter-is-a-plea-for-country-before-party/

National Center for Education Statistics. (2019). *Enrollment and percentage distribution of enrollment in public elementary and secondary schools, by race/ethnicity and level of education: Fall 1999 through fall 2019* [Data set]. U.S. Department of Education. https://nces.ed.gov/programs/digest/d19/tables/dt19_203.60.asp

National Council for the Social Studies. (2012). *The College, career, and civic life (C3) framework for social studies state standards: Guidance for enhancing the rigor of K–12 civics, economics, geography, and history.* https://civxnow.org/wp-content/uploads/2021/09/c3-framework-for-social-studies-rev0617.pdf

Pew Research Center. (2019) *Trust and distrust in America.* https://www.pewresearch.org/politics/2019/07/22/trust-and-distrust-in-america/

Putnam, R. T., & Borko, H. (2000). What do new views of knowledge and thinking have to say about research on teacher learning? *Educational Researcher, 29*(1), 4–15. https://doi.org/10.3102/0013189X029001004

Stein, M. K., Smith, M. S., & Silver, E. A. (1999). The development of professional developers: Learning to assist teachers in new settings in new ways. *Harvard Educational Review, 69*(3), 237–269. https://doi.org/10.17763/haer.69.3.h2267130727v6878

Tichnor-Wagner, A., Kawashima-Ginsberg, K. & Hayat, N. (2021). *The state of civic education in Massachusetts: A report prepared for the Massachusetts Department of Elementary and Secondary Education.* https://circle.tufts.edu/latest-research/state-civic-education-massachusetts

CHAPTER 3

Supporting Civic Discussions With Younger Students

Terence A. Beck

Scenario: Fourth-grade students are discussing whether there should be a constitutional right to legal representation when people are accused of a crime.

> *Carl:* What if they proved he murdered someone? I mean, do you think he should deserve a lawyer?
>
> *Celeste:* Let's say Randy, if you're being accused for stabbing someone and you didn't do it, and you get a lawyer and you didn't have the money to pay for it? How would you get a lawyer?
>
> *Randy:* I couldn't. That's why I think everyone should get one.
>
> *Carl:* What if they knew he did? What if like, someone saw him?

There is much that is notable about this excerpt from a much longer exchange (Beck, 2003, p. 337). Let us focus on the engaged nature of the students' talk. This exchange feels personal, like it is more than an academic exercise. Students talk as if they care about this issue, and they use tools of persuasion ("What if . . ." and "Let's say. . . ."). They seem to be listening to each other. Celeste's example of someone who can't afford a lawyer directly refutes Carl's assertion that some people aren't deserving of a lawyer. Randy responds in a way that supports Celeste's question, and Carl seeks to undermine Randy's assertion. The students use what the other has to say rather than simply making a previously determined point. In other words, the students are talking to each other—throughout the extended exchange, the teacher's voice is absent.

This exchange came late in a 12-day intervention designed to support 4th-grade students as they deliberated about civic issues. The intervention was designed with the belief that even young children are capable of engaged talk around civic issues when they are provided with the tools they need. In this chapter, I look across methods that have demonstrated impacts on young students' abilities to engage in productive discussions and consider ways that teachers can support student discussion.

Throughout this chapter, I make assumptions that are best revealed here. First, as I noted, I assume that with the appropriate supports, even children in the earliest grades are capable of engaging productively in a discussion. Just because students are unable to do something today doesn't mean they can't do it at all; that's why they have teachers. I trust students. With support, time, instruction, and experiences, students can engage in complex activities like discussion.

Second, I assume that leading a productive civics discussion is one of the most difficult things we ask teachers to do. There are dozens of ways a discussion can go wrong, and there are so many variables that teachers simply don't control, like the mood of the class, the time of day, and social dynamics between students. Teaching with discussion can be an exercise in humility, and it can be some of the most rewarding and memorable time teachers have during the school day.

Third, I assume a functioning classroom with a basic level of safety for students (two pre-requisites for a good discussion). Paradoxically, discussion both needs a relatively safe community and it builds such communities (e.g., see discussions on cooperative learning in Chapter 1). Teachers need to attend to issues of safety for discussion to flourish, but since Part III of this volume discusses this perquisite in depth, I do not describe how teachers might create safer classrooms here.

Fourth, I assume a sociocultural approach to discussion. That is, I draw on James Wertsch's (1998) idea of mediated action. Wertsch posits that any activity (such as a discussion) requires both actors (in this case students) and tools. Tools can be physical (e.g., a computer or a document) or cultural (e.g., beliefs, ideas, ways of speaking deemed appropriate in school). Actors and tools are both necessary for people to act—people cannot act without tools and tools cannot act on their own. The important point is this: Wertsch notes that if you want to change action (for example, a teacher wants to change how students engage in academic discussions), the most productive route is to focus on changing the tools being used, not trying to change the people. In other words, I assume that supporting students in discussion is not about exhorting them to try harder or to speak up but is about providing them with new tools (e.g., ideas, ways of speaking). Changing the tools changes the action, and it can change the actor (but be aware that the students will also change the tools and use them for their own purposes).

Fifth, while teachers often understand discussion is a powerful way to teach many types of social studies content (Brookfield & Preskill, 1999; Wilen, 1990), I assume that the goals of civic discussion are not only to learn content but to also learn how to discuss (Parker & Hess, 2001). Civic discussions give students "practice in entertaining multiple perspectives and viewpoints on important issues that affect our lives" (Westheimer, 2015, p. 12). Civic discussions are concerned with creating dispositions in students to act democratically when they are no longer under the gaze of the teacher—to be willing to listen respectfully, make arguments thoughtfully and humbly, and consider points of view other than their own. These dispositions are not created through exhortation. Instead, dispositions are "patterns of thinking and behaving that are not learned through transmission but rather through practice in a supportive social environment" (Reddy et al., 1998, p. 16). Fostering democratic dispositions requires teachers to regularly conduct civic discussions so that students experience the power of engaging skillfully in a discussion.

In this chapter, I consider how teachers might support students as they learn and appropriate the tools necessary to engage in civic discussions. I focus on civics because our society is increasingly unable and unwilling to engage with each other (Pew Research Center, 2017). Schools must respond. Democracy requires citizens who can talk across difference in order to deliberate about what we should do about the considerable problems we face (Parker, 2003, 2005). Young students are emphasized here because learning to deliberate as citizens requires practice over time—we can't afford to wait until high school to introduce these ideas (Parker, 2006). My emphasis is on young students, but these ideas can support students of all ages who are engaging in a discussion.

I begin by thinking generally about the tools students need in order to engage in civic discussions. From there, I illustrate how teachers might support students in acquiring and using these tools in seminars and deliberations, two types of civic discussions that I consider in this chapter.

GENERAL TOOLS TO SUPPORT CIVIC DISCUSSIONS

Supporting a discussion requires that we provide students with the tools they need to engage respectfully with others. At its most basic, discussion demands that we have three types of tools: (1) something to talk about, (2) a reason to talk about it, and (3) a way to talk about it. When we neglect one of these areas, the discussion is unlikely to go well.

A rich and interesting topic is the "something to talk about" tool required for a good discussion. If the topic is uninteresting or unimportant, there is little reason to engage. Not everything in the civics curriculum is deserving of discussion. Figuring out what students might talk about can be difficult for adults. It can be difficult to see the world from the students' point of view. Teachers know what we find interesting but anticipating what our students might be willing to talk about requires knowledge of students, knowledge of content, and some imagination. And students might find something interesting but feel like they don't have the authority to say anything about it. Adults know so much that we often don't remember what it was like to not know (Feiman-Nemser & Buchmann, 1985). Having something to talk about means finding the sweet spot where curriculum expectations meet student knowledge and student interest.

Discussants need a reason to talk with each other. Most of us have experienced discussions that amble from one topic to another and seem to accomplish little more than wasting time. Discussions work best when we grasp why they matter. With a terrific topic, that reason can be self-evident, but teachers shouldn't assume that students see the purpose. When it is made clear, the goal of a discussion can be a tool that students use to participate. The goal shapes what students talk about. For example, if students are trying to understand an important and difficult idea, they keep talking about different ways of understanding the idea. If they are trying to decide how to respond to a pressing problem, students think about the nature of the problem and how differing solutions might create additional problems.

The importance of knowing how to talk about a topic should not be underestimated. Participating in a discussion can be socially risky (Hess & Posselt, 2002), and even young children experience this (Hauver et al., 2017). After all, every time we say something, we reveal a bit about ourselves (Gee, 2010), and the judgments of others can be harsh. Even the most experienced discussants need help navigating new discussion situations. We need to know how to safely talk about a given idea *here*, in this place with these people. Provided with these tools, we can engage more freely and more productively.

In what follows, I focus attention on two types of civic discussions—seminars and deliberations—and I illustrate how teachers might support students in the use of good topics, understanding the reasons for engaging with the topic, and learning to talk productively in the academic setting of the classroom.

SUPPORTING SEMINARS: CIVIC DISCUSSIONS THAT ASK, "WHAT SHOULD WE THINK?"

Discussions of what we should think are often most productive when they center around fiction and nonfiction texts that raise important issues, ideas, or values. Looking closely at texts allows students to move beyond their own experiences and imagination and enter the world of another. In social studies, we often refer to discussions of "what should we think?" as seminars (Parker, 2003). Elementary teachers are often familiar with seminars through a variety of literacy techniques—techniques such as literature circles (Brownlie, 2019; Eeds & Wells, 1989), junior great books discussions (Great Books Foundation, 1992), book club (Raphael & McMahon, 1994), Socratic seminars (Strong, 1997), and collaborative reasoning (Beaulieu-Jones & Proctor, 2015; Zhang & Stahl, 2011).

Political philosophers have long argued that democratic citizenship requires a particular set of attitudes and values. Discussion is a powerful place for students to explore civic values like justice, freedom, honesty, and responsibility. In both the social studies and the literacy curriculums there are places where even young students can consider their responsibilities to themselves, one another, and the larger society.

Literacy techniques bring a level of research support that is hard to find when examining social studies seminars (particularly seminars and young children). As a result, I start by exploring some of what we can learn from literacy researchers about supporting skillful seminar discussions. From there, I consider what makes social studies seminars different and what supporting students in social studies seminars might look like.

I begin by examining collaborative reasoning (CR) and the supports that scholars have developed to help students engage with one another. CR closely resembles several seminar techniques aimed at increasing students' discussion of texts (see Part II of this volume for in-depth examples and explorations of these techniques). It has been demonstrated to increase both the quality and quantity of student talk in discussions of texts (Chinn et al., 2001). CR seems to works well across cultural contexts (Dong et al., 2008). And CR seems to be gaining popularity (Chen, 2020) (a recent YouTube search yielded no shortage of videos on the topic with very young students).

In CR, a group of students read a story and discuss a question posed by the teacher (Clark et al., 2003). The question generally involves a dilemma a character in the story is experiencing. Students discuss the question together, and there is a poll at the end of the session where everyone weighs in one final time about the question. The session ends with students debriefing the discussion, making suggestions on how to improve the next one.

In CR, teachers support students' engagement by selecting texts that contain rich, unresolved issues (Zhang & Stahl, 2011) with some "moral or ethical ambiguity" (Beaulieu-Jones & Proctor, 2015, p. 678). That is, the text is not designed to teach a lesson. For example, a text in which the protagonist must make a difficult decision is more likely to inspire conversation than a text like Aesop's "The Boy Who Cried Wolf" that seeks to teach the dangers of lying. When students sense that the story has a right answer, they tend to adopt the "right" stance and the conversation is less likely to take off (Beaulieu-Jones & Proctor, 2015).

Teachers support students' skillful discussion with well-crafted "big questions" that are raised in the text (Clark et al., 2003; Zhang & Stahl, 2011). Such questions become tools students can use—the questions help focus students' attention on that which is meaningful and worth talking about in the text. The teacher's question also suggests why we might engage in a discussion, typically by highlighting something students don't know or giving them a reason to be curious. Questions might, for example, ask students to explore a character's motivation or an author's decision to include a particularly significant detail.

Students' participation is supported by clearly setting norms and expectations (Zhang & Stahl, 2011). Teachers support students both by talking about the relevant skills and by modeling them (Beaulieu-Jones & Proctor, 2015; Zhang & Stahl, 2011). For example, teachers model how they might support an idea using a reference to the text or with expanded explanations, and they communicate that students should do the same.

A key method for supporting young students in CR is building an understanding of what talk sounds like during an academic conversation. Teachers use sentence stems that provide students with parts of sentences they can appropriate and use for their own purposes. Stems such as "I disagree because . . .," "I see why you think that but . . .," [and] "That is a good point, but I have a different idea . . ." (Beaulieu-Jones & Proctor, 2015, p. 681) offer support for the student who has something to say but isn't sure how to say it.

To summarize, CR groups read and discuss a text that raises issues such as fairness or winning and losing. The teacher supports the discussion by identifying in advance the issue in the text and by forming a question that helps students focus on the issue. Teachers set expectations, model how to talk about the issue in the text, and provide sentence stems students can use to put their thoughts into words and engage with one another in reasoning about a text.

FROM COLLABORATIVE REASON TO SOCIAL STUDIES SEMINARS

The supports provided to students to engage in CR move seamlessly into social studies discussions. In a social studies discussion, students engage with issues, ideas, or values directly connected to democracy and their understanding of society and human relationships. Social studies seminars in the youngest grades might explore questions of family obligations or the nature of friendship and trust. Students might consider issues of environmental stewardship or personal responsibility. Social studies seminars typically engage with both stories and informational texts (Beck & Parker, 2022). Like CR, a social studies seminar focuses on deepening our understanding of a text. Students explore meaningful questions that consider what we should think without telling them what to think.

In a social studies seminar, teachers support students through different tools, depending on the type of text and their particular goals. For example, in the Declaration of Independence, Thomas Jefferson lays out an argument for why the representatives of the United States of America must change their government. This argument is rich in political values that can be explored by older elementary-aged students. Supporting students' discussion of this text would require help with some (limited) key vocabulary and modeling of how one makes sense of 18th-century American English. The teacher might model how historians interpret a primary source document by wondering aloud about why the document was written, who the audience is for the document (the English? the Americans? both?), and what the document has to say about King George in contrast to the American representatives. The teacher might ask, "Why do the signers think it is their duty to change their government?" (Beck & Parker, 2022, p. 315). Sentence stems supporting student discussion would move beyond generic statements such as "I disagree" to include moves such as "I think that ____ is one reason the authors say change is needed." Or "Can someone help me understand what this sentence means?" Sentence stems might also include ways for students to engage with others. Stems such as "I'm not sure what you mean by ____," or "I'm interested in knowing what ____ thinks about that." In short, this social studies seminar contains the same general types of supports as we find in CR, but those supports are adapted to address the specific demands of this founding document.

Stories are also rich sources of issues, ideas, and values relevant to social studies seminars, and this is one of many places that literacy and social studies can interact. In what follows, I lay out a process I have used with the folktale *Jack and the Beanstalk* to support students' discussion of the text. I first encountered the power of this story in a workshop created by the Great Books Foundation and have gone on to adapt their approach in order to engage others with the story in a variety of places and contexts. I present my process here as a specific example of how teachers might prepare to support student discussion.

Jack and the Beanstalk Example. For those unfamiliar with *Jack and the Beanstalk*, Jack lives in poverty with his mother and is sent to sell their only asset, a dairy cow who no longer gives milk. Jack sells the cow to a man for magic beans, beans his mother throws out of the window in a rage when she learns of the transaction. Overnight, the beans grow into a beanstalk that reaches to the sky. Jack climbs the beanstalk and encounters an ogre's wife who initially hides Jack from the ogre. During his three visits to the ogre's house Jack steals, first, a bag of gold, second, a hen that lays golden eggs on demand, and third, a very talented harp.

Is there something to talk about here? Supporting students in discussing the issue in this text requires me, as the teacher, to identify those issues. Three issues in this story stand out to me: (1) trust (Jack's trust of the man with the beans, his trust of the ogre's wife, the ogre's wife's initial trust in Jack); (2) when the ends justify the means (Is stealing ever okay?); and (3) risk taking (climbing up the beanstalk not once, but three times). That's a lot to cover for adults, let alone 8-year-olds. There is no need to address every issue in a text. I decide that issues of trust and when ends justify means are those most relevant to civic education. I focus my efforts there.

If students are to talk in ways that deepen their understanding of one of these issues, the text must support differing interpretations—there must be some moral ambiguity. I engage in thinking both about kid-friendly questions I might ask and the extent to which the text lends itself to different answers to those questions.

For the purpose of this example, I focus on trust. Trust is a key aspect of well-functioning societies. And trustworthiness is, in the words of Robert Putnam, a civic virtue (Putnam, 2000, p. 19). Helping young students think about when they should trust, who they should trust, and what it means to be trustworthy is an important democratic goal.

Looking over exchanges in the story between Jack and the man with the magic beans and Jack and the ogre's wife, I consider questions I might ask and the variety of possible answers. In the version of the story with which I'm most familiar, the author describes the man with the magic beans as a "funny looking old man." The man knows Jack's name and he tells Jack, "You look the proper sort of chap to sell cows" (Great Books Foundation, 1992). From a brainstormed list, I select the questions "Why do you think the old man wanted to trade the beans for Jack's cow?" and "Why was Jack willing to trust the funny looking old man? Was that a good idea?"

My questions support conversation because they are kid friendly—with some context, they are easy for young students to understand. My questions also directly support students' consideration of trust by considering motivation and risk. They provide a purpose for engaging with the text.

Brainstorming some possible explanations for why the man wanted to trade for the cow, I come up with at least two: (1) The man might have been looking to take advantage of Jack by trading something he believed to be worthless for a cow he could sell at a considerable profit; (2) the man was in cahoots with the ogre (you might remember that the ogre eats boys—a detail I neglected to mention), recruiting unsuspecting boys by providing them with beanstalks that will entice the boys into the ogre's realm. Both of these interpretations can be supported by the text.

I support students' consideration of the questions by pointing out that the man knew Jack's name and flattered Jack. I start by asking, "Do you think the man ran into Jack by chance? What does the text suggest?"

As the discussion moves forward, I plan to ask the question, "Was Jack smart to trust the man?" Again, I consider the possible answers to this question (and the contextual evidence) before deciding to ask it. I know from experience that students often justify Jack's trust by noting that it all worked out—Jack moved from being on the brink of starvation to being quite wealthy and marrying a princess. The beans were magic as the man claimed—there was no deception here. Other students note the man's clear attempts to manipulate Jack through flattery, the relative inequity between the value of beans and the value of a cow, and the fact that the beans put Jack in considerable personal danger. Things could have easily ended differently. As they discuss these options, students start to see the value and the dangers of trust.

To support students' discussion skills with this story, I model an interest in and an appreciation of what others have to say. I provide sentence stems like, "I think _____ was right/wrong to trust _____ because _____," and "Why do you think _____?"

I support the continual improvement of students' discussion skills by giving them a chance at the end to give new insights and to talk about what went well in the discussion and how we might do better next time.

Literacy strategies like CR tend to provide *general* supports for students to express their opinions and engage with others. The general nature of the process is part of its power because this makes them easier for teachers and students to learn and remember. Yet, social studies educators do well to adapt their supports for students relative to the text they have chosen to discuss and their social studies goals. Supports include selecting texts that explore valuable *civic* issues, ideas, or values, formulating kid-friendly questions, setting expectations for respectful exchange, modeling skills, and providing sentence stems students can use to skillfully contribute to the discussion of the type of text they find before them.

INTELLECTUAL ROLE TAKING TO SUPPORT DELIBERATION

While seminars are important to social studies instruction, democracy ultimately requires that individuals together decide how to act. Considering "What should we do?" is often called deliberation, and it is a key task of democracy (Parker, 2001, 2003, 2010). Students need repeated experience with this task throughout their K–12 lives (Parker, 2006).

A deliberative discussion can be supported using the same tools I outlined—deliberations require something to talk about, a reason to discuss, and a way to talk. In deliberation, the topic is focused on a problem rather than a text, and the question is some variation on "What should we do about this?" (Parker, 2003, p. 131). However, the process of deliberative problem solving engages the following three steps, steps I have adapted from the work of Parker and Zumeta (1999). First, the problem must be identified, and the group members need a common understanding of it. This is a difficult but critical first step because how we frame the problem shapes how we solve it. Is the problem a question of fairness/justice, or is it one of the common good (Hauver, 2017)? Second, the group develops possible solutions and then analyzes the options. What solutions are possible? What are the advantages of each solution? What are a given solution's limitations? Third, the group must agree to pursue a solution that seems likely to address

Table 3.1. Supporting Two Types of Civic Discussion

Cultural Tool	Seminar	Deliberation
A topic worthy of discussion	What should we think? Questions of civic values raised by a text. Issues such as trust, the common good, and individual liberty are often worthy of discussion.	Solving a problem the group faces. Problems of civic concern such as awarding rights or creating laws. Also problems of more local concern such as how to spend money or respond to hate speech in the community.
A reason to discuss the topic	A question focusing attention of an issue, idea, or value the text addresses: What should we think?	A version of the question "What should we (or some democratic body we might want to advise) do about this?"
How we talk about this topic here, in this setting	Clear expectations and norms Teacher modeling Sentence stems: "I disagree because _____."	Clear expectations and norms Teacher modeling Roles and sentences for each step in the process: Framing the problem Examining choices Making a decision and communicating a rationale

the problem—they decide what they should do. Table 3.1 lists the different supports teachers might create for seminars and deliberations.

Engaging in deliberation is complicated by the fact that social problems are typically ill-structured (Voss et al., 1983; Voss & Post, 1988). That is, ill-structured problems do not have one best way of framing them (Kuhn, 2015), and their solutions cannot be easily tested (Voss & Post, 1988). For example, juggling religious liberty with the rights of LGBTQ people is a problem that can be framed in multiple ways, and we can only guess what a given solution might mean in practice.

While deliberations can work well in small groups, a decision impacting the entire group is ideally agreed on by that group. A common practice in schools is to ask students to engage in deliberation in small groups, followed by group reports. Anyone who has participated in this format knows that the small group reports often devolve into a conversation between the small group and the teacher while the remainder of the class quietly thinks of other things (Herrenkohl, 2006). What is necessary to support students in engaging with one another authentically in the large group setting?

Leslie Herrenkohl (2006) developed intellectual role taking in response to the problem of student disengagement in elementary science classes during small group reports. Herrenkohl (2006) found that when elementary students were supported in taking on intellectual roles, they moved from abdicating the task of thinking to the teacher to asking "personally relevant questions and expecting thoughtful answers" (p. 50). Intellectual roles have been demonstrated to work similarly in civic discussions as well (Beck, 2003). Intellectual roles support students' deliberation by providing students with tools they can use when questioning one another about a small group's proposal.

In intellectual role taking, students who are listening to the reports—students in the audience—are assigned roles appropriate to the task and are supported in fulfilling those roles with charts posted in the room that offer suggestions of questions a person might ask in a given situation. These roles create a reason to engage with the small group and provide support for how to engage in this academic setting.

But how are the roles are determined? Intellectual roles are based in disciplinary structures and are intended to communicate the values of the discipline. Table 3.2 provides examples from science, history, and civics to illustrate how the intellectual roles are established and the kind of supports the process offers. As the figure illustrates, the steps reflect the process and the values of people who function as scientists, historians, or civic actors. The intellectual roles assign responsibility to students in the "audience" of what they might listen for during the small group's report. The question stems support students who are assigned a particular intellectual role in forming a question that helps them examine one aspect of the group's report. In the civics example, the group is responsible for examining the pros and cons of the solutions they generate. The intellectual role of the audience member is to question the group to understand what they talked about regarding the different solutions. A possible question they might ask to accomplish this task is "What are the good things about this choice?" The steps, roles, and question stems help students in the small and large group know what to talk about and how to talk in this setting.

To recap, deliberations depend on a problem the group faces. This problem can be of immediate concern to the local setting, or it can involve larger civic concerns such as balancing individual liberty with the common good. The deliberative question focuses on what should be done about the problem. Often the question begins with "should" and invites students to consider whether a particular action should be taken. Students are supported in participating in the deliberation as the teacher introduces and models the process and how participants might listen with care and humility. Charts are widely used and displayed publicly to support students' engagement. Students are assigned intellectual roles with charts that support students in asking questions of small groups.

Table 3.2. Disciplinary-Based Steps in Discussion

Subject	Steps	Intellectual Roles	Question Stems
Science* Conducting and interpreting experiments	1. Predicting and theorizing 2. Summarizing results 3. Relating the evidence or results to the theory and prediction	1. Checking for predictions and theories 2. Checking for a summary of the findings 3. Checking to ensure that the evidence matches the theory	1. What's your theory? 2. What did you find out? 3. Did what you think was going to happen really happen?
History** Analyzing primary-source documents	1. Sourcing—understanding the nature of the artifact 2. Cross-checking 3. Imagining the setting—relevant patterns of belief and thought from the time	1. Checking to see the perspective of the source 2. Checking to see how different sources compare 3. Checking to see what the source tells us about the time period	1. Do you trust this source? 2. Where do the sources agree/ disagree? 3. What does this source tell you about how people thought at the time?
Civics*** Considering what to do about a public problem	1. Framing the problem 2. Examining choices 3. Making and communicating a decision	1. Checking to see how the group defined the problem 2. Checking for the pros and cons of the different choices 3. Checking to see how well the solution solves the problem	1. What do you think the problem is? 2. What are the good things about that choice? 3. Is there anyone who might be hurt by your decision?

* Adapted from Herrenkohl and Gurra (1998); ** Adapted from Herrenkohl (2006); *** Adapted from Beck (2003).

CONSIDERATIONS WHEN APPLYING INTELLECTUAL ROLES TO CIVIC DISCUSSIONS

Up to this point, I have described the process of supporting students to deliberate using intellectual roles. In this final section, I present what I have learned about this method both as a researcher and as one who has used intellectual roles in different classroom settings.

Students often benefit from a clear introduction to the problem, the question, and the process and purposes of the discussion. When starting this process, I relied on well-regarded materials such as those created by the Center for Civic Education (www.civiced.org/). The Center for Civic Education's *We the People* curriculum presents the issues that confronted our founders as they designed the Constitution in formats that lend themselves easily to the kinds of deliberation described here. *We the People* has elementary, middle school, and high school editions that help teachers find materials appropriate to the grade level they are teaching.

With younger students, I introduce intellectual roles gradually. Initial work with deliberation can start in small groups with more traditional reports and exchanges with the teacher. In these early sessions, the teacher models the kinds of questions an engaged audience member might ask of a group.

Problem framing is the most difficult step students take when addressing a civic problem in their small group and when reporting to the larger group. A "problem chart" is helpful here. A problem chart contains the problem statements of the small groups and any notes about the nature of the problem (e.g., is it an issue of fairness or what is best for the majority?). This public chart serves as a reminder to students of how others are framing the question and invites considerations of alternative definitions of the problem. Without the support of a problem chart, students can find problem framing very challenging.

If the steps of defining the problem and generating possible solutions seem overly challenging for students, teachers can temporarily step back and "bind" the deliberation (Hauver, 2017) by offering one or more forced choices for students to discuss. This more restricted form of deliberation still invites students to frame the problem, but it simplifies the task. The solutions tend to suggest a limited variety of problem framings and narrow the possibilities that the larger group will discuss. Bounded deliberations are commonly used in civics classrooms at all levels.

Supporting students as they engage with a civic problem is easier if the teacher has experience with deliberation. Teachers can build their own deliberative muscles by noticing when deliberation is happening in their lives, when it works, and when it doesn't work. The staff at a school often deliberate how to address a problem in the school. Families deliberate when they are faced with various choices. Committees deliberate. City councils deliberate. In contrast to a debate, deliberation at its core is an attempt to work together to make the best choice, not to win an argument (Beck, 1998). The more teachers understand deliberation, the better able they are to help students experience its potential.

Be patient with yourself and with your students. Research into the use of intellectual role assignments suggests the use of intellectual roles requires practice in order for students to begin to see the value of the questions and to ask them authentically (Beck, 2003; Herrenkohl, 2006). As they use and adapt the suggested questions, students start to see their power and change the questions to serve their own purposes as participants in the academic community of the classroom. With practice, students authentically engage with one another to address problems and take on intellectual roles while leaving the charts behind. Students' reliance on the provided questions will subside as they start to adopt and adapt the intellectual tools of a class-wide deliberation.

Similarly, be patient with your students in small deliberative groups. Without a teacher's direct guidance in the small groups, students will initially struggle with the steps of deliberation. However, when small group deliberations are combined with engaged questioning by students taking on intellectual roles, the small group deliberations tend to change. Small groups appear to become accountable to the class when they understand that their classmates will ask about what happened in the group. I've watched small groups that seemed initially unfocused at first develop a sense that time is short and must be used productively. Students say things like, "They are going to ask us about the problems with this choice. What will we say?"

SUMMARY

In summary, I return to where I started: With support, students at every level can engage in meaningful civic discussions. The students at the beginning of this chapter who were discussing when a person should have a right to a lawyer had something to talk about, a reason to talk, and help with knowing how to talk in this place and about this topic. These supports are necessary for all discussions. The supports change as the task changes. Civic seminars engage issues, ideas, and values relevant to democracy. As students experience the power of discussion, they gain knowledge and skills. And as discussion happens over time, students develop dispositions to put their knowledge and skills to work for the common good.

REFERENCES

Beaulieu-Jones, L., & Proctor, C. P. (2015). A blueprint for implementing small-group collaborative discussions. *The Reading Teacher*, 69(6), 677–682.

Beck, T. A. (1998). The music of deliberation. *Educational Leadership*, 55(7), 37–40.

Beck, T. A. (2003). "If he murdered someone, he shouldn't get a lawyer": Engaging young children in civics deliberation. *Theory & Research in Social Education*, 31(3), 327–347. https://doi.org/http://dx.doi.org/10.1080/00933104.2003.10473228

Beck, T. A., & Parker, W. C. (2022). *Social studies in elementary education* (16th ed.). Pearson.

Brookfield, S. D., & Preskill, S. (1999). *Discussion as a way of teaching: Tools and techniques for democratic classrooms*. Jossey-Bass.

Brownlie, F. (2019). *Grand conversations, thoughtful responses: A unique approach to literature circles* (2nd ed.). HighWater Press.

Chen, G. (2020, January 9). How "collaborative reasoning" could be the next public school trend. *Public School Review*. https://www.publicschoolreview.com /blog/how-collaborative-reasoning-could-be-the-next-public-school-trend

Chinn, C. A., Anderson, R. C., & Waggoner, M. A. (2001). Patterns of discourse in two kinds of literature discussion. *Reading Research Quarterly, 36*(4), 378–411.

Clark, A.-M., Anderson, R. C., Kuo, L.-j., Kim, I.-H., Archodidou, A., & Nguyen-Jahiel, K. (2003). Collaborative reasoning: Expanding ways for children to talk and think in school. *Educational Psychology Review, 15*(2), 181–198.

Dong, T., Anderson, R. C., Kim, I., & Li, Y. (2008). Collaborative reasoning in China and Korea. *Reading Research Quarterly, 43*(4), 400–424. https://doi .org/10.1598/RRQ.43.4.5

Eeds, M., & Wells, D. (1989). Grand conversations: An exploration of meaning construction in literature study groups. *Research in the Teaching of English, 23*(1), 4–29.

Feiman-Nemser, S., & Buchmann, M. (1985). Pitfalls of experience in teacher preparation. *Teachers College Record, 87*(1), 53–65.

Gee, J. P. (2010). *An introduction to discourse analysis: Theory and method* (3rd ed.). Routledge.

Great Books Foundation. (1992). *An introduction to shared inquiry* (3rd ed.). Author.

Hauver, J. (2017). "State your defense!" Children negotiate analytic frames in the context of deilberative dialogue. *Democracy & Education, 25*(2), 1–13.

Hauver, J., Zhao, X., & Kobe, J. F. (2017). Performance as pedagogy: Children's trust and the negotiation of subjectivities in the context of deliberative dialogue. *Theory & Research in Social Education, 45*(3), 293–317. https://doi.org/10 .1080/00933104.2016.1258349

Herrenkohl, L. R. (2006). Intellectual role taking: Supporting discussion in heterogeneous elementary science classes. *Theory Into Practice, 45*(1), 47–54.

Hess, D., & Posselt, J. (2002). How high school students experience and learn from the discussion of controversial public issues. *Journal of Curriculum and Supervision, 17*(4), 283–314.

Kuhn, D. (2015). Thinking together and alone. *Educational Researcher, 44*(1), 46–53.

Parker, W. C. (2001). Classroom discussion: Models for leading seminars and deliberations. *Social Education, 65*(2), 111–115.

Parker, W. C. (2003). *Teaching democracy: Unity and diversity in public life*. Teachers College Press.

Parker, W. C. (2005). Teaching against idiocy. *Phi Delta Kappan, 86*(5), 344–351.

Parker, W. C. (2006). Talk isn't cheap: Practicing deliberation in school. *Social Studies and the Young Learner, 19*(1), 12–15.

Parker, W. C. (2010). Listening to strangers: Classroom discussion in democratic education. *Teachers College Record, 112*(11), 2815–2832.

Parker, W. C., & Hess, D. (2001). Teaching with and for discussion. *Teaching and Teacher Education, 17,* 273–289. https://doi.org/http://dx.doi.org/10.1016/S0742-051X(00)00057-3

Parker, W. C., & Zumeta, W. M. (1999). Toward an aristocracy of everyone: Policy study in the high school curriculum. *Theory and Research in Social Education, 27*(1), 9–44.

Pew Research Center. (2017). *The partisan divide on political values grows even wider.* https://www.pewresearch.org/politics/2017/10/05/the-partisan-divide-on -political-values-grows-even-wider/

Putnam, R. D. (2000). *Bowling alone: The collapse and revival of American community.* Simon & Schuster.

Raphael, T. E., & McMahon, S. I. (1994). Book club: An alternative framework for reading instruction. *The Reading Teacher, 48*(2), 102–116.

Reddy, M., Jacobs, P., McCrohon, C., & Herrenkohl, L. R. (1998). *Creating scientific communities in the elementary classroom.* Heinemann.

Strong, M. (1997). *The habit of thought: From Socratic seminars to Socratic practice.* New View.

Voss, J. F., Greene, T. R., Post, T. A., & Penner, B. C. (1983). Problem-solving skills in the social sciences. In G. H. Bower (Ed.), *The psychology of learning and motivation: Advances in research and theory* (Vol. 17, pp. 165–213). Academic Press.

Voss, J. F., & Post, T. A. (1988). On the solving of ill-structured problems. In M. T. H. Chi, R. Glaser, & M. J. Farr (Eds.), *The nature of expertise* (pp. 261–285). Lawrence Erlbaum Associates.

Wertsch, J. V. (1998). *Mind as action.* Oxford University Press.

Westheimer, J. (2015). *What kind of citizen? Educating for our children for the common good.* Teachers College Press.

Wilen, W. W. (Ed.). (1990). *Teaching and learning through discussion: The theory, research and practice of the discussion method.* Charles C. Thomas.

Zhang, J., & Stahl, K. A. D. (2011). Collaborative reasoning: Language-rich discussions for English learners. *The Reading Teacher, 65*(4), 257–260.

Part II

UNPACKING WELL-KNOWN DISCUSSION TECHNIQUES IN THE SOCIAL STUDIES

CHAPTER 4

Socratic Seminar

Learning With and From Each Other
While Interpreting Complex Text

Jada Kohlmeier

"Why hasn't anyone ever taught us this before?" "I wish we would have talked about this long before now." "I feel more motivated to say this now that I understand it more." These are the sentiments of inspiration, surprise, and frustration expressed by six groups of seniors after participating in Socratic seminars on the Pledge of Allegiance in their U.S. government courses. All six classes included mostly Black and White students, evenly divided male and female and race. They were surprised at how little they understood the words and ideas present in the pledge. They were frustrated that they had never been asked to consider, research, analyze or even understand the concepts, values, and facts inherent in the pledge. They were surprised to hear the diverse interpretations of their classmates about what the pledge meant to each of them, why some of them refused to say it, why some of them said it without thinking, and why some of them felt the language was inadequate and should be changed. The previous chapter provided advice on using text to support discussion, and Socratic seminar is a collaborative text interpretation format that generates sharing different ideas, questions, and insights about a complex text. This chapter will explain the purpose, format, and norms of Socratic seminar and highlight evidence from discussions around the U.S. Pledge of Allegiance.

Scholars have been encouraging teachers to utilize the discussion strategy Socratic seminar for over 2 decades (e.g., Parker, 2001). My own studies have found that this discussion strategy is a powerful way to engage students in historical, democratic, and ethical reasoning (e.g., Kohlmeier, 2006; Kohlmeier & Saye, 2014a; Kohlmeier & Saye, 2014b; Kohlmeier & Saye, 2019). The purpose of a Socratic seminar is to engage students in a collective effort to deepen the group's understanding of a complex text. A text can be a reading, poem, piece of art, song, movie, novel, or any form of expression that is rich for a wide variety of interpretations. A seminar differs from a deliberation in that the core purpose is not to persuade or decide but to expand the group's understanding of the ideas in the text. The teacher's role is to facilitate a cooperative effort among a class of students in interpreting the text the group has read/watched/experienced in advance. The teacher should prepare an opening question that requires participants to interpret the text and be authentically puzzling to everyone. The teacher should also prepare additional sub-questions they anticipate will deepen the exploration of the text and to redirect the conversation if the group strays too far from the task of interpreting the text. The norms of a Socratic seminar are simple but important. First, everyone, including the teacher, sits in a circle. Second, no one raises hands. These norms encourage the participants to speak directly to each other and not to the teacher. Third, participants are encouraged to refer to the text or point to a passage in the text to support their interpretation. Printing line numbers down the left margin of a written text makes for easy reference. Fourth, participants should refer to each other by name. It is helpful to have students make and decorate name tents to display on the front of their desks.

When I approached four U.S. government teachers about participating in a 2-year professional development project focused on leading discussions, all were excited about engaging their students in a seminar on the Pledge of Allegiance in their course. They felt this text would be an optimal choice for analysis early in the course because it was short and familiar to everyone but deep in ideas. The teachers believed the conversation would allow them to get to know the lived experiences of their students, for the students to hear aspects of each other's stories, and would introduce the students to the numerous democratic concepts and values they would be exploring throughout the course. The teachers spent the first several days of their courses engaged in ice-breaker activities to create a sense of community and comfort among the students, but this seminar was the first formal class conversation grounded in the core principles of the course. The teachers, a political science professor, and I (teacher educator) spent a week in the summer developing three discussions on three key texts, with the Pledge of Allegiance being the first. In this chapter, I will share the teaching materials and instructional decisions of the teachers and describe how the students responded to the opportunity to interpret the Pledge of Allegiance with their peers as they prepared to deliberate on whether students should be required to recite the pledge in schools.

UNIT AND LESSON DESIGN

The collaborative team built a unit based on an ethical question of fairness and justice (Saye & Brush, 2004; Saye & SSIRC, 2014). The unit was formed on a persistent and topic-specific central question:

Persistent issue: What role should schools play in molding patriotic citizens?

Central question: Should students be required to say the Pledge of Allegiance?

The unit would conclude with students becoming "supreme court" justices hearing a case that was working its way through the federal courts at the time, *Frazier v. Winn*. In the culminating assessment for the unit, students would meet in groups of five and become a mini supreme court under the premise that the case was being appealed to the Supreme Court. The students made a final ruling on whether students should have to have parental permission to opt out of reciting the pledge. The lessons described took three, 90-minute class periods (Appendix A).

In order to prepare for this final assessment, the teacher developed an opener activity in which they asked students to first journal about and then share their feelings on whether students should be required to say the pledge. The discussion centered on the factual, definitional, and value questions inherent in this issue. The teachers were aware that most of the comments would be speculative and ill-informed at this stage. The discussion was intended to engage students in the topic and provide the teachers a window into the lived experiences of their students and insights into misconceptions and/or traumatic incidents they had experienced surrounding issues of patriotic displays and citizenship. Some factual questions they explored were the current practices in their schools surrounding the recitation of the pledge, what students' rights were in terms of refusal or compliance, and what the text of the pledge says. Definitional concepts they discussed included patriotism, rights, freedom, liberty, justice, and republic. Students began to realize they didn't know as much as they thought they did about the law surrounding the pledge, what their rights were, or what the words meant. Teachers also engaged the students in talking about the pros and cons of schools promoting patriotic acts and teaching patriotism. Students were divided on whether this ritual is a healthy exercise in a democracy.

After the opening discussion, which lasted roughly 45 minutes, the students were given a scaffold, which would be their "ticket" into the Socratic seminar in the subsequent class period (Appendix B). This scaffold listed the text of the Pledge of Allegiance at the top and then had spaces for the students to write what words and phrases meant to them. On the back it also included information about the origins of the pledge and its original language. Students submitted this "ticket" to the teacher before leaving class, giving the teacher time to read the comments for misconceptions, stories of hurt or alienation, strong opinions, or other insights into how to prepare to facilitate the seminar the next day.

The second, 90-minute class period featured the Socratic seminar (Parker, 2001) in which students would sit in a circle and collectively interpret the Pledge of Allegiance. The teacher team generated a list of questions to guide their facilitation (Appendix C), but the main questions came from Parker's chapter (2007):

- When you say the pledge, to what are you pledging?
- How do you feel about the phrase "under God" being in the pledge?
- Do you feel the phrase "liberty and justice for all" is descriptive or aspirational?

The seminar conversation lasted about 70 minutes. It began after the teachers reminded the students of the norms of the seminar and reviewed positive behaviors in a class discussion. The students had their "ticket" on their desk. To help students track the conversation, the teachers made a PowerPoint slide to display the three main questions. They also provided, or asked a student to provide, a summary of key ideas that had been shared at various points before moving to the next question. Some teachers had students pause for a few minutes after each of the three questions for quiet written reflection. They encouraged students to write thoughts they were having about a point someone made, language in the text they would like to discuss, or a question they would like to raise. This encouraged more participation from a wider range of students.

STUDENT RESPONSES TO THE PLEDGE

In this section, I will describe the procedures for a seminar and provide sample dialogue from the six seminars on the pledge I observed to "paint a picture" of how to facilitate a seminar with students. The facilitator should open the seminar with the focus question, which should require analysis of the text to answer and invite multiple points of view.

To What Are You Pledging?

The teachers began the conversation by asking students to recite the pledge at the top of their paper (or by memory). Some classes chose to stand, others did not, but they began by saying the familiar words and phrases. Then the teachers asked, "When you say this pledge, to what are you pledging?" In all four classes, this opened a fast-moving conversation with a lot of students sharing phrases like *the flag, the Constitution, the nation, the President.* The teachers then needed to ask follow-up questions to probe some of these ideas. Some of the students (both Black and White) spoke about serving in the Jr. ROTC and the respect they feel for the flag because it connects to military service and sacrifice. Other students said they were pledging to the president, which generated some challenge from other students. In each class, there were always a small number of students, sometimes Black but also often White, who voiced comments that shared criticisms of the Constitution and democracy and even disengagement because the Constitution was written by slave holders. All four teachers posed questions that asked students to connect their feelings about the pledge to the grammar and structure of the text. The opening question brought to the surface many feelings, emotions, and understandings about the government, the Constitution, and military and social issues such as racial inequality and injustice. It became evident very quickly which students felt connected to political institutions and to the government and which were indifferent, resistant to, or alienated by the government. Many shared direct connections with members of the military, and many shared stories of how they felt betrayed and ignored by past and current representatives in government positions. One teacher, Janice, allowed students to speak to each other but asked a few questions meant to probe their feelings about patriotism and symbolic language in the text. After Janice asked if you could be patriotic and refuse to say the pledge, students shared a wide range of views related to free speech and the flag and their view that the pledge stands for free speech. Some students were upset by people not wanting to recite the pledge because they felt it offended members of the military, including their family members or themselves serving in Jr. ROTC. Other students shared reasons they did not want to stand for the pledge, and many students defended their classmates' views and decisions. Some of the reasons students did not want to say the pledge had to do with the phrase, "under God," while others shared reasons of feeling excluded from the republic and democracy.

Under God

The two-word phrase *under God* generated spirited conversation and diverse views on the underlying values of the nation, diversity versus unity, and what people actually mean when they say, "under God." After the teacher explained that Francis Bellamy had not wanted any reference to a supreme being in the original pledge because he felt it would be divisive and that the phrase was added in the 1950s to distinguish the United States from the officially atheistic communists, the teachers asked students how they felt about the phrase being included in the pledge and whether it should be removed.

In all six seminars, the first comments were usually made by students providing reasons to keep the phrase. Most argued the phrase should remain because it reminded citizens and elected officials to be humble because God was "in charge" or "in control." Some felt that it was important to remind citizens that elected officials, citizens, and laws should reflect Christian values because "we were founded as a Christian nation." Every teacher would eventually pose a version of the question "The author of the pledge felt that including a reference to a supreme being would divide us, not unite us. His intent of the pledge was to have something all Americans could say without reservation. Are we violating the intention of the pledge if some people don't believe in a god or in a Christian god?" This would usually generate more divergent views and comments. Some of those included ideas that America was founded by people seeking religious freedom, protecting religious minorities, welcoming immigrants from all over the world, and the fact that if the pledge was intended to unify us, then we should take out an inherently divisive phrase that was added later. The majority of students supported keeping the phrase because they felt it bound Americans together as a nation, but the teachers generated a wide range of views on this topic by asking about the original intent of the author and whether the phrase was helpful or harmful. The teachers also began to ask students how they define nation and republic, which generated interesting conversation.

Nation and Republic

Some teachers spent more time on this than others, but Janice's class spent quite a bit of time reflecting on how they defined "nation," which led to a long discussion about a "republic." When the students were discussing the concept of nation, Janice asked questions about whether we could be considered a nation and still disagree with each other or hold different views. The students explored the inherent tension of living in a liberal democracy dedicated to protecting individual liberties and minority rights for a diverse population while at the same time promoting a unifying set of beliefs that knit us together as a nation. One student even pointed to the "under God" discussion in the seminar as an example, highlighting that everyone valued religious freedom, but that some people meant they should keep "under God" in the pledge and others felt it should be removed. Janice asked if a nation meant you could complain about the government or criticize it, and the vast majority of students argued that criticizing the government was a fundamental right in a democratic nation, which led them to talking about a republic.

The students articulated many critical aspects of a republic, but also expressed some misconceptions that would require further examination in the course. Two teachers asked questions related to the grammatical structure of the pledge, which led their students to recognize that they were pledging allegiance to a republic and that they had never really thought as much about the republic as they had about the flag. Most students could talk in general terms about separation of powers and checks and balances, but often they spoke favorably about a strong president and how we are pledging to the president. Because these seminars were held during the first week of the courses, many students had simplistic conceptions and even misconceptions of a republic, which is a useful insight for the teachers in planning for what critical concepts and principles need to be addressed in their course.

Descriptive versus Aspirational?

The teachers asked students to explain what they thought about when they pledged "with liberty and justice for all" and got a wide variety of answers. Students listed freedoms such as speech, religion, assembly, bear arms, remain silent, and press. They said things like "the freedom to live your own life"; "being proud of what you want to do and being able to do it"; "not being forced to something you don't want to do"; and "go the way you want to." They defined justice in phrases such as "equal treatment for everyone"; "not being put in jail without a trial"; "innocent until proven guilty"; "having the police treat everyone equally"; and "getting the punishment you deserve—not more and not less." The teachers then asked the students if they felt this phrase described America as it is now or as it should be. This question seemed to create a moment of pause in the conversation and even a bit of uncomfortable silence. Unfortunately, often this question came too late in the class period to warrant the deep conversation it deserved. The teachers wished they had spent less time on the nation/republic discussion to leave more time for this powerful question, since the tone often shifted from defending the United States and the pledge to a more careful analysis of how the United States is not living up to its ideals. Students cited examples of racial minorities being treated differently by police and the courts, LGBTQ members being discriminated against, racial or gender minorities being denied jobs or educational opportunities, and economic inequality, and some felt strongly that only the rich and powerful really have much voice in our republic. The students articulated more understanding and consideration for people who couldn't say the pledge because our society doesn't live up to its ideals. They also expressed a desire to keep pushing our society to work toward more liberty and justice for all Americans.

STUDENT REACTIONS TO ANALYZING THE TEXT OF THE PLEDGE

At the end of a Socratic seminar, it is important to have the participants go around the circle and share their experiences during the seminar. The debriefing of the seminar is intended to encourage student ownership. Students often suggest areas for improvement for closer listening, asking more follow-up questions, encouraging wider participation, and even suggestions for different questions or texts. In the case presented, these seminars were the first discussion of the course for these teachers and students. The students consistently shared appreciation of the opportunity to analyze and reflect with their peers on the meaning of the pledge, especially since they are asked to say it every day/week for their school career. Students praised the respectful and welcoming atmosphere of the seminar and said things like, "I like this because the other opinions affect the way you think"; "They said something I never would have thought of and I thought it was really good"; and "I liked that we could throw an opinion out there and we could agree or disagree with people. I liked that you [teacher] didn't restrict what we could or couldn't say." One student commented on why the seminar was a powerful way for her to learn when she said, "I like this method of learning better than you writing on the board because I wouldn't remember that later, but I'll remember this longer."

This final student comment summarizes the powerful learning that can happen in a Socratic seminar where students build their knowledge through the cooperative interpretation of a complex text. Many students expanded their view of how people think about the pledge and also to what extent our society is living up to its ideals. Many students expressed frustration that they had been saying the Pledge of Allegiance since kindergarten and had never been asked to think about the history of its creation, the meaning behind the words, or whether they should be required to say it in school. The subsequent lesson would ask the students to begin examining arguments for and against requiring parental permission for students to refuse to say the Pledge of Allegiance in school.

CULMINATING ACTIVITY

Once the students had interpreted the pledge with their classmates, they were ready to turn to the policy question, "Should students be required to have parental permission to refuse to say the pledge?" The teacher introduced this question after the grabber on the first lesson and then re-stated it to begin this lesson. They put the students into pairs and gave the students a scaffold with information on two Supreme Court cases from the 1940s about whether students should be required to say the pledge in schools (Appendix D). Jehovah's Witness students in the 1940s were objecting to saying the pledge in schools on religious grounds. In 1940, the Supreme Court ruled the state could compel a student to say the pledge (*Minersville School District v. Gobitis*, 1940). However, after watching the rise of fascism spread across Europe, the Supreme Court reversed itself in the landmark case *West Virginia State Board of Education v. Barnette* (1943) in which it said democratic societies should not compel citizens to express views related to politics, religion, or belief. Despite this ruling, schools and teachers have continued to compel students to recite the pledge.

After students worked through the two historic cases in pairs, they were put into groups of five to become small "supreme courts" in which they would rule on a case that has never come to the Supreme Court but was ruled on by the 11th Circuit Court of Appeals in 2009, *Frazier v. Winn*. Following the *Barnette* decision, Florida passed a law in 1943 requiring students to recite the pledge unless they had parental permission to refuse. Even with permission not to recite the pledge, the students still had to stand for it. In 2008 Frazier refused to stand to recite the pledge or get his parents' permission, citing both violated his First Amendment freedom of speech. In *Frazier v. Alexandre*, in 2008, the Court ruled that Frazier did not have to stand for the pledge, but he did have to have his parents' permission. Frazier sued again regarding the necessity of having his parent permission. This became *Frazer v. Winn*, the case the students would decide. The students were given a scaffold (Appendix E) to guide their deliberation through the arguments on both sides of the case and make a ruling. After they revealed their rulings to the rest of the class, the teacher revealed that the circuit court had ruled parental permission was constitutional but requiring students to stand was unconstitutional. The teacher then allowed the students to discuss their reactions to that decision as a class.

CONCLUSION

It is clear from our research that having students interpret the Pledge of Allegiance in a Socratic seminar was a powerful example of students socially constructing a broader and deeper understanding of the democratic concepts and values inherent in our liberal democracy. These same students analyzed two other documents in two additional units, Martin Luther King, Jr.'s "Letter from a Birmingham Jail" and the Supreme Court case *Texas v. Johnson* (1989) (which upheld flag burning as protected speech (Kohlmeier & Saye, 2014a; Kohlmeier & Saye, 2014b; Kohlmeier & Saye, 2019). In all cases, we found the Socratic seminars provided a rich opportunity for students to learn the factual, conceptual, and ethical components of key democratic principles such as the rule of law, just laws, liberty, general welfare, and patriotism from the text and from their classmates. We found similar results using seminars to facilitate student analysis of historical documents of all types.

In an increasingly polarized political climate, having students work together to interpret complex texts provides powerful opportunities for students to learn from and with each other about democratic principles, values, and concepts. Students consistently report enjoying seminars because they learn from and about their peers. Members of our democratic society need more practice with deep analysis of complex ideas and values in a cooperative, conversational format. This discussion technique works well because the norms of sitting in a circle, collectively working to listen carefully and empathize with various interpretations of a complex text, promotes the types of civil discourse necessary for a liberal democracy to function.

REFERENCES

Frazier v. Alexandre, 555 F. 3d 1292 (Court of Appeals, 11th Circuit 2008). https://
law.justia.com/cases/federal/appellate-courts/ca11/06-14462/200614462
-2011-02-28.html

Frazier v. Winn, 535 F. 3d 1279 (Court of Appeals, 11th Circuit 2008)

Kohlmeier, J. (2006). Couldn't she just leave? The relationship between consistently
using class discussions and the development of historical empathy in a 9th grade
world history course. *Theory and Research in Social Education, 34*(1), 34–57.

Kohlmeier, J., & Saye, J. W. (2014a). Ethical reasoning of U.S. high school seniors
exploring just v. unjust laws. *Theory and Research in Social Education, 42*(4),
548–578. https://doi.org/10.1080/00933104.2014.966218

Kohlmeier, J., & Saye, J. W. (2014b). Ethical reasoning of high school seniors exploring issues of free speech. *Social Studies Research and Practice, 9*(2), 33–47.

Kohlmeier, J., & Saye, J. W. (2019). Examining the relationship between teachers' discussion facilitation and their students' reasoning. *Theory and Research in Social
Education, 47*(2), 176–204. https://doi.org/10.1080/00933104.2018.1486765

Minersville School Dist. v. Gobitis, 310 US 586 (Supreme Court 1940)

Parker, W. C. (2001). Teaching teachers to lead discussion: Democratic education in
content and method. In J. J. Patrick & R. S. Leming (Eds.), *Principles and practices of democracy in the education of social studies teachers: Civic learning in
teacher education* (Vol. 1; pp. 111–133). ERIC Clearing house for Social Studies
Social Science, Education.

Parker, W. C. (2007). Pledging allegiance. In J. Westheimer (Ed.), *Pledging allegiance:
The politics of patriotism in American's schools* (pp. 71–72). Teachers College Press.

Saye, J. W., & Brush, T. (2004). Promoting civic competence through problem-based
history learning experiments. In G. E. Hamot, J. J. Patrick, & R. S. Leming
(Eds.), *Civic learning in teacher education: International perspectives on education for democracy in the preparation of teachers* (Vol. 3; pp. 123–145). Social
Study Development Center, University of Indiana.

Saye, J. W., & SSIRC. (2014). Achieving authentic pedagogy: Plan units, not lessons.
Social Education, 78(1), 33–37.

Texas v. Johnson, 491 US 397 (Supreme Court 1989). https://www.oyez.org
/cases/1988/88-155

West Virginia State Board of Education v. Barnette, 319 US 642 (Supreme Court
1943). https://www.oyez.org/cases/1940-1955/319us624

CHAPTER 5

Structured Academic Controversy
What It Can Be

Walter C. Parker

Language is one of the most potent resources each of us has for achieving our own political empowerment.

—Danielle Allen

In this chapter,[1] I offer an appreciation of the instructional strategy called structured academic controversy (SAC) and detail the revisions I have made to it. I have taught with it, using it in my own teaching. I have taught for it, teaching novice and experienced teachers to use it in their teaching. And I have studied it, inquiring into its purposes, principles, and procedures. I am delighted by the depth of thinking it often provokes and reassured by the cooperation it brings about. I am impressed by the linguistic work it gets done and buoyed by its utility. I appreciate its relative ease of implementation, even for novice teachers; its suitability to rigorous curriculum goals; and its responsiveness to the demands placed on education in a liberal democracy, especially its promotion of knowledge growth, reasoning with evidence, respect, and civil discourse. Here, I review SAC's development as a cooperative learning strategy and then detail the modifications I have made to sharpen its effect. These address three outcomes: content selection for deeper learning, literacy development, and cultivating student voice. In my judgment, they are important additions to the model, and they work in concert to prepare students to take their place on the public stage.

The revised SAC aims to be effective socially, academically, and civically. In a SAC, students develop knowledge while learning to use language and information to engage with others on controversies of fact, definition, and values. To its credit, SAC goes beyond mere *exposure* to multiple views on these controversies to having students actually grapple with these views. This is because in SAC participants must role-play, exchange views, and determine if what others are saying requires them to adjust their own beliefs.

The chapter is informed by a 10-year research-and-development study of the high school government course[2] as well as my experience teaching SAC to secondary school and college students, and their teachers, for over 30 years. My graduate students across these years have been collaborators. As teaching assistants in social studies curriculum and instruction courses at the University of Washington and as copresenters at inservice workshops and academic conferences, they have fueled my thinking about SAC—its strengths and weaknesses, its nooks and crannies.[3] Still, the conclusions presented here are my own.

COOPERATIVE LEARNING AND SAC

Before we can make sense of the revisions, let us look at traditional SAC's legacy and structure. SAC was developed by two scholars of cooperative learning, David Johnson and Roger Johnson (1979, 1985, 1988). SAC has elements in common with other types of cooperative learning, but it is unique, too. Let's begin with the broader concept.

As detailed earlier in this volume, cooperative learning became a popular instructional strategy in the 1980s when a disparate group of educational psychologists and sociologists turned their attention to learning in small groups or teams. Prominent among them in addition to the Johnsons were Elliot Aronson (1978), Robert Slavin (1985), Yael Sharan and Shlomo Sharan (1976), and Elizabeth Cohen (1986). Together, they found positive outcomes: increased school attendance and motivation to learn, and greater academic and social learning by a wider range of students.

Common elements across the several types of cooperative learning are positive interdependence, individual accountability, face-to-face interaction, and teacher-assigned heterogeneous learning groups. The first of these speaks to the need for a group-worthy task. The task *requires* the group if the work is going to get done. The goal is to accomplish the task by way of everyone doing their job and encouraging others to do theirs. The second prohibits group grades. Individuals are to be held accountable for doing their part and learning. If formal assessments are to be done, they are for individual learning. However, group recognition and rewards are common alongside individual accountability, especially when competition between groups is included. Students encourage one another in the group to succeed so that the group can earn whatever group rewards are available. The third common element is captured by Cohen's (1986) observation that the process of group interaction is "enormously interesting" (p. 3) to young people. There's something about the group dynamic that motivates students to learn to cooperate successfully and achieve the group's goal. They become a team. Further, "students who usually do anything but what they are asked to do become actively involved with their work and are held there by the action of the group. . . . Face-to-face interaction with other group members demands a response or, at least, attentive behavior" (p. 3).

The fourth similarity across types of cooperative learning concerns equity pedagogy and group composition: Teachers aim to achieve in each small group the greatest heterogeneity possible given the student population at hand. Teachers achieve this mix in small groups of two to five, purposefully mixing whatever student differences are at hand—social status, academic ability, attendance record, interpersonal skill, gender, race, religion, learning challenge, talent, personality, skill set, first language, and so forth. In this way, small groups are as heterogeneous as the whole class. Ability grouping, along with other segregating schemes, is rare because it minimizes rather than maximizes the mix, and "there is no evidence that putting low-achieving students into a homogeneous ability group is effective" (Cohen, 1986, p. 22). Further, the teacher emphasizes to students that cooperative groupwork is work, not play. Friends are not allowed to choose one another for small group work—friends tend to play rather than work. Random assignment may be used to assign students to small groups in a new class where the teacher has little knowledge of students' strengths, social status, identities, and background. Groups can be purposefully mixed once the teacher is more familiar with the individuals in the classroom. Roles can be assigned (e.g., Cohen's group harmonizer, group facilitator, and group timekeeper), and everyone will have a particular part to play.

SAC

SAC shares these attributes with other types of cooperative learning but uniquely joins language to cooperative learning on controversial issues. These controversies can be ethical (issues of right), conceptual (issues of definition), or empirical (issues of fact). The selected controversy is SAC's subject matter, and students play the role of an advocate for one side of the issue.[4]

The entire procedure typically occurs in a single small group of four, divided into two pairs. Consequently, the teacher in a typical classroom is coordinating six or seven SAC groups at once and twice that number of pairs. SAC also centers on the study of texts and other resources (e.g., maps, photos), student–student discussion, role playing, and advocating competing positions on a controversial issue. The controversial issue can be historical or current—from "Should the Parthenon Marbles be returned to Athens?" to "Should our state's law on police use of deadly force be changed?" While these two examples are mainly ethical, controversies that are mainly empirical are common too—from the historical stalwart, "Which side fired the first shots at Lexington Green?" to the current issue "Is mass incarceration of African Americans the new Jim Crow?" And conceptual issues are ubiquitous. Was the American Revolution really a *revolution*? When does a military action become a *genocide*?

SAC is an ambitious classroom practice. The subject matter is rigorous, requiring scaffolds to build the prior knowledge students lack as well as strategies to connect with the funds of knowledge they bring. The pedagogy, too, can be challenging, requiring not only small group management but also supports for reading comprehension and productive face-to-face discussion. Furthermore, teachers must monitor their own convictions and biases, deciding whether to present as controversial an issue on which they have already reached a position (Hess & McAvoy, 2015). Yet, SAC is worth the trouble. It is pertinent to civic learning outcomes and also to disciplinary content and skill objectives (hence "academic" in its moniker). SAC is both a discourse structure and an instructional procedure. Johnson and Johnson's starting point is that when students are put in small groups and asked to interact with other students while they learn, conflicts among their preferences and perspectives are likely. Rather than avoiding such conflict, SAC mobilizes it as a learning opportunity. The Johnsons (2009) write, "Intellectual conflict is not only highly desirable but also an essential instructional tool that energizes student efforts to learn. . . . Ideas in the classroom are inert without the spark of intellectual conflict" (p. 37).

First, the teacher assigns students to mixed teams of four, which are then subdivided into two pairs. Each pair is assigned to a position on the controversy and asked to role-play advocates of that position. Next, each pair is told to prepare a presentation of its position and reasons to the opposite pair. The two partners work alone and together to study the information provided, and then together they plan a brief presentation to the other pair. After this preparation, the pairs take turns making their presentations, and then a general discussion unfolds, each pair still advocating its position and asking the other side for the key facts that support its position. What happens next is crucial: The pairs reverse perspectives. Each pair presents the other's argument to its satisfaction. The point here, of course, is to grasp the facts and logic used by *both* sides. Then comes the final phase of the SAC where the two pairs join together to summarize the best arguments for both points of view, and then to reach a consensus on a position that all can support.[5]

THE REVISED MODEL

I have made three revisions to traditional SAC. Each is an addition. I call the result SAC+. These additions address content selection, reading comprehension, and political autonomy. They are needed because they address problems that arise in the course of a SAC: They help teachers select the most powerful (educative, generative) controversies for study, deepen students' understanding of the selected controversies, and develop students' capacity to make uncoerced (independent) judgments. The third modification emphasizes political autonomy over consensus, as we shall see. Altogether, and this is key, the revisions mobilize schools' unique character as mediating institutions where young people encounter the broader public. According to developmental psychologist Connie Flanagan (2013), schools are "mini-polities" where young people "work out what it means to be a citizen of the larger polity" (p. 229). Schools have the necessary assets for this work, as I have shown elsewhere (Parker, 2005, 2010). Briefly, they have diverse schoolmates (more or less), problems (academic, social, and civic), "strangers" (schoolmates who aren't friends or family[6]), and curriculum and instruction (schools are educative places). For even the youngest students, school is a public place, not to be confused with a home, temple, workplace, or market. "The children I teach," wrote kindergarten teacher Vivian Paley (1992), "are just emerging from life's deep wells of private perspective: babyhood and family. Then, along comes school. It is the first real exposure to the public arena" (p. 21).

Publics come in all sizes and shapes: the classroom and school, the town and nation, the neighborhood, the peer group, the bowling alley, the pub. These are social spaces—beyond the family—where a "we" is deciding what to do about a shared problem. Language is joined with cooperation. This is Habermas's (1984) "communicative action" (p. 1) and Dewey's (1985) "conjoint communicated experience" (p. 93). The essence of discussion, as Bridges (1979) wrote, is "to set alongside one perception of the matter under discussion the several perceptions of other participants, challenging our own view of things with those of others" (p. 50).

1. Content Selection

Despite the challenges, SAC is not too difficult to pull off, even for a beginning teacher. The structured group work is not hard to manage, and it is more or less the same procedure each time. What is difficult is *planning* a SAC, and content selection is at the center of this work. Known also as curriculum decisionmaking, content selection is the practice in education whereby declarative and procedural knowledge are selected for instruction. It entails choosing from a universe of possibilities a small sample of subject matter suitable for teaching and learning in a particular course and context, with students of a particular age, culture, and history. The process is problematic because class time is limited while the subject matter possibilities are vast and the students diverse.

The Johnsons paid scant attention to the matter. Yet, choosing the controversy and the ideas it features is a crucial undertaking for teachers, especially if the SAC is to be a workhorse. Accordingly, this first revision suggests that a SAC should not be marginal to a course's central purposes or done simply to engage students. SACs *are* engaging (the Johnsons' "spark"), but this spark should be mobilized to help students achieve a course's core subject matter.

Two principles can steer this work. One involves identifying a course's most important concepts and skills; the other deepens learning through learning cycles.

Identifying Central Concepts and Skills. While content selection can mean that one topic is selected instead of another (e.g., *migration* over *region* in geography), or one perspective over another (e.g., centering the United States' founding on 1619 rather than 1776), it more subtly refers to a *relationship* among subject matters: Some subject matter is prioritized over others, and instruction is orchestrated for both. As Bruner (1960) said in an earlier era, "To learn (a discipline's) structure, in short, is to learn how things are related" (p. 7). This means that a course's subject matters need to be orchestrated to achieve deeper learning of prioritized material and somewhat superficial learning of needed but peripheral material. In this way, depth and breadth are treated not as opposites but as partners. Let me explain, and to do this I will introduce concept development.

To achieve the vaunted "curriculum of ideas" rather than the pilloried curriculum of "names and dates," concepts need to be the mainspring of a course. Concepts are ideas, and ideas are abstractions that apply to several or many concrete instances (cases, examples). In a conceptual curriculum, the abstract and the concrete work together. To learn a concept is to learn its critical attributes *and* to see how they operate in an array of examples. Examples will differ from one another, but each has the concept's critical attributes along with many facts. There are different kinds of music, each with lots of factual detail, yet they are all music; many kinds of government, but all are governments.

Consider *federalism*, the organizing concept of the U.S. government and, by extension, the high school government course. To learn the concept superficially is to learn its definition, that is, to learn that the concept's name "federalism" refers to (1) a way of organizing a nation, (2) in which power is distributed or shared between national and subnational units of government (states, provinces). In other words, there are numerous ways to organize a nation, and federalism is the one where two or more levels of government have formal authority over the same land and people. Notice how abstract this definition is; no examples yet. To learn this (or any) concept deeply requires multiple examples. *The examples are also part of the curriculum.* Without them, the concept is only a definition to be memorized, an abstraction without legs. A deeper understanding of "federalism" will include, in addition to its definition, knowledge of a diverse set of on-the-ground examples that display the definition in an array of concrete circumstances (federalism in the United States, India, Mexico, etc.).

A course can meaningfully contain only a handful of central concepts because each of them has to be exemplified to be understood. The identification of these concepts and their examples becomes, then, a primary focus for content selection. Only then, to return to SAC, does SAC become meaningful, for SAC can be deployed to teach these examples. Examples of federalism take us quickly to both contemporary and historical policy controversies, from state-by-state marijuana legislation back to the famed Jefferson–Hamilton conflict over the legitimacy of a national bank, and many in between: Obamacare, same-sex marriage, and abortion policy.

Skills, too, need to be selected—reduced in number from all the possibilities and related to the focal concepts. *Deliberation* is the critical thinking skill that SAC teaches along with the broader social skills of cooperation. Skills, like concepts, develop iteratively across multiple trials. To learn to deliberate (to weigh alternatives in discussion with others) requires modeling, practice, and feedback. This takes us to the second principle for content selection.

Deeper Learning Through Looping. Meaningful learning requires that a limited set of powerful ideas and skills is selected for study and that these are studied and applied in multiple examples and scenarios. This emphasis on multiplicity is not a matter of repetition but complexity. Bransford et al. (2000) call it cyclical learning. Bruner (1960) had a similar idea and called it a "spiral" curriculum (p. 52). High school teachers I work with call it "looping." It entails revisiting ideas and skills in different contexts, cyclically, in order to know them differently and comparatively, and therefore deeply. Learning is deepened—made more complex and applicable—thanks to revisiting the same idea or practicing the same skill, but in multiple, novel problem spaces (examples, cases). Each cycle is different. Students see the differences, but they aren't derailed by them because they see the similarities too, which are the critical attributes of the concept.

Returning to our illustration, teachers of the U.S. government course might plan three SAC cycles on federalism. Further, they might select law-related controversies that center on the delicate balance of power between the national government and state governments. In this way, *federalism* would be developed across three examples. Their similarities and differences will deepen students' understanding of the concept's critical attributes; meanwhile, myriad peripheral knowledge will be gleaned from the human and institutional dramas of each case, the branches of government involved, and the relevant clauses from the Constitution. Examples can be selected that are spread across the centuries:

1829. In *McCulloch v. Maryland* the Supreme Court decides that a national bank is legal under the Constitution's "necessary and proper" clause, and that the national government is supreme over the states.

1995. In *United States* v. *Lopez*, set in Texas, the Supreme Court strikes down Congress's Gun-Free School Zone Act of 1990 on the grounds that the federal government violates reserved powers of the states with this legislation.

2005. In *Gonzales v. Raich*, set in California, the Supreme Court decides that, under the Constitution's Commerce Clause, Congress can criminalize the production of cannabis and its use even if states have legalized it.

Teachers likely would re-mix the SAC groups in each cycle—the four-person teams and their constituent pairs—thereby looping the cooperative learning experience, the skill of deliberation, and the peer context for each student's political autonomy moment (more on this in section 3, Student Voice). These learning cycles build transfer of knowledge (application) into the bones of instruction as the concept is applied to one novel scenario after another.

Looping multiple SACs on a perennial controversy, as in this illustration, is not a requirement of SAC pedagogy, but we can see how this kind of course design would contribute to a more complex understanding of the subject matter. Furthermore, perennial issues recur—students will face them in the future. Meanwhile, multiple SACs on unrelated controversies, which are more common, still have the advantage of sharpening students' skill of deliberation, since that (the skill as opposed to the content) is what is looped.

2. Learning From Text

We turn now to literacy development and zero in on reading comprehension. There are two reasons to do this. First, a SAC is a language- and text-dependent learning activity. A SAC cannot be pulled off successfully without students completing its reading tasks with decent comprehension. Middle and high school teachers know that many reading assignments are given but fewer are completed, and fewer still are comprehended. Without comprehension, what we get in SAC is, at best, naïve opinion formation. Second, reading comprehension is not easy for adolescents—including students admitted to advanced courses (Parker et al., 2018). We know that adolescents generally are not gaining adequate levels of literacy skill, and this directly impinges on SAC. Greenleaf and Valencia (2017) summarize the stark reality: "Few students reach literacy levels that enable them to develop interpretations, think critically about texts, make evidence-based arguments, or assemble information from multiple texts into a coherent understanding of a topic" (p. 235). Few adolescents can do it, yet it is precisely what SAC requires.

Many secondary school teachers support their students' reading, actually requiring it and bringing it to the center of instruction. What this second addition does is build this support into the structure of SAC rather than leaving it to chance. At stake is access to the learning outcomes of a SAC—its academic, social, and civic goals. SAC requires the reading *and* comprehension of informational texts so that students' opinion formation is flush with facts—juicy facts about the historical context of the controversy, the participants and their perspectives, the alternatives being considered, the interest groups behind these alternatives, and so forth. This addition to SAC attends both to text selection and comprehension.

Text Selection and Modification. A SAC is a deliberation—this is its central skill. This means that teachers must select texts that present two sides of the selected controversy. These are the positions on the controversy that students will read and discuss within the pair, and present to the other pair, and then weigh as they form their own opinions on the matter. Background information on the controversy is also needed. This is typically presented in a third text that both pairs read first. Often, it is a section from the course textbook or a story from a reputable news source. Or teachers can present it orally or by other means. Students do need background information on the controversy in order to make sense of the position (the "side") they have been asked to present.

Before selecting this background text or the texts presenting the two sides, teachers need first to hone the SAC question, for this focuses the reading activity: Students read to answer this question. Returning to *federalism* and the second SAC example, the court case about guns in schools, a teacher might frame the controversy like this: "Is the 1990 Gun-Free School Zones Act, forbidding individuals from knowingly carrying a gun in a school zone, unconstitutional because it exceeds the power of Congress to legislate under the Commerce Clause?" (Oyez, 1995). But a simpler question could focus more tightly on the two levels of government: "Does the national government have the power to regulate school gun policies in the state of Texas?"

Once the question is honed, texts can be selected. For Supreme Court cases, the two sides are likely to be abridged versions of the decision and the dissent. Streetlaw.org and Landmarkcases.org are deservedly popular sources for such adaptations. But most SACs are not dealing with controversies that come before the highest court in the land, and so texts must be found elsewhere. Consider these four SAC controversies:

- Was Lincoln a racist?
- Why did the United States drop the atomic bombs on Japan?
- Should our state's law governing police use of lethal force be changed?
- Should human consumption of Chinook salmon be outlawed, reserving the fish for Orca whales who otherwise face starvation?

The first two are historical, and abridged texts for them are freely available from the Stanford History Education Group (SHEG, 2020) at sheg .stanford.edu. For many historical controversies, however, a well-chosen section from the course textbook may have to suffice for the background information because it is readily available; meanwhile, the alternative positions will come from primary and secondary texts. The latter two controversies refer to current events—one across the nation and one specific to the Pacific Northwest. The needed texts for the current controversies will be found in various media—alternative positions in editorials, op-eds, blogs, and interest group websites; background information in news reports.

Text selection is complicated by the need to modify texts so that struggling readers, along with their more accomplished classmates, actually attempt the reading and then comprehend it. Organizations like Streetlaw and SHEG often do the modifying, saving teachers the trouble. One of their most important adaptations is to shorten the text to a reasonable length, and then surround the print on a page with calming white space. This builds compliance (students will be more likely to do the reading) and comprehension too. A reading specialist at the first school where I taught called it "reducing" the text. "If you want them to read it closely, reduce it" was her gentle command. Whether the course textbook or a primary document, reduction of the amount of print and simplification of the prose will be needed. Wineburg and Martin (2009) write

> The real question for teachers is not whether to use or not to use primary sources. The crisis in adolescent literacy is too grave and the stakes too high for such neat choices. Rather, the question for teachers must be: How can I adapt primary sources so that all students benefit? (p. 212)

To summarize, when we select texts for SAC, we align them to one or more of the course's central concepts. In this way, we get the SAC to do the basic work of the course, serving its main learning goals. Second, we frame a pertinent SAC question. It presents the controversy as an open question, and it focuses the reading and group work plus the follow-up activities (writing, oral presentations). Third we choose a text for each of the two positions—one for each pair—and, typically, we choose also a third, impartial text that is read by both pairs and gives needed background information. Fourth, we modify the texts as needed to increase the likelihood that struggling as well as proficient students will read and comprehend them. Overall, the point is to use texts to teach students about the controversy and then to elicit students' own positions on the controversy. All this matters because middle and high school students have surprisingly few opportunities and little support to *use texts for purposeful learning in the subject areas* (Greenleaf & Valencia, 2017). Happily, SAC is a near-ideal activity for it: The purpose for reading is clear, the amount of text is limited, and the information in the text is needed for the tasks that follow—the pair presentations, the discussion, and students' decision about how to decide the controversy.

Comprehension. For some, text selection is the essence of content selection, but experienced teachers of middle and high school students know that their students' reading comprehension must be supported explicitly. It cannot be assumed that students will do the assigned reading, let alone comprehend it. Fortunately, SAC paves the way for teachers to scaffold reading comprehension because key supports are built into SAC's structure. Once teachers enter the structure, they find themselves engaging in three practices that facilitate better comprehension. These three distill a good deal of reading research:

1. Before reading begins, teacher provides a purpose for reading the selected text.
2. Teacher specifies ways of interacting with the text during reading.
3. Teacher makes clear how the information taken from the text will be used after reading.

The needed support occurs in three phases. The crucial *before*-reading support occurs when teachers present an unambiguous statement as to why students need to read the text: "Read this to learn the side of the controversy you will present to the other pair and the arguments you and your partner will make." *During* reading, the teacher supports comprehension by having students work with their partner to mark up the text, talk about its position, facts, and arguments, and anticipate the arguments the opposing pair will make. This is similar to the annotation strategies students may learn, but it is active and conversational rather than passive and silent. *After* reading, the partners plan their presentation, sequencing and prioritizing the points they will make and dividing the speaking time. Then, they proceed to the presentations and the reversal of perspectives, and then the pairs join together to evaluate the arguments. This takes us to the third revision.

3. Student Voice—Political Autonomy

Danielle Allen (2014) focuses on the role of language in political maturation, calling it "one of the most potent resources each of us has for achieving our own political empowerment" (p. 21):

> When we think about how to achieve political equality, we have to attend to things like voting rights and the right to hold office. We have to foster economic opportunity and understand when excessive material inequality undermines broad democratic political participation. But we also have to cultivate the capacity of citizens to use language effectively enough to influence the choices

we make together. The achievement of political equality requires, among other things, the empowerment of human beings as language-using creatures.

Language development was explicitly the concern of the second revision. The third revision goes further, using language to express one's own claims and preferences. This revision promotes political autonomy, which is the capacity to make an uncoerced decision. This is required if students are to take their place on the public stage, giving voice to their own thinking about public affairs.

But this is a debatable revision. Educators argue, as they should, about whether in a liberal democracy it is more important to teach the young to make independent decisions or to work with others to reach decisions acceptable to all (consensus and compromise). Liberal democracies[7] value both, but in SAC+ I emphasize the cultivation of students' autonomy. The Johnsons, recall, opted for consensus. The main reason for my decision is that, especially in middle and high school classrooms, which is to say especially with teens, responsible individuation from peers and parents is a developmental imperative. Adolescents need opportunities to clarify their own values and take responsibility for their own convictions, not rejecting peers or family but growing their own wings, finding their own voice.[8] Language is essential—articulating one's own thinking and listening to others' thinking. As Flanagan (2013) shows in *Teenage Citizens*, this is the critical period of life when political ideas are born. Nurturing independent judgement during this period will embolden adolescents to follow neither the crowd nor the demagogue, but to think for themselves.

Consequently, this revision adds another step to the SAC procedure, and it skips over the consensus prompt that ends the Johnsons' model (see Figure 5.1).

Figure 5.1. SAC+ Model

1. Students are assigned to teams.
2. Teams are divided into pairs, and each pair is assigned a position and directed to study their text(s) in order to prepare a presentation on the pair's position, reasons, and supporting facts.
3. Pairs study their text(s) and prepare a presentation. Comprehension is not assumed but encouraged and facilitated by the teacher.
4. Pairs present to one another, listening carefully to the arguments given.
5. Pairs reverse perspectives, feeding back what they have heard to the satisfaction of the other pair.
6. Discussion still in roles: The two pairs join together to summarize the best arguments for both points of view.
7. Genuine discussion. Students are invited to drop the assigned positions and see if the team can reach a decision on the question or, if not, clarify the points of disagreement. Each student clarifies and expresses their own position and argument.

In SAC+, students are quickly led into the issue's contested space. This occurs at steps 1 and 2. Before they have studied the controversy, they are placed in a team and divided into pairs representing competing positions on the issue. They are told they will be presenting their position and argument to the other pair, and then are given time to study the issue and prepare an argument. This enacts what I call the "engagement first" principle (Parker et al., 2018): Steps 1 and 2 engage students and create a need to know the background of the controversy and the position-specific information and reasoning that they will read at step 3. There is a kind of productive anxiety (Cohen's "the action of the group"). During the paired presentations and what follows, steps 4–6, students are responsible for articulating and listening to one another's reasons. Then comes the final step where students are given the opportunity to drop the position to which they were assigned. At this point, students search for their "own" position and reasons. They decide whether to stick to the assigned position they had been presenting and defending or abandon it in favor of the one argued by the opposing pair, or a hybrid or something altogether different. They may have developed some investment in the assigned position by now (this is common); or, if they had a pre-SAC position on the issue, they may seize the opportunity to assert it now if they still favor it. Either way, students might switch from a defensive stance (in role) to an inquisitive one (free of role). They might become curious about what position to adopt as their own now that they know something about the controversy, enough to be a reasonably informed participant in that space—a legitimate player. This is an accomplishment. With the pairs now having studied the texts, presented, and listened to one another, the discussion can be an intelligent one, and individuals' opinion formation can take off from there. "Do we need to agree?" someone asks, just to be sure. "No, you don't," is the reply.

The prompt "Feel free to drop your assigned position. What do you really think?" creates a moment where students may abandon the assigned position and reasons, yet they are not asked to do so; they are provided the opportunity to do so. Consequently, the opportunity is fresh, a sort of reset moment. Following the structured role playing of preparing, sharing, and listening to positions, there is an opening. Why? The listening and feedback process at steps 4 and 5 matters. This is what Waks (2010) calls "giving ear to" the other argument and "waiting in suspense . . . with attentive expectation or anticipation" (p. 2744). Having prepared, presented, and defended a position, and then having given ear to the "other" position, not one's "own"; and then, on top of this, being liberated from the assigned position— all this may leave the student wondering just where their "own" mind is on the issue. This is the political autonomy moment.

It is important to see that respect is implicated along with language. Both come with the territory of exchanging reasons. Listening to one another is initially structured (steps 4–6), and then loosened when the role requirement is dropped. Listening continues at step 7 as students gather material from one another to form their own opinions. Free now to believe what they want, participants must determine if what others are saying requires them to adjust their own opinion. They sort through what others are thinking/saying as they shape their own thinking/saying. Laden (2012) shows that this kind of responsiveness is inherent in reasoning. This is why exchanging reasons (deliberating) promotes mutual respect. When I give you my reasons and ask you for yours, I acknowledge that you too are a thinker, a reasoner, not a cardboard character. Sharing reasons implicitly recognizes the inner life, the dignity, of our interlocutors.

Using SAC+ to cultivate voice *rather than* consensus-building skills is debatable, as noted. Learning to speak one's mind, expressing one's preferences and objections, is crucial to young people's maturation as individuals and citizens. Voice is *the* elemental form of civic engagement and empowerment. But both independence and cooperation are necessary, and they operate in tandem. After all, we think better about problems when our partners are capable of thinking for themselves. Schools should cultivate both as part of their civic mission. As we loop students through a number of SACs, we can alternate at step 7 so that students one time are directed to reach a consensus (per the Johnsons) and, next time, to express to one another (the "public stage") their own view. Or we could do both in the same lesson: press for consensus during the discussion, and press students to argue for their own position during follow-up writing and presentations. At any rate, the combined effect of teaching for consensus *and* autonomy is sure to make for more robust deliberations as the course progresses.

CONCLUSION

As our democratic experiment falters, strong civic pedagogies are needed in schools. SAC+ is one such pedagogy. It aims to teach cooperation (its social goal), the course's central concepts and controversies (its academic goal), and deliberative skill along with political autonomy (its civic goal).

Time for teachers' instructional planning and collaboration is the key resource here. Ideally, teachers will talk with one another about the handful of concepts that could effectively anchor a course, the handful of related controversies and texts that will be targeted for study, and the learning cycles that will deepen learning. All this is too difficult and too interesting to be done alone. Argument is needed to get it right.

SAC+ is not a value-free pedagogy. It especially promotes five goods: knowledge, critical thinking, literacy, multiple perspectives, and student voice. More generally, SAC+ values liberal democracy and the principles that define it—popular sovereignty, equality, liberty, pluralism, evidence-based reasoning (science), and respect. The latter, respect, underpins the

listening, speaking, and argument—the language—that constitute deliberation. This same cluster of values rejects indoctrination and coercion, for
these negate critical thinking and liberty, and they are fundamentally disrespectful. Accordingly, SAC+ is centrist in the manner of Dewey's (1902)
middle way. It is a pragmatic path between the extremes of traditional and
progressive pedagogies. Students are encouraged to make up their own
minds rather than toe a line. This makes a deliberative pedagogy like SAC+
too radical for some conservatives (e.g., Kurtz, 2021) and too conservative
for some radicals (e.g., Gibson, 2020). On one side are those concerned that
students will be drawn away from their parents' values or that social studies
education will be politicized; on the other are those concerned that so-called
impartial deliberations perpetuate inequities by concealing them. This is a
juicy controversy, worthy of looped SACs in a teacher education course.

Let me return, finally, to the appreciation I began with. Incisive research
by early cooperative learning researchers was consequential. A sustained
school reform movement was launched, instruction was reimagined along
the lines of social interdependence theory and equity pedagogy, and educators were shown that they could have their cake and eat it too: School
attendance and academic achievement were strengthened thanks to dynamic social interaction among diverse students, not sacrificed to it. Here I
have presented principled modifications to sharpen the effect of the earlier
model. These address problems that will surely confront teachers who want
to implement it: choosing and then framing the right controversy, getting
students to understand it by reading and talking about it, and helping them
form and express their own views.

NOTES

1. For helpful comments on an earlier draft, I am grateful to Pat Avery, Mary
Anne Christy, Jenni Conrad, Carole Hahn, Jane Lo, and Sheila Valencia.

This chapter draws at points, with permission, from Parker (2011); and Parker
and Lo (2016).

2. See Parker et al. (2013, 2018).

3. I am referring particularly to Terry Beck, Afnan Boutrid, Steven Camicia,
Mary Anne Christy, Carol Coe, Jenni Conrad, Wendy Ewbank, Sibyl Frankenburg,
Tina Gourd, Diana Hess, Khodi Kaviani, Bruce Larson, Jane Lo, Natasha Merchant,
Jonathan Miller-Lane, Shane Pisani, and Lisa Sibbett.

4. Most controversies have more than two "sides," of course. SAC simplifies
the controversy to two, making it more accessible. The controversy can always be
complicated after the SAC lesson, at which point students, thanks to the SAC, will
have enough background knowledge to make sense of the additional information.

5. Variation in the procedure is common and accepted. See Avery et al. (2013).

6. See Parker (2010), on the distinction between friends and kin, on the one
hand, and acquaintances and strangers—the "public"—on the other.

7. Liberal democracies have elections and representative governments (this is democracy) that protect civil rights and liberties (this is liberalism).

8. See Article 12 of the United Nations Convention on the Rights of the Child.

REFERENCES

Allen, D. (2014). *Our Declaration: A reading of the Declaration of Independence in defense of equality.* W.W. Norton.

Aronson, E., Blaney, Nancy T., Stephan, C., Sikes, J., & Snapp, M. (1978). *The Jigsaw classroom.* SAGE.

Avery, P. G., Levy, S. A., & Simmons, A. M. M. (2013). Deliberating controversial public issues as part of civic education. *The Social Studies, 104*(3), 105–114.

Bransford, J., Brown, A. L., & Cockling, R. R. (2000). *How people learn: Brain, mind, experience, and school.* National Academies Press.

Bridges, D. (1979). *Education, democracy and discussion.* Humanities Press.

Bruner, J. (1960). *The process of education.* Harvard University Press.

Cohen, E. G. (1986). *Designing groupwork: Strategies for the heterogeneous classroom.* Teachers College Press.

Dewey, J. (1902). *The child and the curriculum.* University of Chicago Press.

Dewey, J. (1985). *Democracy and education.* Southern Illinois University Press.

Flanagan, C. A. (2013). *Teenage citizens: The political theories of the young.* Harvard University Press.

Gibson, M. (2020). From deliberation to counter-narration: Toward a critical pedagogy for democratic citizenship. *Theory and Research in Social Education, 48*(3), 431–454.

Gonzales v. Raich (Syllabus), 545 U.S. 1 (U.S. Supreme Court 2005)

Greenleaf, C., & Valencia, S. W. (2017). Missing in action: Learning from texts in subject-matter classrooms. In K. A. Hinchman & D. Appleman (Eds.), *Adolescent literacies: A handbook of practice-based research* (pp. 235–256). Guilford.

Habermas, J. (1984). *Theory of communicative action.* Beacon.

Hess, D. E., & McAvoy, P. (2015). *The political classroom: Evidence and ethics in democratic education.* Routledge.

Johnson, D. W., & Johnson, R. (1985). Classroom conflict: Controversy vs. debate in learning groups. *American Educational Research Journal, 22*, 237–256.

Johnson, D. W., & Johnson, R. T. (1979). Conflict in the classroom: Controversy and learning. *Review of Educational Research, 49*, 51–61.

Johnson, D. W., & Johnson, R. T. (1988). Critical thinking through structured controversy. *Educational Leadership, 45*(8), 58–64.

Johnson, D. W., & Johnson, R. T. (2009). Energizing learning: The instructional power of conflict. *Educational Researcher, 38*(1), 37–51.

Kurtz, S. (2021, March 15). The greatest education battle of our lifetimes. *National Review.* https://www.nationalreview.com/corner/the-greatest-education-battle-of-our-lifetimes/

Laden, A. (2014). *Reasoning: A social picture*. Oxford University Press.

McCulloch v. Maryland, 17 US 316 (Supreme Court 1819)

Oyez. (1995). United States v. Lopez, 514UW549. www.oyez.org/cases/1994/93-1260

Paley, V. G. (1992). *You can't say you can't play*. Harvard University Press.

Parker, W. C. (2005). Teaching against idiocy. *Phi Delta Kappan, 86*(5), 344–351.

Parker, W. C. (2010). Listening to strangers: Classroom discussion in democratic education. *Teachers College Record, 112*(11), 2815–2832.

Parker, W. C. (2011). Feel free to change your mind. A response to "The Potential for Deliberative Democratic Civic Education." *Democracy and Education, 19*(2). http://democracyeducationjournal.org/home/vol19/iss2/9

Parker, W. C., & Lo, J. C. (2016). Reinventing the high school government course: Rigor, simulations, and learning from text. *Democracy and Education, 24*(1). http://democracyeducationjournal.org/home/vol24/iss1/6

Parker, W., Lo, J., Yeo, A. J., Valencia, S. W., Nguyen, D., Abbott, R. D., Nolen, S. B., Bransford, J. D., & Vye, N. J. (2013). Beyond breadth-speed-test: Toward deeper knowing and engagement. *American Educational Research Journal, 50*(6), 1424–1459.

Parker, W. C., Valencia, S. W., & Lo, J. C. (2018). Teaching for deeper political learning: A design experiment. *Journal of Curriculum Studies, 50*(2), 252–277.

Sharan, S., & Sharan, Y. (1976). *Small group teaching*. Educational Technology Publications.

Slavin, R. E. (1985). *Learning to cooperate, cooperating to learn*. Plenum.

Stanford History Education Group. (2020). *Reading like a historian*. https://sheg.stanford.edu/history-lessons

United States v. Lopez, 514 US 549 (Supreme Court 1994)

Waks, L. (2010). Two types of interpersonal listening. *Teachers College Record, 112*(11), 2743–2762.

Wineburg, S., & Martin, D. (2009). Tampering with history: Adapting primary sources for struggling readers. *Social Education, 73*(5), 212–216.

CHAPTER 6

Structure Matters

Comparing Deliberation and Debate

Paula McAvoy and Arine Lowery

When teachers decide to introduce a political issue in the classroom, one important decision they will make is how to structure the discussion. Discussions can take many forms. Sometimes pairs of students are in a 5-minute "turn and talk." At other times, the teacher uses more complex strategies that may require students to take on particular roles, assign students to temporarily defend views they do not endorse, and put limits on who participates and for how long. The structure of the discussion can greatly affect the experience for students, including how many participate, the tone of the discussion, and what students learn.

In this chapter we compare two different strategies commonly associated with the democratic aims of social studies. The first is a small group deliberation that encourages students to consider a set of policy proposals that address a social problem, come to a consensus, and then present their proposal. The second is a team debate in which participants try to convince a panel of their peers to declare their side the winner. Both strategies can be used to engage students in discussions of public policy issues, and both require students to weigh competing values, consider new evidence, and give reasons to one another. We compare these strategies to show that the design of the activities, specifically the difference between working toward agreement versus trying to win, activates different discussion skills and promotes different democratic dispositions. These differences affect how students experience the activity and how their political views change as a result of the discussion. Understanding these differences will help teachers make more informed decisions about when, why, and how to use a deliberation versus a debate.

THE STUDY

We compare deliberation and group debate using evidence from a study of students participating in a civic education program that engaged them in both strategies. Data was collected in fall 2019 from 165 high school participants involved in the Close Up Washington program, which brings high school students from around the county to DC for a week-long, place-based study of the federal government. Participants travel to DC as a school group, but upon arrival they are put into geographically diverse groups of 20–24, led by a Close Up trained instructor. This group stays together for the program week. Our surveys showed that students in this sample were politically diverse but leaned slightly conservative, majority white, and majority middle class or higher. The program offers a lab-like setting to study discussion, because we are able to see large numbers of students in classroom-size groups engage in the same strategies.

Structuring Discussions in Different Ways

In his classic text on classroom discussion, Bridges (1979) defines discussion as a type of collective inquiry into a question, and it is the act of inquiry that facilitates learning. In our work with teachers, we notice they often think about discussion as a set of individual contributions and do not see it as a collective act. As a result, teachers rely too heavily on whole class, teacher-centered approaches that often fall short of actual discussion. Strategies like the ones we describe here are designed to engage the students in collective inquiry by introducing a compelling question, preparing students with background materials, and providing a structure so that they productively engage with one another.

On two of the evenings at Close Up, leaders (who act as facilitators) engage students in discussions of controversial issues using different structures.[1] Table 6.1 presents the key differences in each design.

Table 6.1. Key Differences Between Structured Deliberation and Group Debate

Characteristics	Structured Deliberation	Group Debate
Open public policy question	Framed to invite a **range of options**. Example: What actions (if any) should the government take to address climate change?	Framed to set up **two sides** (pro/con). Example: Should our state's minimum wage be raised to $15/hour?
Background materials	Students receive materials that explain the issue and **multiple policy options**.	Students receive materials that explain the issue and read **reasons for and against**.
Groups	Students work in randomly assigned **small groups** or groups purposefully assigned to include students who will likely disagree.	Students first divide into two like-minded teams to develop their best reasons and arguments. They then engage in **whole class debate** between two groups.

(continued)

Table 6.1. (continued)

Characteristics	Structured Deliberation	Group Debate
Moments of required participation	Opening share out and closing share out.	Each person must stand and speak for 1 minute.
Aim of the activity	**Consensus:** To develop a policy that the small group can all endorse.	**Win:** To be on the team that is declared the winner.

Both of these strategies are highly structured and move students from learning about an issue to engaging in a student-centered exchange of ideas. Both strategies also have moments of required participation. Teachers often worry about expecting all students to verbally participate in discussion, believing that it is too uncomfortable for some. Structured discussion strategies scaffold participation so that students know when and how to participate. Requiring everyone to participate also has the effect of requiring everyone to listen.

In what follows, we provide more detail about each activity and discuss how asking students to come to a consensus or attempt to win the argument alters the experience and effect of the discussion. We also present findings that show that students do not experience the same discussion in the same way. In particular, we found that girls reported more discomfort, particularly in the debate.

PUBLIC POLICY DELIBERATION

Within democratic theory, deliberation is a specific type of discussion directed at coming to a decision about an issue (Gutmann & Thompson, 1996). Juries deliberate to determine innocence or guilt, a Congressional committee deliberates proposed legislation, and the student government deliberates how to raise money for activities. Providing students with opportunities to experience deliberation in the classroom is often a recommended component of democratic education, because it allows students to learn about issues, practice reason giving, expand their understanding, and think about solutions with an eye toward the common good (Gibson & Levine, 2003; Gutmann, 1999; Hess, 2009; Levine & Kawashima-Ginsberg, 2017; Parker, 2003).

Beyond the classroom, deliberations within social and political organizations result in actionable decisions. Usually, the goal is for participants to move toward consensus about what to do, which requires participants to compromise and think creatively about how to reach a solution that is acceptable for all. Within the classroom, deliberative activities invite the participants to practice working collaboratively while evaluating possible solutions to a policy issue. As Levine (2018) notes, classroom deliberations about policy issues "are better described as simulated deliberations, in which the students pretend to be deciding on behalf of the United States" (p. 2). Some deliberative classroom activities are designed to have students find consensus and others stop short of this, a decision that makes the activity more focused on individuals formulating their own view about the issue and less about coming to a collective decision.

The structured deliberation at Close Up is designed so that participants work in small groups to come to agreement about a policy that they all endorse. The design is highly student centered, with the leader playing the role of "guide on the side" (King, 1993), cuing groups when it is time to move to the next part of the activity. We found that culminating with a consensus position tended to result in students modifying their views toward more agreement about the issue and contributed to generally positive feelings about the discussion.

Structured Deliberation

1. The Set Up. Establishing clear norms for the classroom is important for this design. Students spend most of the time in small groups, with minimal intervention by the teacher. For this reason, students need to trust each other to be fair and attentive to how people are differently positioned related to the issue at hand. Close Up begins the process of norm setting on the first night of the program, when each workshop group establishes agreements for the week. Prior to the deliberation activity, students have spent the day being mixed into a variety of short paired and three-person discussions as they tour Washington, DC. These low-risk discussions serve to reinforce the norms by helping students get to know one another, establishing the expectation that everyone needs to participate, and providing practice with respectfully listening and responding to differences of opinion. Similarly, teachers wishing to engage in deliberation should begin the year with norm-setting activities and work toward building the skills and trust necessary for having students work in productive small groups.

Deliberations begin with a clearly stated question of public policy. Ideally, these are current, relevant to students, and open to multiple interpretations. For example, during the program week we studied, different groups of students deliberated, "What actions, if any, should the government take to address the issue of homelessness?" and, in the example we present here, "What actions, if any, should the government take to address climate change?" Notice that these are not framed as yes/no; instead, the question is designed so that students have room to explore many options. Certainly, people in democratic society do deliberate yes/no questions, such as "Should our state raise the minimum wage to $15/hour?" Indeed, this is a good question for the structured academic controversy model, described in Chapter 5. Yet, this deliberation activity is designed to have students consider many options and collaboratively craft a policy they all can endorse. The open framing of "What actions, if any . . ." creates more opportunity for finding points of agreement.

Last, teachers should explain the purpose of deliberation. During our observation of the climate change activity, the leader began by naming deliberation as the type of discussion that they would be engaging in and explaining that its purpose is to "examine an issue and consider many different policies." She foreshadowed that they would be working in small groups as they "attempt to come to a consensus" on a policy that the government should pursue. She also set the tone for the activity by explaining that deliberations are an opportunity to "collaborate," to develop a shared understanding, and to provide everyone a chance to hear others' viewpoints.

Taking the time to set the norms, identifying an open policy question, and explaining the purpose and outcome is an essential, and often neglected, first step in getting all students ready to deliberate.

2. Share Out. After the setup, students are sorted into groups of six. To set the appropriate tone for deliberation and to give the group a moment to get comfortable with one another, the teacher should pose a question or set of questions related to the topic that allows all students to share a view without comment or questioning from others. Consider, for example, beginning a deliberation on environmental issues with the share out prompt, "When I think about climate change, I feel [blank], because [blank]." The openness of this prompt allows students to choose a range of reactions, which could include personal experiences. A required share out immediately puts all voices into the group and gives students practice with an important deliberative skill: listening. In our own work with deliberative activities, we have observed that inviting group members to share something about how they are affected by the issue creates an open deliberative climate (McAvoy et al., 2020).

Close Up designs their share out as a 10-minute "focus group" activity. Each group receives one copy of a list of several survey items related to the topic they are about to discuss. The survey uses a Likert scale of "strongly disagree" to "strongly agree." One student is assigned to be the recorder and asks everyone to respond to each question and marks the answer on the sheet. For example, students were asked to what extent they agree with the following statement: "I live in a home where we actively combat climate change." Recording these answers on a single sheet creates a quick visual that allows the group to see where there is agreement and disagreement. This also promotes participation, as each person must share their responses to several questions.

In the climate change discussion we observed, the focus group questions unearthed disagreement about whether climate change was caused by human activity. This began when participants were asked to respond to the statement "I live in a household that recycles as a way to combat climate change." Brett and Joe explained that they were not sure how to answer, because they recycle but insisted it was not to stop climate change. Both seemed to be climate change skeptics. Brett clarified, "I want to keep things clean. I just don't think it really helps the climate." As the group worked through the sheet, Brett and Joe continued to qualify their answers, because the questions took as a given that climate change is real and caused by human activity, and they wanted to say it isn't. Nevertheless, they cooperated with the activity, and hearing from everyone resulted in the group appearing more relaxed with one another. As they waited for other groups to finish, Mike, another participant, asked, "So what do you all actually think?" Brett jumped in to explain that he thought temperatures on Earth naturally rise and fall over time, "But I don't think it's a frantic, 'We're all going to die' situation.'" Rather than push against this view, Mike simply clarified, "So you don't believe man-made climate change is happening." Brett reiterated that he thought this was part of Earth's natural cycles, and Mike simply nodded. Brett then added, "But I do believe in clean energy."

This moment illustrates several important effects of having students begin by sharing initial reactions before moving into deliberation. First, the survey format communicated that this was not a moment to debate, and that they were being asked to listen to one another as preparation for a collaborative work. Second, knowing where everyone stands helps people to identify their differences, commonalities, and to what extent the question is personal for group members. For example, during the focus group for the homelessness deliberation, some students shared that they had family members who had experienced housing insecurity. Knowing that some participants are directly affected by an issue helps everyone engage with sensitivity. Last, Brett's clarification that he does believe in clean energy suggests to us that he wanted to signal he was willing to cooperate with his peers. Perhaps allowing his minority view to be voiced without pushback made him open to finding common ground. Importantly, the overall effect of a share out is that everyone experiences feeling heard.

3. Background Materials. Deliberations need participants to have some background understanding of the issue. Providing background is important to get the group on the same empirical starting point for the discussion and helps foster participation by giving students evidence and reasons to draw upon. To that end, Close Up provides time for everyone to read a background brief. In a classroom setting, teachers should clarify terms and ensure comprehension of the issue before beginning the deliberative process. Alternatively, classroom teachers could pre-assign a reading so the students arrive prepared to discuss.

Background materials need to be closely vetted by teachers, because they shape what reasons and evidence come into the discussion. The climate change case provides a clear example. Close Up models good practice by presenting background materials that treat the empirical question of whether climate change is caused by human activity as settled by science but leaving open the question of what to do about it (Hess & McAvoy, 2015; McAvoy & Ho, 2020). Yet, as we saw with Brett, students may still enter the conversation as climate change skeptics. The materials acted as a buffer against the deliberation shifting toward a debate about the scientific evidence. In a different small group, we observed a girl do just that when she countered a climate skeptic:

> I get what you're saying [about there being more important issues], but . . . let's assume all of this [gesturing to the background sheet] is legit and climate change is real and polar ice caps are melting. . . . Wouldn't you consider that to be a more pressing issue when it comes to just living on the planet, not just as Americans but as the entire world?

Although this comment was met with a smile from the skeptic, he did not try to argue against the science and was willing to grant that there could be dangers that need to be addressed. Despite what looks to be intractable differences of opinion about the reality of a warming planet, students in all of the small groups were able to identify a common policy position by the end of the activity, and this was in large part because the background sheet set parameters around discussion.

4. Small Group Deliberation. At the root of all deliberations is the question "What should we do?" If the class is deliberating the question "What should the dress code at our school include?" they will be able to come up with many policy options on their own. When teachers ask students to deliberate questions of public policy, students will need to learn more about possible choices.

Close Up provides this through a second handout with a matrix of policy options regarding the issue. The policy matrix guides the options that the students consider, but they are not limited to the information in the evidence packets. The climate change matrix included six options that ranged from "The government should research the issue more" to a carbon emissions tax that would hasten independence from all fossil fuels. Each option included a statement explaining "what supporters say" and "what opponents say." Students were directed to discuss each option and come to consensus about a policy, or set of policies, they all endorse. They could also choose to take no action at all.

Sorting through these options engages students in what Parker and Hess (2001) have labeled "teaching with discussion." In other words, students are reading new information with the intention of discussing it. This prompts them to learn, for example, what the Paris Climate Change Accord is, think about whether they support the United States rejoining, and then articulate that view to others. In this way, discussion motivates learning about the content.

In our observations, the groups stayed on task and engaged respectfully as they discussed the provided options. Across all groups, we saw students ask others to clarify ideas, they kept interruptions to a minimum, and they gently offered rebuttals. However, we also noted that participation became uneven during the 30 minutes of less-structured deliberation about the policy matrix. In most groups, two or three people did the bulk of the talking.

In the last 10 minutes of the deliberative time, the instructor handed each group a piece of chart paper and directed them to record the options that they endorse. This direction to come to consensus moved the discussion from talk about "What do I believe?" to "What can we all accept?" The leader also explained that each person would be sharing their group's proposal in the next part of the activity. This collective responsibility reengaged those who had participated less and created what Parker labels in Chapter 5 of this volume "productive anxiety," as everyone suddenly felt the need to have something to say.

5. Sharing Decisions. One ending to a small group deliberation is to have a member of each group present their policy to the entire room. If there are five small groups, five people will present. Close Up's approach is to reconfigure the room for the last 15 minutes so that students move to a new group composed of a representative from each of the original deliberation groups (i.e., the jigsaw method). Each person takes a turn explaining the policy that their previous group developed. The result is that every person in the room shares their group's decision and has to be ready to answer questions. This becomes an opportunity for everyone to make one last statement and reinforces what they just learned.

In our observation, all groups agreed that at a minimum the United States should rejoin the Paris Climate Agreement, one of the least aggressive of the options. This choice appealed to some because of their concern for the dangers associated with climate change. Others were persuaded by the view presented in the materials that participating was important to maintain the United States' role as a superpower. We note that while there was consensus around the Paris Agreement, groups differed in the additional policy ideas they endorsed, with some advocating more immediate action. Again, the materials were essential to the outcome. The range of options, which included the "for" and "against" opinions, gave students room to find points of agreement, including students who entered as skeptics.

6. Reflection. Giving students time to reflect on what they experienced is a valuable way to conclude a deliberation. Teachers might ask a question, such as "Did anyone change their view about this issue?" Teachers can also ask students to reflect on the process of deliberation and ask, "What did we do well as a class during this activity, and what could we improve on?" This meta talk about discussion helps students to come to a better understanding about the skills necessary for good discussion.

The Effect of Coming to Consensus

In the study, we found that students' views about the topic changed significantly after engaging in the deliberation (McAvoy & McAvoy, in press). This does not necessarily mean that they fully reversed their opinion, but they might have moved a position or two along a scale. When we investigated how those views changed, we found that the trend across rooms was for the participants to move toward consensus (McAvoy & McAvoy, in press). In other words, there was more agreement among the students after the deliberation than before the deliberation. This suggests that asking students to identify a consensus position does create a willingness to modify one's views.

Lo (2017) cautions that this may not be good news. While consensus promotes the democratic values of political tolerance and open-mindedness, Lo (2017) argues that encouraging students to seek common ground might obscure important disagreements—especially those voiced by marginalized communities. We see something like this in climate change deliberation. The few students who were deeply concerned about climate change often accepted a consensus position that was less grounded in the reality of a rapidly growing climate crisis. In fact, the survey data showed that the consensus position for the room was to become a little less supportive of the idea that "the government should do more to stop climate change" from pre to post, though the mean score was still on the side of taking action. It is possible that through deliberation some students became less convinced that climate change is an urgent issue.

PUBLIC POLICY DEBATE

Debate is another skill often associated with democratic life. Candidates debate to convince voters to support them, legislators engage in floor debates, and lawyers debate guilt or innocence during trials. Unlike the act of deliberation, which seeks common ground and finds value in compromise, the purpose of a debate is to win through the art of argumentation. In short, deliberation is collaborative and debate is adversarial.

Debate also has academic value. Teachers have long used debate as an activity to promote critical thinking about an issue. When students prepare for debate, they must consult evidence, construct arguments, and formulate rebuttals. These skills are also part of deliberation, but because debate positions students to defend their views, it requires them to be oppositional in a way that is not present in a deliberation. The defensive stance of debate also requires students to be somewhat inauthentic during the activity. If, during the course of a debate, a student feels persuaded by the other side, they are expected to remain committed to their original position until the activity is over.

The Close Up activity that we observed engaged students in group debate in which two teams engage in a back-and-forth exchange of ideas, with the goal to win over a panel of peers. The structure was used to simulate a Congressional committee hearing as part of a larger activity modeling the legislative process. The three or four students who were undecided volunteered to serve as the judges who acted as moderators and chose the winner. In this section, we explain the activity and how the competitive aspect affected the student experience.

Structured Group Debate

1. The Setup. As in deliberation, selecting the right kind of question matters, and this activity requires a question that invites a yes/no answer. In the case we describe here, the group was asked, "Should Congress allow those who are permitted to carry concealed weapons in one state to carry concealed weapons in all states?" Other possible questions include "Should the voting age be lowered to 16?" or "Should our state raise the minimum wage?" Ideally, teachers select questions that divide the class fairly evenly.

Some students become quite competitive in debate situations, so it is important that the setup also includes reminding students of the classroom norms. During the concealed carry debate, the leader asked students to review the poster of community agreements they had created on the first evening and then addressed the adversarial nature of debate by trying to set a tone of mutual respect. She explained:

> I really want to make sure that . . . we're keeping an open mind, respecting other people's opinion, being courteous to others when they're talking, being involved, and using your inside voice. As well as . . . [making sure] we're not personally attacking other people but we are countering their argument. It's a very different feel. We want to make sure we're not interrupting, we're not berating other people's opinion . . . we just have to be mindful of how this might be uncomfortable, but it shouldn't be disrespectful.

This leader also invited students to generate ideas about what a good argument is, cuing them to think about evidence, reasons, and clear examples. Importantly, this activity occurs on the evening after the aforementioned deliberation, so students have had a collaborative experience before moving into debate.

2. Background Materials. As with deliberations, a common set of materials will put students on a more even starting point and allow the teacher to exercise some control over the set of reasons that get introduced during the debate. Close Up first provides a background sheet that sets up the problem by explaining terms, current policy, the proposed policy change, and why there is disagreement. After students have processed the issue and asked clarifying questions, students review reasons for and against the proposed policy.

We note one other use for background materials: They should make the issue complicated. Debate can have the effect of making an issue appear easy to solve if students are asked to defend views that they already feel certain about. Using so-called "wedge issues" that divide the American public may invite students to make snap judgments and then engage in an activity that simply affirms their views. Selecting topics that are either less familiar to young people (e.g., mandatory minimum sentencing for drug convictions) or presenting an unexpected question to a familiar topic is less likely to ignite partisan incivility. It is also more challenging. In this case, we heard many students during the week express support for protecting the right to own a gun, but the question of whether a state must recognize another state's concealed carry permit put into tension two traditionally conservative values: states' rights and gun rights. Consequently, as students read the materials, we overheard one student sigh, "This is hard."

3. Team Preparation. When the activity begins, students are asked to decide which position they most agree with or to identify as "unsure." Students then gather with the others who agree with them and are given 10–15 minutes to organize and decide who is going to make the closing and opening arguments. In this version of the activity, the rules state that every person on the team is expected to stand in front of the group and present an argument for their position. Meg, the group leader, organized the speakers by handing out a game chip to everyone. She explained that the chip should be turned in after each person makes a comment, and no one on a team can make a second comment until all chips have been turned in. This directive clearly heightened the anxiety in the room. Teams quickly huddled and then small groups broke off to gather their thoughts and prepare comments.

While the two sides conferred, Meg prepared the judges for their role. The volunteers were told that each person only gets 1 minute to speak, and it was their job to keep time. Meg also instructed them to think about what they were looking for in a good argument and to make sure they all understood the issue at hand. This is a good example of a "guide on the side" moment (King, 1993). Meg prepared the judges to manage the debate so that she could hand responsibility to them. One way to think about these discussion structures is that they are designed to allow teachers and students to share authority in the classroom.

4. The Debate. The setup for the debate requires each team to sit shoulder to shoulder in a line facing the other team. The judges sit in a row between both teams, forming the bottom of a U-shape. Once the concealed carry room was settled, Meg handed the floor over to the judges and took a seat in a neutral part of the room. She did not say anything throughout the activity other than answer a couple of procedural questions. For the next 30 minutes, the students were in charge.

During the exchange of views, members from each side alternated providing reasons and arguments for the view they endorse, beginning with an opening argument from both sides. The first speaker, Joshua on the pro side, began by sharing that at home he is part of a "Second Amendment activist group known as Open Carry Texas." After describing some of his activism, he delivered his primary point that "the right to keep and bear arms shall not be infringed upon. So . . . not being able to move from one state to another without getting a new permit is infringing that right to keep and bear arms." Trying to parse out whether and why this should be an issue of states' rights or the federal government is the crux of the issue and remains the focus throughout the activity.

Charlotte, the opener from the "con" side countered,

Okay. I'm starting by saying states are so different. They are different from each other, they have different people, they have a different population, they have a different way of living, different cultures, and that means that their gun rules have to be different . . . the states have power over the federal government like it has to be equal it can't just be all the same otherwise it just doesn't work like that.

It was clear from the body language and quivering voices that many of the students were nervous making their comments. Again, the materials provided some support. Most of the reasons offered came from the handouts, and students could opt to quote directly or go off script. Students across all rooms were generally supportive of each other, by respectfully listening and nodding encouragement to teammates. Still, part of the energy in the room is competitive nervousness, and it is often the boys who want to strategize, coach, and occasionally sigh with disappointment. In the other two observed rooms, the debates ended amicably. In the concealed carry debate, two boys from the "pro" team snickered while Ava, on the opposing team, delivered the closing argument, because they felt she was actually supporting their side. Clearly flustered, she abruptly ended her comments and sat down.

After everyone had spoken, the judges exited to decide which side won the debate. When the judges returned, they first praised both sides for "articulating good points," "using facts," and "having a lot of good information." They then announced that those in favor of the law won the debate.

This information was met with disappointment on one side of the room and restrained delight on the other.

   5. Reflection. Providing a moment to reflect on the debate experience is a good way to release students from their adversarial positions. One option is to give every person the opportunity to share where they currently stand on the issue and which arguments they found most persuasive. Teachers might also have students share what they thought about the activity itself or conclude by asking students to write a short reflection about their experience in the activity, explaining their current position and how their view changed over time.

Moving Away From Consensus

As we looked at the video from the three rooms engaging in group debate, it was clear that students were more attentive throughout this activity. This is likely because it has a competitive element and students have less room to hide—all will speak to the entire group. We also see that participation is nearly equal. There is no opportunity for someone to take over the discussion, and it requires students to listen to one another. However, unlike in the deliberation, the survey responses show this format tended to polarize views within each room (McAvoy & McAvoy, in press). This was most clearly seen in the concealed carry debate. Prior to the activity, the students' views clustered around the middle position, and after the debate we could see two opposing groups of beliefs (McAvoy & McAvoy, in press). This aligns with political science research that shows when people engage in political discussions with people who agree with them, views tend to move toward a more extreme position (Mutz, 2006; Schkade et al., 2007). In other words, discussion with like-minded people tends to make participants feel more certain about their views and become more convinced the other side is wrong. Students in this activity spend most of the time working within their like-minded team, and their thinking is directed at rebutting the other side. It makes sense then, that students become more attached to their position.
   There are, of course, good reasons to engage students in debate. In this case, it aligns with the legislative activity they were simulating, and it promotes skills associated with critical thinking. Debate might also be more authentic to the way politics is actually done. We are a country deeply divided, and teaching students to see adversarial disagreement as normal might have democratic value (Lo, 2017). What debate does *not* do is model that changing one's mind in light of new evidence or better arguments is a reasonable thing to do. Philosophical chairs (Seech, 1984) is a discussion strategy that looks similar to the team debate but differs in that there is no winner and because students are invited to switch teams if they change their minds—including moving into or out of the undecided category.[2] Classroom

teachers may want to experiment with this variation if they want students to keep an open mind about the issue.

COMPARING THE TWO STRATEGIES

The post-surveys in our study asked students a series of questions about how they experienced each discussion. Students favored the deliberation a bit more (75% said they enjoyed deliberation versus 70% for the debate). They also felt that both structures made them more interested in the topic (83% for deliberation and 82% for the debate). We also found that students reported more hesitation, disagreement, and anxiety during the debate.

When we looked closer at who was most likely to report feelings of discomfort, we found that for both activities young women were significantly more likely to report that they felt they heard something offensive during the discussion and that they were more hesitant to speak. They were also significantly less likely to say that they felt good about the comments they made. We did not find significant differences by race/ethnicity or social class on the survey questions for either activity, though it is possible that the sample's whiteness and higher social class average was overriding some of these effects.

For most students, the debate activity was more stressful, but we note that it also overcame some of the limitations of the deliberation. The more rigid structure of the activity resulted in all students participating in about equal amounts and did not allow some students (boys) to dominate, because the structure required a lot of listening. Nevertheless, the public declaration of views and competitive aspect to this activity resulted in some students (primarily girls) feeling more anxious about participating. We note that this does not mean that girls do not want to participate in political discussion, as they reported similar levels of enjoyment with the activity, but it does mean that teachers ought to pay attention to the dynamics in the room, use strategies that scaffold the development of discussion skills, and be ready to attend to the emotional aspect of discussion.

CONCLUSION

One of our purposes in comparing these two strategies was to show that discussions need structure. We both work with preservice teachers, and it is quite common to see them try to engage students in discussion by standing in front of the room after a reading or video clip and ask, "So, what do you think?" The hope here is that someone will say anything. As a result, whatever participation happens can feel like filling time and not "real" learning. Both of the activities described were designed to deepen understanding about the issue, while scaffolding participation to ensure that everyone's voice came into the discussion. The structure also moved the teacher away from center stage and allowed students to take responsibility for the activity. The combination of structure plus shared authority is what allows students to experience discussion as collective inquiry (Bridges, 1979).

These two strategies also show that discussions can reinforce different democratic values and skills. Inviting students to deliberate with the intention of coming to consensus modeled an open-minded, collaborative exchange of ideas but resulted in some unevenness in levels of participation. We also found that students' views moved toward more agreement. Debating the issue created an adversarial climate and heightened anxiety but also created more focused attention during the activity and equalized participation. Debating also had the effect of polarizing views within the group. Students also experience these strategies differently. In this set of politically diverse participants, we found that girls felt more discomfort in both strategies but were more supportive of deliberation. Other research has found that topics related to race, sexual identity, gender, and immigration can create negative experiences when students are personally affected by the issue. These interpersonal dynamics make discussion more challenging, but they do not mean students do not want to discuss. Instead, teachers need to be attentive to the ways that they prepare students for discussion, how they frame issues, and how they structure and design the activities so that discussion is inclusive and productive.

NOTES

1. Close Up makes some of its classroom resources free online and others are available for purchase. See https://www.closeup.org/virtual-learning/classroom-resources/.

2. Philosophical chairs was originally designed for the college classroom, but there are many examples of adaptions for the middle and high school classroom. As examples, see Learning Channel (2017) and ProCon.org (2019).

REFERENCES

Bridges, D. (1979). *Education, democracy and discussion*. NFER.

Gibson, C., & Levine, P. (2003). *The civic mission of schools*. The Carnegie Corporation of New York & the Center for Information & Research on Civic Learning.

Gutmann, A. (1999). *Democratic education* (rev. ed.). Princeton University Press.

Gutmann, A., & Thompson, D. F. (1996). *Democracy and disagreement*. Belknap.

Hess, D. E. (2009). *Controversy in the classroom: The democratic power of discussion*. Routledge.

Hess, D. E. (2015). *The political classroom: Evidence and ethics in democratic education.* Routledge.

King, A. (1993). From sage on the stage to guide on the side. *College Teaching, 41*(1), 30–35.

Learning Channel. (2017). *Teaching channel, philosophical chairs, reading like a historian.* https://learn.teachingchannel.com/video/reading-like-a-historian-taking-positions

Levine, P. (2018). Deliberation or simulated deliberation? *Democracy and Education,26*(1),7.https://democracyeducationjournal.org/cgi/viewcontent.cgi?article=1381&context=home

Levine, P., & Kawashima-Ginsberg, K. (2017). *The republic is (still) at risk—and civics is part of the solution.* Jonathan M. Tisch College of Civic Life, Tufts University.

Lo, J. C. (2017). Empowering young people through conflict and conciliation: Attending to the political and agonism in democratic education. *Democracy & Education,* 1–9.

McAvoy, P., & Ho, L. C. (2020). Professional judgment and deciding what to teach as controversial. *Annals of Social Studies Education Research for Teachers (ASSERT), 1*(1), 27–31.

McAvoy, P., Lowery, A., Wafa, N., Byrd, C. (2020). Dining with democracy: Discussion as informed action. *Social Education, 84*(5), 289–293.

McAvoy, P., & McAvoy, G. (in press). Can debate and deliberation reduce partisan divisions? Evidence from a study of high school students. *Peabody Journal of Education.*

Mutz, D. C. (2006). *Hearing the other side: Deliberative versus participatory democracy.* Cambridge University Press.

Parker, W. C. (2003). *Teaching democracy: Unity and diversity in public life.* Teachers College Press.

Parker, W. C., & Hess, D. (2001). Teaching with and for discussion. *Teaching and Teacher Education, 17*(3), 273–289.

ProCon.org. (2019, May 1). *Philosophical chair lesson plan.* https://www.procon.org/background-resources/philosophical-chairs-lesson-plan/

Schkade, D., Sunstein, C. R., & Hastie, R. (2007). What happened on deliberation day. *California Law Review, 95,* 915–940.

Seech, Z. (1984). Philosophical chairs: A format for classroom discussion. *Teaching Philosophy, 7*(1), 37–41.

CHAPTER 7

Document-Based Discussions in History

Orienting Students to the Discipline

Abby Reisman

In social studies classrooms, discussions are as valuable as they are rare. The College, Career, and Civic Life (C3) framework for social studies promotes discussion as an essential ingredient in instruction that promotes knowledge building, argumentation, and civic discourse (National Council for the Social Studies [NCSS], 2013). Recent research has found effects for discussion in social studies classrooms on student political knowledge and involvement (Hess & McAvoy, 2015), while across subject areas classroom discussion has been shown to foster young people's subject matter learning, engagement, conceptual understanding, reading comprehension, and epistemic reasoning (e.g., Duschl & Osborne, 2002; Engle & Conant, 2002; Nystrand, 2006). It is therefore doubly troubling that discussions are all but absent in history classrooms (Reisman, 2015; Saye & Social Studies Inquiry Research Collaborative [SSIRC], 2013).

It's no mystery *why* discussions are so rare: They're hard! Most preservice teachers enter teacher education with a preexisting vision of what discourse in history classrooms sounds like: at best, teacher-centered recitation; at worst, straight lecture. Successful discussions demand that teachers orchestrate the social dynamics of the classroom, that they understand the subject matter deeply enough to pose compelling, open questions, and that they can improvise both, often in response to student comments that threaten to veer the discussion off course. Blank stares and awkward silences threaten to undermine any attempt. Such challenges exist for teachers across subject areas who attempt to facilitate discussions.

In my work with preservice and inservice teachers, I focus on a specific type of discussion: *whole class document-based historical discussion*, an instructional activity that engages students in the work of historical interpretation and argumentation. In prior work, my colleagues and I defined whole class document-based discussion in history classrooms as

> those activities in which the teacher and all the students negotiate historical questions or controversies using each other's ideas and historical texts as resources. The purposes of such discussions are to *build collective knowledge* and allow students to practice listening, speaking, and engaging in historical interpretation. In instructionally productive discussions, the teacher and a wide range of students contribute orally, listen actively, and respond to and learn from others' contributions. (Reisman et al., 2018, emphasis added)

In this chapter, I attempt to explain and illustrate what it means to build collective knowledge in history in the context of whole class document-based discussions.

FRAMEWORK FOR FACILITATING HISTORICAL DISCUSSIONS

A whole class document-based discussion in history represents the culminating activity of a document-based lesson: a lesson that prompts students to use historical documents—primary and secondary sources—to answer a central historical question (CHQ) about the past (Reisman, 2012). Document-based lessons have a predictable activity sequence in which the teacher first establishes background knowledge, then supports student historical reading of two to three documents, as students work either independently or in small groups. Finally, the teacher facilitates a whole class discussion in which students attempt to answer the CHQ using evidence from the lesson's documents.

In working to support preservice teachers' facilitation of discussions, my colleagues and I developed a framework that broke down the complex endeavor of whole class document-based discussion facilitation in history (Reisman et al., 2018). The framework for facilitating historical discussions comprises four practices: (1) engaging students as sense-makers, (2) orienting students to the text, (3) orienting students to each other, and (4) orienting students to the discipline. As I will discuss, we found that novice teachers were able to do the first three to varying degrees; that is, they learned to pose open questions and encourage students to elaborate on their reasoning; they started to prompt students to support their claims with evidence; and they encouraged students to respond to and build on each other's ideas. But the fourth practice, orienting students to the discipline, remained elusive (Reisman et al., 2018, 2019). I think the reason, in part, was our uncertainty about what the practice entailed and what it looked like in practice. This absence has meant that we do not have illustrations and examples of what orienting students to the discipline should look like in whole class document-based historical discussions.

Figure 7.1. Revised Framework for Facilitating Historical Discussions

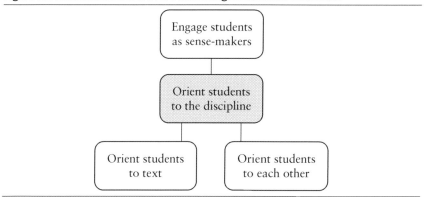

In this chapter, I suggest my colleagues and I were thinking about "orienting to the discipline" in the wrong way in our original framework. Rather than searching for discrete examples of the teacher orienting students to the discipline, we should consider orienting students to the discipline as a practice that emerges over the course of the entire discussion, beginning with planning—in the design of the CHQ and selection of documents. Rather than having four distinct practices, the revised framework depicted in Figure 7.1 showcases how the first three practices should be depicted as all contributing to orienting students to the discipline (see Figure 7.1).

When reconfigured in this way, we have to reenvision how the other three practices—engaging students as sense-makers, orienting students to the text, and orienting students to each other—contribute to orienting students to the discussion. In this chapter, I first present an example of a teacher orienting students to the discipline in whole class discussion, and then discuss why I believe she succeeded in doing so. I then flesh out how the three supporting practices contribute to orienting students to the discipline. Finally, I offer some common pitfalls and helpful tips for enacting each of these practices. I draw from data collected in my own teacher education courses and prior research projects to illustrate my points. I close with a comment on why I remain committed to such discourse despite its evident challenges.

ORIENTING STUDENTS TO THE DISCIPLINE

What does it mean for a teacher to orient students to the discipline in the course of a document-based history discussion? Here, I share an excerpt from a discussion led by Jen, a teacher candidate in her first semester of a 1-year master's program. Each year, I ask preservice teacher candidates in my social studies methods course to record themselves facilitating a document-based historical discussion and to write a two-page memo in which they analyze two of their instructional decisions in that discussion. Jen facilitated a discussion about Chinese immigration and, specifically, anti-Chinese sentiment that resulted in the restriction of Chinese immigration in 1882. The lesson is part of Stanford History Education Group's "Reading Like a Historian" curriculum,[1] and the CHQ for the lesson asks "Why was Chinese immigration restricted in 1882?" The four documents in the lesson, ranging from a letter by a prominent Chinese American merchant to a newspaper article about the economic panic of 1873, offer two distinct interpretations in response to the CHQ: economic anxiety and racism. Unlike most document-based lessons that appear online, this lesson plan includes a passage by historian Beth Lew-Williams (2011) to guide teachers' understanding of how the documents answer the CHQ:

> Why did the federal government pass the Chinese Restriction Act in 1882? Scholars agree that the answer lies in economics, politics, and prejudice—although they differ on which motivation was most salient. . . . *Economics played a significant part in the formation of the anti-Chinese movement, but only because the economic situation was viewed by white westerners through a lens of racial assumptions.* During a time of market booms and busts in the 1870s, white westerners believed that 'cheap' and abundant Chinese labor would be used by American monopolists to undercut the wages of white workers. Since white westerners assumed that the Chinese were inassimilable outsiders—instead of potential proletariat allies—they saw the Chinese as a significant threat to the American worker and to the American family. (p. 21, emphasis added)

In other words, Lew-Williams argues that we can't understand the origins of anti-Chinese immigration by solely focusing on economic anxiety *or* racism; we need to see those two forces as related—that white westerners' racist assumptions prevented them from seeing Chinese immigrants as potential allies. For the purpose of this discussion, we should consider Lew-Williams's complex interpretation of the causes of anti-Chinese immigration to be the learning goal.

The episode of discussion excerpted occurred right after students read the first document of the lesson: an 1878 flyer by the Pioneer Laundry Workers Assembly in Washington, DC (see Figure 7.2). The group was affiliated with the Knights of Labor, a labor federation that has a mixed record on inclusion and solidarity. They were known for their inclusion of skilled and unskilled workers, and for organizing across race and gender lines, but they vehemently opposed Chinese immigration. A close reading of the flyer reveals an economic argument: The authors claimed that Chinese workers were taking work from "our labor" and driving down wages. But, as Lew-Williams argues, this economic argument is filtered through a racist assumption that Chinese laborers are fundamentally "undesirable" outsiders.

Figure 7.2. Pioneer Laundry Workers Flyer From Stanford History Education Group Lesson on Chinese Immigration

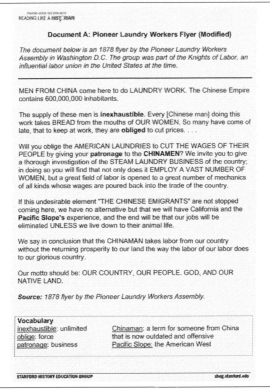

Jen opened the discussion with 11th graders by asking how the document answered the central question "Why was Chinese immigration restricted in 1882?":

S1: I was gonna say that jobs and employment is the biggest reason.

T: Okay, where did you see that?

S1: They say "the Chinaman takes labor from our country without the returning prosperity to our land the way the labor of our labor does to our glorious country."

T: So you're saying it's an economic justification. Does anyone else agree with that?

S2: They're basically saying they come to do work, but there's so many of them over there. "The Chinese Empire contains 600,000,000 inhabitants. The supply of these men is inexhaustible. Every [Chinese man] doing this work takes bread from the mouths of our women."

T: So we're kind of hearing that they feel like there's a threat to something that people here could have, whether that's the actual jobs or the profit from the jobs, right?

S3: Yeah, similar to what she said, they're taking the money from them. And it's also part of the third part when it talks about if there's no changes they say "the end will be that our jobs will be eliminated unless we live down to their animal life."

T: Right. One thing I heard you say when you said "their animal life." Does that further the economic answer to this question, or does that bring in a different line of reasoning? We're trying to answer this question [Why was Chinese immigration restricted in 1882?]. And we just kind of heard three people talk about maybe economic reasons and a shortage of jobs. But now just introducing this other sentiment, "animal life," and I wanted to know if that changes our answer to this question or introduces another line of reasoning?

S4: I think that sounds a little racist.

T: Okay yeah.

S5: Oh, well, for me, it changes my opinion on the historical question. At first, I thought it was linked to racism. But now I think they felt as though Chinese men that came there was kind of exploiting them on their jobs. So they probably thought, if they're doing it to us, why not do it to them to even the playing field?

T: So what do you think? Jamie is saying this is about jobs and more of an economic issue. And Cathryn says it's more racist. Could it be both?

S6: I think it could be both. Because they're saying "our jobs will be eliminated" so that's the economic reason but it also changes the tone or voice that they're using like "animal life"—it sounds racist to me.

[Bell rings]

T: Thank you guys. What Isabel was just saying about tone is really good close reading. We'll pick this up tomorrow.

Although this discussion only focused on one document, Jen did a number of things—namely, *engaging students as sense-makers, orienting students to the text,* and *orienting students to each other*—that allowed students to move collectively toward a complex historical learning goal.

1. Engaging Students as Sense-Makers

Jen framed discussion around an open-ended question and invited students to wrestle with the lesson's central problem. In prior work, I argued that the ultimate goal of document-based historical discussions is to bring students into a *historical problem space* (Reisman, 2015) and that teachers achieve this by rendering the past puzzling, and in ways, unknowable, even as they push students to engage more deeply with the documents. The historical problem space is a site of tension that resists pat answers and simple explanations. As teachers facilitate document-based historical discussions, they must continually surface, highlight, and focus students' attention on this problem space, inviting students to do the cognitive work of resolving it. In this case, the lesson's documents and CHQ established a historical problem space: Was Chinese immigration restricted for economic or racial reasons? Jen returned to this CHQ and continually highlights the tensions in the document throughout this brief excerpt.

Teachers can further engage students as sense-makers by expressing interest and genuine curiosity in their ideas (e.g., "I'm curious to hear why you think that"), and by prompting students to elaborate on their reasoning (e.g., "Tell us more about why you see it that way"). Jen could have further probed students' reasoning in the excerpt. For example, she was quick to tell the first student that her claim constituted an economic reason. Ideally, this classification could have emerged from the students themselves. When engaging students as sense-makers, teachers treat students as full participants with legitimate ideas.

2. Orienting Students to the Text

Historical documents obviously represent an essential element of document-based discussions, and for such discussions to be successful students should use those texts as evidentiary warrants to support their claims about the past. For that reason, a key factor of orienting students to the discipline is engaging students in the interpretive work of historical analysis. Wineburg (1991) distilled three heuristics historians draw on when making sense of the partial and often-contradictory documentary record: (1) sourcing, or considering a text's provenance and purpose; (2) contextualization, situating a document in its historical context; and (3) corroboration, synthesizing evidence from multiple sources to arrive at a plausible claim about the past. A teacher can orient students to these disciplinary practices by highlighting the way a student engaged in a disciplinary practice (e.g., "Notice how Hannah just sourced the document by observing that it was written before the boycott") or framing a particular elicitation in the language of historical thinking (e.g., "Remember, as historians, we always try to understand historical accounts within the time and place they were created—to contextualize. Can someone help us contextualize Frick's interview?").

I would argue that Jen missed some opportunities to engage students in historical thinking around the document. When students supported their claims with evidence from the text, she didn't ask them to consider whether that evidence was reliable. Specifically, she could have asked students to consider the perspective of the Pioneer Laundry Workers Assembly and the purpose of the flyer. To her credit, Jen acknowledged as much in her reflection memo:

> Another component of the discussion that I want to make improvements on next time, is to not only have students use the text, but to actively challenge the text. The document states many grievances that my students interpreted as fact. For example, many times, my students pointed to economic grievance that Chinese immigrants were taking jobs. . . . Although in the moment, I saw this as a good use of text-based evidence to explain an economic line of reasoning, and let students run with it, I really should have pressed students to be critical of the fact that we don't actually *know* if this was true. Next time I would have added a caveat, saying something along the lines of '[Students] have pointed to x in the text that talks about Chinese immigrants taking jobs. . . . We have to remember that we don't necessarily know that this is the case, as we have not seen any sources yet that might corroborate that claim.'

3. Orienting Students to Each Other

Finally, Jen oriented students to each other as a means of helping them build a more complex response to the central historical question. Complex understandings of the past represent substantive historical content and reflect core historical concepts such as historical significance, evidence, continuity and change, cause and consequence, historical perspectives, and the ethical dimension (Seixas & Morton, 2013). Learning goals in document-based historical discussions are, in effect, answers to the central historical question that take into consideration the historical context and the multiple perspectives evident in the documents. In that sense, the learning goal is an *interpretation*—one that students need not accept but should understand. When a teacher orients student to each other, it is to help them collectively build this complex learning goal.

The learning goal of the lesson was for students to formulate a response to the CHQ that incorporated both the obvious economic anxiety that was evident in the documents *and* the undeniable racism. Because the segment doesn't capture what students continued to discuss the following day when they read the remaining documents, it's a bit unfair to evaluate the extent to which Jen supported students in achieving this goal. However, we can see that Jen worked to highlight and orient students to the key arguments raised by their classmates. A satisfying answer should integrate these two themes, though to get to this state of convergence the teacher first must establish that each exists. Impressively, Jen succeeded in eliciting both arguments with students only having read the first document. Furthermore, we can see that Jen was partially successful in achieving her learning goal, given S6's final comment and Jen's attempt to highlight it as students packed up. Had the students read all four documents, the two arguments would likely have emerged even more clearly.

As this example illustrates, orienting to the discipline does not appear as a discrete teacher move. Rather, it's the result of a coordinated set of moves by which the teacher engages students as sense-makers, orients them to the text, and orients them to each other *in disciplinary ways*, that is, in ways that direct students toward (1) the historical problem space, (2) disciplinary reading practices, and (3) the lesson's historical learning goal. The challenge then, is to engage in these three supporting practices in disciplinary ways. Next, I discuss some common pitfalls and helpful tips that could help teachers use these three supporting practices to orient students to the discipline.

ENGAGING STUDENTS AS SENSE-MAKERS

Engaging students as sense-makers begins at the planning stage. Without an open historical question that invites students into a legitimate historical problem space, teachers are limited in their capacity to engage students as sense-makers and therefore orient students to the discipline. The good news is that teachers no longer need to design such questions from scratch! A slew of classroom-ready, document-based history lessons are available to teachers online.[2] Many teachers choose to modify the central historical questions in these existing document-based lessons (see Fogo et al., 2019), but adapting existing materials is easier than designing them from scratch. Armed with a compelling and open central question and a legitimate historical problem space, teachers can begin to transform the nature of classroom talk, opening the floor to student voice and participation.

In one of my early studies on discussion, I found that teachers had an easier time eliciting student participation when they posed evaluative (i.e., requesting that students judge historical actors or events; e.g., Was the New Deal a success?) rather than interpretive (i.e., requesting that students describe and/or explain historical events; e.g., What happened at the Battle of the Somme?) (Haroutunian-Gordon, 2009; Reisman, 2015). But I often remind teachers that certain precautions must be taken in formulating evaluative historical questions. The goal of historical discussion is to better understand the past and to ground one's understanding in the documentary evidence.

Common Pitfall

Certain evaluative questions don't invite students into a historical problems space. For example, if we pose questions that ask students whether a particular event was *justified*, we're asking them to judge that event on the basis of their own moral convictions. In all cases, such questions (e.g., Was Truman justified in dropping the atomic bomb on Hiroshima?) make it exceedingly unlikely that students will ground their claims in evidence or, if they do, that they will engage analytically with that evidence (e.g., if they use Truman's words to support their claim, they're unlikely to consider the reliability of his arguments). A slight adjustment to the question (e.g., Why did Truman decide to drop the atomic bomb on Hiroshima?) invites students into the historical problem space by forcing them to reimagine Truman's mindset and context in 1945.

An even greater risk of posing such evaluative questions is that they might open the door to claims that are morally untenable. A common example that I regularly encounter is when teachers ask students whether Indian removal, a 19th-century policy of forced relocation of Indigenous people in the United States, was justified (e.g., Reisman, 2017). A preservice candidate in my methods class recently submitted a video in which he attempted to facilitate a discussion of this question, using Andrew Jackson's 1830 State of the Union address, where Jackson makes the case for Indian removal. As students attempted to parse the text, the teacher was at pains to frame Jackson's arguments as morally reprehensible, lest students accept his arguments. Needless to say, the teacher's (warranted) interjection in the discussion squelched student discourse. A different CHQ—for example, "How did Andrew Jackson justify Indian removal?"—would have pointed students toward the text and a deeper understanding of the 1830s without framing the tragedy of Indian removal as potentially justifiable. With this alternative question, the teacher could have engaged students as sense-makers and, as they wrestled in a legitimate problem space, expressed genuine curiosity about their interpretations of the text and historical context. In other words, in this instance it would have been preferable to choose an interpretive question over an evaluative one. Ethical evaluations of historical events represent an important goal in social studies instruction and discussion because they engage students in questions about our collective responsibility to account for past injustice (Seixas & Morton, 2013). But my stance is that students are better positioned to judge historical actors when they first understand what happened.

Helpful Tip

Although the work of designing a generative and open CHQ occurs *before* one enters the classroom, the teacher must revisit the CHQ throughout instruction to further engage students as sense-makers as they encounter each new piece of evidence. The purpose of organizing instruction around a single question is to force students to generate answers that attempt to reconcile contradictory evidence and competing interpretations. In doing so, students are truly positioned as sense-makers and oriented to the discipline.

ORIENTING STUDENTS TO THE TEXT

We saw in the previous example that Jen missed an opportunity to orient students to the text when she didn't prompt them to question the pamphlet's reliability. She did, however, prompt students to support their claims in evidence (e.g., "Where did you see that?"). The standard "move" that teachers use to prompt such reasoning is "textual press" or asking students to find evidence in the text to back their claim. Teachers also orient students to text when they check that students comprehend texts at a literal level and have a foundation on which to develop interpretations (e.g., "Take 5 minutes to work out with your neighbor what you think Frederick Douglass is trying to say in this address. Circle any words you don't recognize").

These three aspects of orienting students to the text—literal comprehension, text as evidence, and historical thinking—illustrate the balancing act that teachers must play while facilitating document-based historical discussions. Ideally, students should have an opportunity to read and comprehend the texts *prior* to participating in the whole class discussion. However, it's inevitable that issues related to comprehension will emerge. The challenge for teachers, then, is to support student comprehension of the text without solely focusing on comprehension or missing opportunities for critical interrogation of the document's claims.

Common Pitfall

My research with preservice and inservice teachers has found that they quickly adopt "textual press," though they typically use it when asking students to summarize a given document. We were far less likely to see teachers prompting students to use the text as *evidence* in making claims related to the CHQ or inferences about the author's reliability or the historical context (Reisman et al., 2018, 2019).

For example, the following teacher candidate described her effort at facilitating discussion with 11th graders as "pulling teeth." I watched her video, in which she attempted to facilitate discussion about two competing interpretations of the New Deal,[3] and found that she mostly prompted students to summarize the texts and clarify relevant terms and concepts.

> *T:* I want someone to summarize for me what is Carl Degler saying about the New Deal.
> *S1:* Basically he's saying that the New Deal made it so Americans could trust the government with the economy.
> *T:* Ok. So where in the text do you see that idea of trust?
> *S1:* Oh—Americans began to expect the government to act in times of economic troubles and intervene to help make things better.
> *T:* Good. So, [it] was the role of government to provide this assistance. What about this idea of, revolutionary; what does he mean by that?

S2: Change.

T: Exactly. It's a drastic change in how Americans viewed the government. And in the last paragraph he uses the word *shift*. What kind of shift does he say happens as a result of the New Deal?

S3: A permanent shift.

The teacher continued this self-described dental work for over 8 minutes. Then, with 90 seconds remaining in class, she asked students to *evaluate* each historian's argument: "Okay, so, to wrap up the discussion, who do you think is more valid? Whose argument is stronger?" Without further prompting, three students offered animated arguments defending one or the other historical interpretation of the New Deal. A fourth student started to speak when the bell rang. This example highlights the value of framing the discussion with open questions. Had the teacher started the discussion with the question she posed at the end, it's quite likely that she would have surfaced whether students understood Degler's argument about the New Deal.

Helpful Tip

Instead of centering the discussion on summarizing the lesson's documents to ensure comprehension, teachers could choose to *stabilize the content* (Reisman, 2015) when they encounter widespread misunderstanding. In the following example, a teacher facilitated a discussion about Texas independence[4] with 11th graders and discovered that few students in the class understood one of the documents, a pamphlet by an abolitionist who opposed independence. Though students had been engaging freely in the discussion, the teacher paused the open discourse and assumed control:

T: Let's look at it all together then. Okay, who can read the sourcing information for me?

[S reads sourcing information on abolitionist Benjamin Lundy. T reminds class what abolitionism means.]

T: What do we think this author's perspective is? Does he think [Texans] are justified in taking Texas, or they're greedy?

Ss: Greedy.

T: They're greedy. And why does he think they're greedy?

S1: Because they're taking Texas to make it a slave state.

T: What do we know, looking at a map of Texas?

S2: It's below the line.

T: Okay. What do we know about our discussion of the Missouri Compromise and 36°30′? What would happen if Texas were added? What kind of state would it be?

S4: It would have to be a slave state.

T: It would have to be a slave state. Okay? So when he talks about "we have been asked to believe that the inhabitants of Texas have been fighting to maintain the sacred principles of liberty and the natural, inalienable rights of man, whereas their motives have been exactly the opposite." So does he think they're fighting for liberty?

Ss: No.

In this example, the discussion centered on an open-ended historical question: Why did Texans revolt against the Mexican government? This question invited students into a historical problem space as they tried to determine whether the Texas revolutionaries were fighting for self-determination or to preserve slavery. However, when the teacher discovered that students didn't understand the perspective of the document written by the abolitionist—and therefore had no access to the argument that Texans revolted to preserve slavery—she paused the discussion to stabilize their understanding of the authorship and perspective of the source. Once this was established, the teacher returned to facilitating the document-based historical discussion, with students working together to build a collective understanding of why Texans revolted against the Mexican government.

ORIENTING STUDENTS TO EACH OTHER

We also saw in the first example that Jen oriented students to each other. That is, she signaled that multiple legitimate interpretations can coexist and that complex, nuanced interpretations require collective construction. In many ways, this aspect of discussion facilitation is the most challenging because it requires teachers to relinquish control and encourage students to engage directly with one another. Jen oriented students to each other using two common moves. The first, "uptake," refers to when a teacher incorporates a student's prior comment into a subsequent question (Nystrand et al., 1997). Jen did so when she asked whether students agreed with S1's claim, and again when she picked up on the prior student's mention of the phrase "animal life" (i.e., "One thing I heard you say when you said 'their animal life'"). The second move, "expose the discussion structure," refers to when the teacher helps students track and align themselves with the various perspectives raised in the discussion. In Jen's discussion at the start of this chapter, she exposed the discussion structure when she asked, "So what do you think? Jamie is saying this is about jobs and more of an economic issue. And Cathryn says it's more racist. Could it be both?" To "expose the discussion structure," the teacher needed to track, distill, and restate the core axes on which the discussion revolved. Doing so required candidates not only to follow the lines of argument that students had raised, but also to organize these arguments in relation to the central question of the lesson.

Common Pitfall

One of the greatest challenges in orienting students to each other is figuring out how to move beyond an impasse and direct students toward a historical learning goal. If the purpose of whole class document-based discussion is to engage students in collective knowledge construction, then we want students to at least attempt to articulate why they can't arrive at a shared interpretation. Even more valuable would be for students to arrive at a complex answer that incorporates all the perspectives on the table.

For example, in the discussion that follows, a teacher facilitated an animated discussion with 7th graders about the 1892 Homestead Strike for which students read two documents that offered conflicting accounts of who was to blame for the violence that ultimately killed several strikers and private Pinkerton agents who were dispatched to help break the strike: a 1922 autobiography by labor activist Emma Goldman and an 1892 interview with plant manager Henry Frick.[5] The interpretive CHQ for the lesson asked "Why did the Homestead Strike become violent?" The discussion began after students read the second document, the interview with Henry Frick. The excerpt starts after one student quoted from Frick to argue that he intended for things to remain peaceful. I've italicized all the instances where the teacher oriented students to each other in this short discussion:

> T: So Kyle is saying that Frick says, "We didn't want a confrontation. We are doing this as peacefully as possible." *How many of you agree with Kyle that they were not trying to be confrontational?*
>
> S1: I was going to say, they were entering the factory like as quietly as possible as if they were planning something. Why would they do that? I didn't fully believe what he was saying.
>
> T: So Allison is saying, "Wait a minute. Why the need to come in in the middle of the night? There's something fishy going on." *Do you agree with that?*
>
> S2: To be honest, I think that Frick is actually trying to make himself look like he's not a monster. And he's actually trying to make it look like the employees and the [union] is the bad. What if Frick is just accusing them to make himself look better?
>
> T: *Does anybody agree that Henry Frick is just accusing them in an effort to make himself look better?* What do you think, Mike?
>
> S3: In this document, it says that the association started the fire but in the first document it says that the Pinkertons did . . .
>
> T: Okay, so we have two different accounts. I only have a couple of minutes left. But what we were trying to get at through both these documents is why did it turn violent? Can you walk out of here and tell me 100%? *Give me a poll. If you think that the Emma Goldman document is more reliable, raise your hand. If you think*

that the Henry Frick document is more reliable? And Adam, I hear you saying no. Why are you saying no?

S4: Well, to be honest, I don't know. Because the Emma Goldman document is actually just really not that reliable and the Henry Frick one isn't either.

T: If I take Emma Goldman and I take Henry Frick and they both have, you know, a dog in this fight, am I going to get a reliable account? They want to paint themselves in a positive light. So if we can come up with a neutral perspective, that would help us decide why it turned violent (emphases added).

The students in this class offer sophisticated arguments about Frick's account of the confrontation, most of which they ground in the text, a testament to the teacher's prior success orienting students to the text. Moreover, the teacher actively oriented students to each other, prompting them at nearly every turn to respond to the prior comment (see italics). However, at the end of the discussion, students were no closer to formulating an answer to the CHQ. Indeed, the teacher explained the impasse as a matter of irreconcilable perspectives and suggested that only a "neutral" perspective could help students answer the central question. I would argue that this conclusion represents exactly the wrong take-away from such a discussion, as it reinforces the notion that such neutral historical texts exist in the first place. Even with these two flawed sources, students are in a fairly good position to begin to paint a picture of the broader historical context that gave way to this violence (e.g., tension between labor and industry; the growing strength of the Amalgamated Association Union; the attempt to circumvent strikers in the dead of night). It's important to note the CHQ did not ask "Who shot the first shot?"—a question that would have, indeed, been more difficult to answer with the available texts. Rather, the question asked "Why did the Homestead Strike become violent?" Students could have used the documents to surface ways that labor and management disagreed about workers' rights and what constituted fair compensation. The larger point here is that when teachers orient students to each other in a disciplinary way they do so as a means of supporting collective knowledge construction of a historical learning goal.

Helpful Tip

Using visual tools, for example, a graphic continuum that arranges students' names along a spectrum representing their responses to the CHQ, can help expose the discussion structure. Such tools allow students to see where they stand in relation to their classmates on a given question and relieves the teacher of needing to constantly "expose the discussion structure." Moreover, such tools also make clear that students' views can change (e.g., move on the continuum) as they encounter new evidence and persuasive counter-arguments.

CONCLUSION

Like Socratic seminars, structured academic controversies, or debates, document-based discussions in history are instructional activities that open the classroom to student voice, textual analysis, and argumentation. By framing history as a space for formulating and challenging interpretations, they offer a radical alternative to business as usual in history classrooms.

In this chapter, I have attempted to describe what *orienting students to the discipline* looks like in the context of whole class document-based historical discussions. In other words, I have tried to articulate what makes a historical discussion *historical*. I began by suggesting, in contrast with prior work, that orienting students to the discipline is not a discrete teacher move. Rather, it's the result of a coordinated set of moves by which the teacher engages students as sense-makers, orients them to the text, and orients them to each other *in disciplinary ways*. I then illustrated what it might look like to enact these practices in disciplinary ways. For example, to engage students as sense-makers, the teacher must pose a CHQ that opens a legitimate historical problem space, and then continually revisit this CHQ throughout the discussion. To orient students to the text in disciplinary ways, the teacher must attend to students' historical thinking so that they move beyond literal comprehension or pulling decontextualized quotes to support their claims, and also critically attend to the author's perspective and historical context. Finally, the teacher must strive to orient students to each other, such that the discussion moves toward a complex historical learning goal that represents an answer to the CHQ.

I know from years of supporting preservice and inservice teachers that orienting students to the discipline in these ways is not easy. But I remain committed to the notion that historical discussions must develop students' capacities to tolerate historical complexity. It's worth noting that these complex understandings of the past have profound implications for how we understand our present. Consider the topics discussed: how the growing success of labor organizers in 1892 and the power of industry exploded in violence during the Homestead Strike; how the institution of slavery was inextricable from the calls for Texas independence; and how economic anxiety and racism fueled 19th-century anti-immigration movements. Not only do these complex historical understandings run counter to the pat, white-washed narratives touted by textbooks, the underlying themes echo across time.

We have an urgent responsibility to prepare students to resist simple explanations to the complex problems they encounter and witness in their lives.

NOTES

1. The document-based lesson can be found here: https://sheg.stanford.edu /history-lessons/chinese-immigration-and-exclusion.

2. For example, Stanford History Education Group's Reading Like a Historian Curriculum, University of Michigan's Read.Write.Inquire project, UCLA History Geography project curriculum resources, and Berkeley's History-Social Science project lesson database.

3. These resources can be found here: http://historicalthinkingmatters.org /socialsecurity/1/resources/interpretation1/.

4. This document-based lesson is available here: https://sheg.stanford.edu /history-lessons/texas-revolution.

5. The document-based lesson can be found here: https://sheg.stanford.edu /history-lessons/homestead-strike.

REFERENCES

Duschl, R., & Osborne, J. F. (2002). Supporting and promoting argumentation discourse in science education. *Studies in Science Education*, *38*, 39–72.

Engle, R. A., & Conant, F. R. (2002). Guiding principles for fostering productive disciplinary engagement: Explaining an emergent argument in a community of learners classroom. *Cognition and Instruction*, *20*(4), 399–483.

Fogo, B., Reisman, A., & Breakstone, J. (2019). Teacher adaptation of document-based history curricula: Results from the *Reading Like a Historian* curriculum-use survey. *Journal of Curriculum Studies*, *51*(1), 62–83.

Haroutunian-Gordon, S. (2009). *Learning to teach through discussion: The art of turning the soul*. Yale University Press.

Hess, D. E., & McAvoy, P. (2015). *The political classroom: Evidence and ethics in democratic education*. Routledge.

Lew-Williams, B. (2011). *The Chinese must go: Immigration, deportation and violence in the 19th-century Pacific Northwest* [PhD dissertation, Stanford University].

National Council for the Social Studies. (2013). *The college, career, and civic life framework for social studies state standards: Guidelines for enhancing the rigor of K–12 civics, economics, geography, and history*. Author.

Nystrand, M. (2006). Research on the role of classroom discourse as it affects reading comprehension. *Research in the Teaching of English*, *40*(4), 392–412.

Nystrand, M., Gamoran, A., Kachur, R., & Prendergast, C. (1997). *Opening dialogue: Understanding the dynamics of language and learning in the English classroom*. Teachers College Press.

Reisman, A. (2012). The "document-based lesson:" Bringing disciplinary inquiry into high school history classrooms with adolescent struggling readers. *Journal of Curriculum Studies*, *44*(2), 233–264.

Reisman, A. (2015). Entering the historical problem space: Whole-class, text-based discussion in history class. *Teachers College Record, 117*(2), 1–44.

Reisman, A. (2017). Integrating content and literacy in social studies: Assessing instructional materials and student work from a Common Core-aligned intervention. *Theory and Research in Social Education, 45*(4), 517–554.

Reisman, A., Cipparone, P., Jay, L., Monte-Sano, C., Kavanagh, S. S., McGrew, S., & Fogo, B. (2019). Evidence of emergent practice: Teacher candidates facilitating historical discussion in their field placements. *Teaching and Teacher Education, 80*, 145–156.

Reisman, A., Kavanagh, S., Monte-Sano, C., Fogo, B., McGrew, S., Cipparone, P., & Simmons, E. (2018). Facilitating whole-class discussions in history: A framework for preparing teacher candidates. *Journal of Teacher Education, 69*(3), 278–293.

Saye, J., & the Social Studies Inquiry Research Collaborative. (2013). Authentic pedagogy: Its presence in social studies classrooms and relationship to student performance on state-mandated tests. *Theory & Research in Social Education, 41*(1), 89–132.

Seixas, P., & Morton, T. (2013). *The big six historical thinking concepts.* Nelson Education.

Wineburg, S. S. (1991). Historical problem solving: A study of the cognitive processes used in the evaluation of documentary and pictorial evidence. *Journal of Educational Psychology, 83*(1), 73–87.

CHAPTER 8

Embedding Discussion Throughout Inquiry[1]

María del Mar Estrada Rebull, Chauncey
Monte-Sano, Amanda Jennings, and Jeff Kabat

There are many reasons it is important for all students to participate regularly in discussion in social studies. As mentioned through previous chapters, students build social studies knowledge and understandings through dialogue: Making sense of social and historical issues requires that we put forth our own perspectives, alongside other—often contrasting—perspectives, and process them through conversation (Hess & McAvoy, 2014; Reisman, 2015). Thus, discussion creates the space for students to build social studies knowledge and understandings in authentic ways. There are also cognitive benefits: Students learn through discussion because it gives them a chance to connect their existing knowledge to new content in meaningful ways, and it helps them develop the necessary language that comes along with it (Jones & Hammond, 2018; Kramer-Dahl et al., 2007; Mercer, 2000; Schleppegrell, 2004). Moreover, when students participate in dialogue, they learn in ways that are consistent with the democratic and civic purposes of social studies education by navigating different ideas, listening to others, and working toward conclusions collectively (Hess, 2009; Parker, 2006). Even with compelling reasons for classroom discussion, it's not always clear how to foster regular discussions that allow *all* students to share in these benefits.

Our view of discussion differs from common framing in several important ways. We see discussion as an everyday practice, with a role at every stage of the inquiry process, not as a special or rare event. It is also important that a wide range of students participate consistently; not just the same few over and over (e.g., Kelly, 2007). This includes students with different academic profiles; different cultural, linguistic, and racial backgrounds; and different levels of propensity to share their thoughts. When discussions only include a few student voices, the group only benefits from limited perspectives. This can lead to skewed or incomplete social studies knowledge and understanding, which can prevent many students from reaping the learning benefits of participating in discussion. Inclusive discussions enable the diversity of perspectives required for meaningful social studies and extend the benefits of discussion to all students. Lastly, instead of limiting students' roles in discussion to brief comments, "right answers," or serial sharing of disconnected ideas, discussion-rich classrooms offer students opportunities to contribute substantive thinking through extended turns of talk and creatively build on each other's ideas (e.g., Mercer, 2000). It is this building and responding that we aim to support because it is an integral part of collective sense-making, knowledge construction, and civic education in social studies. In other words, students' thinking and participation drives the discussions, and inquiry, forward.

READ.INQUIRE.WRITE

In this chapter, we draw ideas from our time working together at Starling Middle School over a 4-year period during which we developed, tested, and revised the Read.Inquire.Write. curriculum for 6th–8th grades.[2] Our coauthor team for this chapter is a small subset of the many amazing people we've been privileged to work with on this research project (for a more complete account, see the Read.Inquire.Write. "About" page[3]). Throughout this chapter, we use "we" to share ideas that reflect our collective thinking and refer to "Mr. Kabat" or "he" when sharing examples from his classroom.

The Read.Inquire.Write. curriculum is organized into a series of "investigations," 1- or 2-week units each divided into four phases (see Figure 8.1 for more detail about each phase). The investigations are focused on a debatable central question, multiple sources with contrasting perspectives, and a writing task with an authentic purpose. Together, these investigation components offer an overarching purpose for ongoing discussion.

The remainder of this chapter is divided into four parts. First, we draw on an investigation about post-apartheid South Africa to show how Mr. Kabat uses discussion to drive inquiry learning in each of the four phases of the investigation. Second, we look more closely at phase 2 of the investigation to describe how Mr. Kabat's use of rotating participation structures (i.e., direct instruction, individual, pair/small group, whole group) can support discussion throughout inquiry learning. Third, we focus on one participation structure from phase 2, whole group, and provide examples of teacher facilitation moves that can support inclusive whole group discussions. Finally, we show how establishing classroom norms and expectations early in the year lays the foundation for productive discussions that support all students' learning. Figure 8.1 gives a visual overview of the layered work of leading inclusive discussions throughout an inquiry and depicts how each part of the chapter draws on and is related to the other parts.

Figure 8.1. Overview of Leading Inclusive Discussions Throughout Inquiry

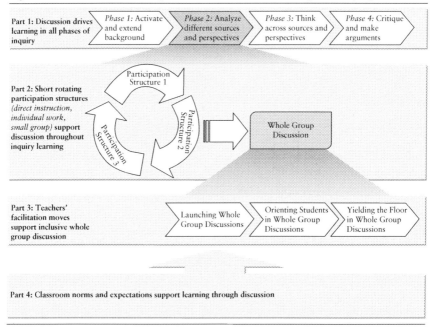

1. DISCUSSION DRIVES LEARNING IN ALL PHASES OF INQUIRY

One way to think about discussion in the social studies classrooms is to hold formal, lengthy events such as seminars, debates, or lesson-culminating whole group conversations. We offer an alternative perspective: an *inquiry approach*, in which discussions are not only a culminating event, but also an everyday means of collective sense-making (see Monte-Sano et al., under review).

We understand inquiry as a process of learning through asking questions, analyzing information from different perspectives, making sense of the issues alongside others, and forming conclusions to orient thought and action. Similarly, the inquiry arc in the college, career, and civic life (C3) framework contemplates four dimensions: (1) developing questions and planning inquiries, (2) applying disciplinary tools and concepts, (3) evaluating sources and using evidence, and (4) communicating conclusions and taking informed action (National Council for the Social Studies [NCSS], 2013). The components of this process can give students and teachers a lot to talk about. Therefore, discussion is not simply a final event to build toward, but a constant feature that permeates the entire process of inquiry.

We look at how discussion can be situated within social studies inquiry in the context of the South Africa investigation in Mr. Kabat's 7th-grade class.[4] In the first phase, students connected to the topic, and they extended their background knowledge in preparation for the inquiry. They analyzed different sources and perspectives on the central question ("Is post-apartheid South Africa living up to its promises?"). The sources for this investigation included the following:

1. An interview with Zondwa, a Black South African woman who remembers life during apartheid and compares it to the present day, highlighting significant improvements.
2. An interview with Pieter and Brandon, two young white South African men, who say Black people have been favored more than white.
3. An *Economist* article that reports on inequity and unemployment figures in South Africa 18 years after the end of apartheid.
4. An NPR news story that reviews the book *South Africa @20: For Better or For Worse.*[5]

Students read and analyzed each source and reflected on how it could help them think about and respond to the central question. In the third phase, they reflected on what claims in response to the central question could be best supported by the evidence. In the fourth and final phase, students critiqued speeches by then-presidential candidates Jacob Zuma (who emphasized South Africa's strengths under the rule of his party, the ANC), and Helen Zille (who denounced ANC's shortcomings and called for a change). They drew from these critiques to argue why *The New York Times* should *not* endorse one of those candidates in the 2014 South African general election; that is, they critiqued one of the presidential candidates based on their speeches.

Students had frequent discussions as they worked through each of the phases of this investigation, but not all of these interactions were culminating discussions in which they proposed conclusions in response to the central question as we often find in the social studies education literature (e.g., Reisman, 2015). We have identified "sense-making discussions" as those interactions that happened while students analyzed and made sense of sources (Monte-Sano et al., under review). In such discussions, students consider or analyze details about and within a source in order to understand the source's meaning; this work sets them up to develop interpretations later. We distinguish sense-making discussions from "argumentative discussions," where students consider the reliability of sources, corroborate and synthesize sources, or identify claims that are supported by evidence and reasoning, which are all aspects of developing an argument in response to a central question, and similar to the kinds of discussion discussed in the literature (e.g., Reisman, 2015). We found that some argumentative discussions are culminating moments in a lesson and others happen in the

Figure 8.2. Examples of Discussions in Each Phase of the South Africa Investigation

	Phase 1: Activate and extend background	Phase 2: Analyze different sources and perspectives	Phase 3: Think across sources and perspectives	Phase 4: Critique and make arguments
Phase Descriptions	Review knowledge of South Africa and engage with the central question.	Read and analyze sources as they think about the central question.	Think about the range of responses to the central question that are plausible given the available evidence.	Critique interpretations of the CQ offered by others and/or develop their own evidence-based response to the CQ.
Examples of Discussion from Mr. Kabat's South Africa Investigation	1. Individually, then in small groups, then in whole group sense-making discussion, predict what happened in post apartheid South Africa. 2. Whole group sense-making discussion about the promises of post apartheid South Africa and students' reflections on them. 3. Pairs and then whole group sense-making discussion of the significance of the past apartheid South Africa new national anthem and project. 4. Individually take notes during a video, then whole group sense-making discussion about what statistics about post apartheid South Africa tell us.	1. In pairs or small groups, mark the genre and date of each source and who created it. Then in a whole group sense-making discussion share what they marked and why. 2. In pairs, annotate sources to develop comprehension and consider how the source relates to the central question. Share developing understandings in a whole group sense-making discussion. 3. Whole group argumentative discussion of the reliability of each source in relation to the central question.	1. Individually, identify possible claims and evidence/reasoning to support the claims. 2. In whole group argumentative discussion, discuss, challenge, and add to each other's thinking.	1. Individually, read candidate speeches, then in pairs share what they critiqued. Debrief in whole group argumentative discussion. 2. In pairs, share which candidate they did not want the New York Times to endorse. In whole group argumentative discussion, justify claims with evidence and reasoning. 3. Write individually, then in pairs talk about what they need to do to wrap up their writing. 4. In whole group, share what helps them learn and write during the investigation.

course of a lesson. These distinctions reinforce the notion that students think together through discussion throughout the inquiry. Figure 8.2 offers a summary of the phases of this investigation, followed by examples of the discussions—both sense-making and argumentative—students had within each of Mr. Kabat's class.

Engaging in inquiry gives students a lot to talk about as they interpret complex sources with contrasting perspectives, respond to a debatable central question, and craft an argument. During this 1-week inquiry, Mr. Kabat used discussion as a regular tool for collaborative sense-making and deliberation of arguments through all the different stages of inquiry. But how did the teacher help make it work?

2. SHORT ROTATING PARTICIPATION STRUCTURES THAT SUPPORT DISCUSSIONS

The Read.Inquire.Write. curriculum breaks complex inquiries down into phases of disciplinary work. Each phase encompasses a meaningful disciplinary goal that contributes to developing and making an argument in response to the central question (like identifying useful parts of a source or finding evidence to support a claim). Dividing inquiry into phases offers students a chance to process each aspect of the disciplinary work needed to produce a written argument based on sources. Additionally, each phase is further broken down into activities. During each activity teachers use multiple participation structures to support students. For example, phase 2 focuses on analyzing a set of sources, and one activity within that phase might focus only on analyzing the headnote and attribution of *one* of the sources. For that one activity, a teacher might employ multiple participation structures and facilitation moves. This breakdown of inquiry combined with rotating participation structures supported students' work during each phase of inquiry (e.g., see Figure 8.2).

Multiple opportunities during each phase of work for discussion further support students' progress. Mr. Kabat's overall strategy for promoting inclusive discussions throughout these inquiries was to have students work on each phase through a rotation of some or all of these participation structures: (a) whole group explicit instruction/modeling, (b) individual work, (c) pair or small group discussion, and (d) whole group discussion.

By starting with explicit instruction and modeling, the teacher makes the disciplinary strategies accessible for all students. Then, a moment to work and think individually (usually less than a minute) gives every student a chance to consider the material and formulate a point of view or question to contribute. Next, as Mr. Kabat shared during one of our debriefing conversations, pair or small group talk "gives [students] ownership, gives them interest, gives them more ideas than they would ever get calling one on one." Students get the chance to try out their ideas and refine their understandings in a safe environment. Small groups help multilingual learners as well. They have the option to, as Mr. Kabat said in a debrief, "gently join" or "gently not join" in small groups or pairs, instead of the hard dichotomy of raising or not raising their hand in a large group setting. In a survey, many of the students said it helped to talk with their group, because it allowed them to hear what other people have to say, to see that their ideas could be challenged, and to know that they could revise their thinking. Having prior moments of individual and/or pair or small group talk increases the chances that more—and more varied—students will contribute during whole group discussions. Lastly, whole group discussions are moments in which students' insights are put forward for the rest of the group to learn from, consider, build on, or push back.

Let's look more closely at one segment from phase 2 of the South Africa investigation and notice the rotation of the different participation structures Mr. Kabat uses and how discussion is incorporated within this phase of the investigation (refer to Figure 8.2). During phase 2 of the investigation, students work with source 1: the interview with Zondwa, a Black woman who remembers life during apartheid, compares it to the present day, and evaluates how the government is doing. In this phase of the inquiry, students annotate the source to pinpoint how Zondwa feels about the post-apartheid government (thus informing the response to "Is post-apartheid South Africa living up to its promises?"). Through a video, students get explicit instruction on annotating the source with attention to how an author thinks or feels; then they talk in pairs; then they shift to whole group discussion. On this day, students spent 1–4 minutes in each participation structure.

Students experienced this particular sequence of participation structures (explicit instruction/modeling, individual work or pair talk, whole group discussion) three times in a row. Each sequence of participation structures focused on a particular activity connected to analyzing the interview with Zondwa (e.g., analyzing the headnote and attribution, making sense of what Zondwa was saying, and evaluating the source). Different combinations of participation structures were repeated, with some alterations, across multiple activities in each lesson.

3. Teachers' Facilitation Supports Inclusive Whole Group Discussions

After pair or small group talk, whole group discussions are usually the last participation structure in each of the phases of disciplinary work. Teachers involved in creating the Read.Inquire.Write. curriculum developed a pattern for these discussions. Initially, several students share from their independent, pair, or small group work to launch the discussion. Then, teachers offer orienting follow-ups and remarks that help build common understandings and scaffold student thinking. This moment of substantial teacher facilitation often leads to a third, final moment, in which teachers yield the floor and students take the lead in furthering their ideas and building off of each other. Let's see how Mr. Kabat's facilitation of a whole group discussion played out when students worked with the Zondwa source during phase 2 of the South Africa investigation.

Launching Whole Group Discussions

In whole group discussions that draw from students' previous work, one of Mr. Kabat's first goals is for one or several students to share some of the thinking they have been doing. This share out is valuable in itself, because it makes the contributions visible for the rest of the group. Sometimes a simple share out can suffice as a whole group moment, especially if there isn't time for more. But this initial share out can be the launching pad for further collective sense-making.

So, how do teachers launch whole group discussions and promote initial contributions from a range of students? Mr. Kabat often begins with low-stakes, open-ended invitations to share from the work they just completed, rather than posing a question that feels like a quiz that can be passed or failed. For instance, he has asked questions like, "What is something you noticed/underlined/wrote?" instead of "Who is this author?" Mr. Kabat also prompts students to share from the pair or small group discussions by asking "Who can share something they thought, heard, or said at their tables?" These kinds of prompts open the door for a wide range of contributions coming from students at any level of attainment. For Mr. Kabat, even contributions that show misunderstandings are valued: "We're gonna steer it, we're gonna thank you for saying that, because it's gonna make us think of something that'll maybe get us to the right place." Knowing their comments will be well received likely makes students more willing to talk in the whole group, and misunderstandings can create good opportunities to talk through points of confusion.

Teachers can bring diverse voices into the initial share outs in other ways. Instead of relying on volunteers (who may tend to be the same students over and over again), Mr. Kabat has used random calling to invite *other* students to speak or called on specific students he noticed had useful contributions as he circulated during independent work or small groups earlier. In Figure 8.3, we share examples of how Mr. Kabat launched a whole group sense-making discussion about the Zondwa interview.

Figure 8.3. Examples of Launching Whole Group Sense-Making Discussions

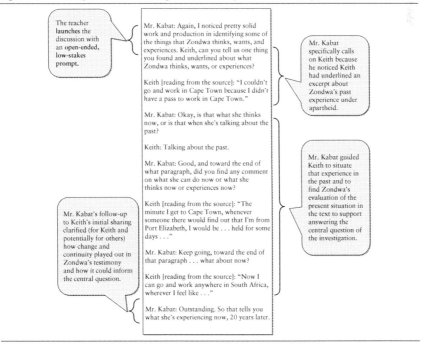

"Orienting Moves" in Whole Group Discussions. With students' initial contributions as starting points, teachers follow up with purposeful moves to further the process of thinking together and extending student thinking. We use Reisman and her colleagues' (2017) four practices to analyze the instructional work that goes into discussion facilitation. Mr. Kabat used several of these moves as they discussed the ideas Zondwa shared in her interview (see Figure 8.4):

1. Engaging students as sense-makers. Teachers *engage students as sense-makers* by asking open-ended questions with multiple plausible responses, listening carefully to students, and taking up or responding to students' ideas. Sometimes this means following up on students' initial ideas by prompting them to elaborate, explain their meaning or reasoning, or push their ideas further. This sends the message that the discussion is not about "a right answer," but about students' own thinking about the issues. Often, just providing ample wait time invites and allows students to participate.

2. Orienting students to each other. Teachers *orient students to each other* by prompting students to recognize each other's contributions and make connections between them, rather than just issue a series of isolated comments. Sometimes students themselves signal that they're building on someone else's ideas or agreeing or disagreeing with them; if they're not, teachers point it out. Some teachers also provide sentence stems to this end. Another option is for teachers to ask everyone to show their stance physically and notice others' stances (holding up a different number of fingers for different options, thumbs up or down, or moving to different parts of the room).

3. Orienting students to the text. Teachers *orient students to the text*. In social studies inquiries, students regularly work with written and visual texts (i.e., sources). When students share their thoughts or conclusions about a text, they often do so without explicit references to these texts. This makes it challenging for students to collectively consider an idea without its basis or assess the justification for a claim. We've regularly seen teachers ask students to point out specific parts or details of the sources relevant to their points. Orientating to the text can help clarify ideas, or help students better inform and ground their thinking. This move reinforces an important disciplinary practice of grounding interpretations in documentary evidence. This discussion move can also promote inclusivity by helping make the connections to the texts accessible for all students.

4. Orienting students to the discipline. Teachers *orient students to the discipline* by highlighting disciplinary ways of thinking or working

Figure 8.4. Examples of Orienting Moves in Whole Group Discussions

This moment is a continuation of the discussion in Figure 3. Before this moment, students had read and annotated the Zondwa source, then the teacher had launched the whole group discussion, asking them to share what they found and underlined about what Zondwa thinks, wants, or experiences.

Adam and Lacie here include direct quotations in their comments after seeing Mr. Kabat **orient Keith to the text** during the initial launch.

Mr. Kabat **engages** Adam and Lacie as **sense-makers** by prompting them to elaborate on what their chosen quotes mean to them.

Mr. Kabat: Alright, Leah.

Leah: Um, I wrote on the side margin that she can work wherever she wanted.

Mr. Kabat: Okay. And again, that was in the past, comparing that with now? Good.

Jaspan: See that? I had already thought of that.

Mr. Kabat: Adam.

Adam: She said "old government was just around to give people hardship, hurt them, and oppress them."

Mr. Kabat: And when she's saying now, saying that's what the old government was doing, does that give you a feeling about what she might think about the new government?

Adam: Yeah, because they built houses [inaudible].

Mr. Kabat: So, it makes you feel that now, if she saying that's what they used to do, makes you feel that, now it's different, right? Nice. Lacie.

Lacie: Oh, so I underlined, "you just need to be a little bit more patient," and wrote, "does she feel like more could be done than what's alreay going on?"

Mr. Kabat: So, you're asking, could more be—it's generally positive, right?

Lacie: Yeah, but like she's like, I don't wanna . . . the negative, but she was like, oh, we just need to learn to be a little bit more patient.

Mr. Kabat: Excellent. That's a great question and comment, you know, mmm, beautiful.

Mr. Kabat's prompts and comments also **orient students to the discipline** by directing them to notice the differences between then and now in Zondwa's testimony (thinking in terms of change and continuity is key in history and for this central question in particular).

embedded in social studies inquiry. In whole group discussions, we've seen teachers build off students' comments to guide the whole group toward new understandings about the social or historical issues and about the ways in which we construct our knowledge about them.

Yielding the Floor to Students. In our work together, we have seen many whole group discussions in which moments of students sharing from their individual and small group work, followed by moments of teachers' purposeful facilitation, led to whole group discussion with a wide range of participants. In these moments, a range of students—including multilingual learners and less advanced readers—take extended turns of talk and build off of each other's contributions without much teacher mediation. At junctures like this, we've seen teachers yield the floor to students so that their ideas and exchanges can take center stage.

Yielding the floor to students can be hard, because students' ideas can take unexpected turns, and teachers may feel the need to redirect, clarify, evaluate, or provide concluding remarks. Yet, teachers can be purposeful and selective about their interventions. This entails letting students speak at length, avoiding interrupting or weighing in, and protecting sufficient wait time for students to finish their comments before others have a turn.

By yielding the floor to students, teachers honor the core of inquiry-oriented social studies: students' sense-making about historical and social issues. However, we have found that these student-centered whole group discussion moments don't just happen spontaneously: they are built toward through independent work, small group talk, and teachers' whole group facilitation.

Let's go back to Mr. Kabat's whole group sense-making discussion about the meaning of the Zondwa interview to see how several students took the floor. After Lacie's comments (in Figure 8.4), each student wrote a sentence to sum up their interpretation of Zondwa's views about the new South African government. After a few minutes of writing, students started sharing their interpretations of the source in a whole group discussion (see Figure 8.5).

In this last section of the whole group discussion as it relates to the central question of the investigation, we can see students taking their time in long turns to share what they've gradually come to through the different participation structures: their interpretations of Zondwa's stance, grounded in evidence and reasoning. The teacher's role at this point was mostly to yield the floor to them.

This whole group discussion moment was the final stage of this particular activity, which included explicit instruction, individual work, pair talk, whole group sharing, and teacher facilitation. Subsequent disciplinary activities also featured rotating participation structures in which opportunities for all students to talk were, once again, key in their learning. It's important to note that this was not the culminating discussion—this was just one of the activities, and as they moved to other activities within this phase of the inquiry (where they analyzed sources) the teacher cycled through participation structures once again to support students' continued involvement in analyzing sources. After several rotations of participation structures focused on different aspects of analyzing sources (each with embedded short discussions), the class participated in a culminating whole group discussion.

Figure 8.5. Examples of Yielding the Floor in Whole Group Discussions

Students are sharing, testing, and further developing their interpretation of the source as it relates to the central question, "Is post-apartheid South Africa living up to its promises?"

Mr. Kabat doesn't call on the new hands when Jaspan gets stuck, allowing him to finish his thought.

Adam: Yes, she does. Um [long pause, Adam apparently looking for what he was going to say]. Never mind. Oh, yeah yeah: She, um, because, yeah, she does, but not enough, because she said that she sees some of the positives, but not all of it so we have to wait for someone like to do other good things.

Adam had ample time to figure out what he wanted to say.

Mr. Kabat: [Gives a thumbs up, points to Jaspan to go next].

Jaspan: She didn't back then, 'cause she said that the old government was just around to give people hardship and hurt them and oppress them. But then, now, um, yes, they're living up—or what? [Several other hands go up at this point] What? Yeah, living up to its promises because they said that if people [reading from source] . . . "Yes, people are in need of houses now, but if you could just have a look at how many houses have been built. There has been a lot."

Mr. Kabat doesn't add anything; he just calls on the next student.

Mr. Kabat weighs in to orient students to each other by directing them to listen to Leah's comment, which turned out to be an agreement with Jaspan's thinking.

Mr. Kabat: Okay, while you were reading, I don't think you heard, you may have heard Leah, what were you saying? [To Leah] Say it loudly, what you said.

Leah: I was gonna say that.

Mr. Kabat: You said "I was gonna say that," good. Shaimaa.

Shaimaa: Uh, I said yes, because I quoted what she said: "I can go anywhere in South Africa whenever I feel like," so basically there's like a little bit of good.

Shaimaa gives her interpretation of Zondwa's stance and supports it with a quote and reasoning, all on her own. Mr. Kabat doesn't add on.

Mr. Kabat: Jordan.

Leah orients herself to other students: She positions her interpretation of the source in contrast to what others have said, grounds it in textual evidence, and offers her reasoning.

Jordan: I said "Zondwa thinks it's living up to the promises. She looks like, for the positives, and is always finding them." She says patience is the key and she hopes that—and she has hope for her country.

Mr. Kabat: Beautiful. Andrew, Leah.

Andrew: Um, Zondwa believes that it's better, but it could still use some work. She says, you just have to be patient.

Mr. Kabat: Leah.

Leah: Okay, so, I don't know why anyone's saying that, uh, she doesn't think that things are getting better, because she says, "I don't wanna dwell on the negative—I see the positives," and like, and like there's like a positive but there's literally a sentence in it that says "I feel government has done a great deal. . . . Things have become better." And that shows that her perspective is that they are living up to the promises.

Jordan also provides a text-grounded interpretation, which Mr. Kabat praises briefly before calling on other students.

4. Classroom Norms and Expectations for Inclusive Discussions

As we have shown, social studies inquiries provide regular occasions for substantive discussion. However, students might not automatically be keen to participate. When we saw how often and how many students participated in discussions throughout Mr. Kabat's inquiries, we spent time in his 6th-grade classroom at the beginning of the school year to learn more about how he establishes a supportive classroom environment with students when they first start middle school. We found that the robust, inclusive whole class discussions we observed rely on established norms and routines for a healthy learning environment. Mr. Kabat's priority during the first 2 weeks of school is to establish the conditions that enable and sustain broad student participation and regular opportunities to talk by fostering community and establishing expectations. His 6th-grade teaching partner does similar work in the first 2 weeks of school, and then they reinforce those norms and routines throughout 6th and 7th grade. By the time we observed what was originally a 7th-grade South Africa investigation, students were accustomed to and a part of a supportive learning community.

Fostering Community

A strong community is the key underlying condition for inquiry and on-going talk in Mr. Kabat's classroom. Such community relies on everyone knowing each other's names and personalities. At the beginning of the year, Mr. Kabat prioritizes getting to know each other during the first week of school. It's important both to the community building and to the interactive style that supports inquiry. In one activity, for example, Mr. Kabat shares his personal background and then asks students to share something about themselves at their tables. Other activities during this first week aim for everyone to learn everyone else's names. Additionally, he takes time to make sure he calls each student by the name or nickname of their preference, and that he's pronouncing each one correctly. Pre-assigning students to specific pods of three to five members also helps him learn names quickly: He keeps a seating chart with him during class, and he calls on different students by name. Mr. Kabat greets everyone by name in the hallways and expresses he's happy to see them. A strong community also entails a safe environment. As Mr. Kabat shared in a debriefing conversation, this means that students know "that everybody's working on the same team in this room, that I'm not gonna be teased or disrespected in this class, at least when the teacher's paying attention. . . . That no matter what I say, there's value to it in this room." They know that even if they give the "craziest, most off-topic, most wrong answer possible," Mr. Kabat's response is going to be positive.

In one example of this community building during the South Africa investigation, we saw Mr. Kabat reinforce this notion of being on the same team and being positive with students: Jaspan got frustrated that Lacie shared a comment with the whole class that he had wanted to share. Mr. Kabat affirmed both students and diffused the frustration by saying, "You're both very sharp thinkers and you're on each other's wavelength." Later in the lesson, Lacie wanted to share again. Instead of calling on her right away, Mr. Kabat checked with Jaspan first: "Jaspan, I'm about to call on Lacie; should I call on you first?" In so doing, Mr. Kabat built that sense of community and trust that everyone had a place in their community.

Setting Expectations

In Mr. Kabat's room, each participation structure has its own set of expectations, and there are expectations for how to transition smoothly between them. Students are familiar with the term *expectations*, and Mr. Kabat uses it to cue students at different moments. He might say, "Group work expectations will be in place for this activity. Can someone remind me what the expectations for group work are?" or "You're doing a great job following discussion expectations."

Group Work Expectations. Mr. Kabat's expectations for small group talk include students focused on their own table groups rather than on other tables; a volume level that allows their group to hear them, but not others; and participation from everybody in the group. This last one is not a strict requirement, especially during the first days of middle school, but a goal. Mr. Kabat explained the following when we debriefed during the first week:

> I will notice kids that are listening but not talking, and I get a sense that maybe that's their personality, they're introverted. I might give them a week or two before I go up to them during small group talk and say [whispering], 'How come you're not talking? Think of something.' And I might get them to tell me something and I'll say, 'Beautiful. When he (another group member) stops talking, I want you to tell everybody.' I try to encourage them to join that way. . . . As the community is built, and as the students feel comfortable and safe, they're much more likely to talk. . . . And sometimes I have to talk to other kids and say, 'Alright now, you're talking a lot and it's fantastic. But part of your job in a group is to make sure everyone talks.'

Mr. Kabat has experimented with small groups over the years, and he has come to some configurations that work best for him. He sets up the room with permanent pods for three to five students of mixed ability. Leaving furniture this way, instead of moving it each time for small group work has several advantages: (1) It prevents hassle, noise, and distraction; 2) it promotes more frequent small group work; (3) students are used to sitting in groups all the time—they don't feel like it's a special, social moment in which they can have unrelated talk or ignore directions. We see groups of three or four members (or even five) enhance group inquiry. With this range of participants, multiple perspectives emerge. Students who might be shy not only benefit from this, they are also more likely to participate than if they were in pairs. (Other Read.Inquire.Write. teachers prefer pair talk.)

Mr. Kabat doesn't always assign different roles to students within a group, but he gives groups a common task, such as answering a question to elicit prior knowledge, coming up with possible claims for an argument, or finding evidence in a source. He makes sure that everyone has the materials they will need and that the directions are clear. He may also indicate the duration of the talk (for example, 30 or 60 seconds) before signaling for the students to start. If there are worksheets involved, some students may tend to fill them out individually, so he signals that the priority is that they actually talk to each other and that the worksheets and graphic organizers are just supports. Mr. Kabat takes advantage of the fact that everything about middle school is new to incoming 6th graders. When he asks students to talk in groups, they do it, and it gets established as a normal routine.

Whole Class Discussion Expectations. Each day, Mr. Kabat's goal is that every student speaks out loud at least once. If a student or a group hasn't spoken, he'll call on them even if they don't raise their hands. By starting on the first day of class, students take it as the normal routine, and they learn that they can be called on anytime. Also, as Mr. Kabat shared in a debrief that students "quickly learn that they have the total power to say, 'I'm not sure,' or 'I wanna pass today,' or whatever, for whatever reason, because it's a safe and comfortable environment: it's all good." But because students' participation is scaffolded with earlier individual and pair or small group work, they are typically prepared to share an idea in whole class conversation.

CONCLUSION

Frequent discussions embedded in the process of inquiry can provide opportunities for *all* students to build social studies knowledge and understandings, consider different perspectives, and practice dialogical skills that are essential in a democracy. Building a welcoming community and setting up routines and expectations for discussions early in the year is key to attaining classrooms in which fruitful, inclusive discussions take place regularly. Mr. Kabat and other teachers have found success in promoting talk on a day-to-day basis by breaking up inquiries into smaller disciplinary segments, in which students engage through rotating participation structures. Students process their ideas individually and through small group talk and then share them in a whole group discussion, where the teacher's purposeful facilitation can help further and connect these ideas just as much as their purposeful yielding of the floor to students. With these and similar strategies, teachers can turn their social studies classrooms into communities where students collectively make sense of historical and social issues through dialogue and drive an inquiry forward.

NOTES

1. We are grateful for the teachers, school leaders, students, and researchers who contributed to this work and made it possible. We are also grateful to Jane Lo and Abby Reisman for their feedback on this chapter. This work was generously funded by the Library of Congress Teaching With Primary Sources program and the James S. McDonnell Foundation. The authors alone are responsible for the ideas in this chapter. The recently launched Read.Inquire.Write. curriculum embodies this work and has been generously supported by the Braitmayer Foundation, the James S. McDonnell Foundation, the Library of Congress, and the Spencer Foundation.

2. See https://readinquirewrite.umich.edu/.

3. See https://readinquirewrite.umich.edu/team/. Specifically, the ideas in this chapter are based on the following: (1) Chauncey's and Jeff's early collaboration in developing, assessing, and revising inquiry-oriented social studies investigations to support students' analytical thinking and argument writing; (2) Chauncey's article with Schleppegrell et al. (article in review) analyzing data to understand how teachers support inclusive and substantive student participation in discussions while using the Read.Inquire.Write. curriculum; (3) Jeff's approach to establishing routines and norms for discourse in his middle school social studies classroom at the beginning of the year and Mar's documentation of his work. Claims about discussion facilitation in this chapter are grounded in students' discourse and teachers' instructional moves (as captured and analyzed in video-recorded class sessions), regular conversations with participating teachers and students, and analysis of classroom artifacts (e.g., a handout or set of slides).

4. Originally, the South Africa investigation was written for and implemented with 7th graders, so we refer to Mr. Kabat's 7th-grade classroom here. However, we have since revised this investigation and now include it in the Read.Inquire.Write. curriculum that is freely available online as a 6th-grade investigation.

5. We have since updated the source set to include a perspective from a South African news agency.

REFERENCES

Hess, D. E. (2009). *Controversy in the classroom: The democratic power of discussion*. Routledge.

Hess, D. E., & McAvoy, P. (2014). *The political classroom: Evidence and ethics in democratic education*. Routledge.

Jones, P., & Hammond, J. (Eds.). (2018). *Talking to learn*. Routledge.

Kelly, S. (2007). Classroom discourse and the distribution of student engagement. *Social Psychology of Education: An International Journal, 10*(3), 331–352.

Kramer-Dahl, A., Teo, P., & Chia, A. (2007). Supporting knowledge construction and literate talk in secondary social studies. *Linguistics and Education, 18*, 167–199.

Mercer, N. (2000). *Words and minds: How we use language to think together*. Taylor & Francis.

Monte-Sano, C., Hughes, R. E., & Thomson, S. (2019). From form to function: Learning with practitioners to support diverse middle school students' disciplinary reasoning and writing. In B. Rubin, E. Freedman, & J. Kim (Eds.), *Design research in social studies education* (pp. 31–57). Routledge.

Monte-Sano, C., Schleppegrell, M., Sun, S., & Wu, J. (in review). Discussion in diverse middle school social studies classrooms: Promoting all students' participation in the disciplinary work of inquiry. *Teachers College Record.*

National Council for the Social Studies. (2013). *College, career, and civic life: The C3 framework for state social studies standards.* Author.

Parker, W. C. (2006). Public discourses in schools: Purposes, problems, possibilities. *Educational Researcher, 35*(8), 11–18.

Reisman, A. (2015). Entering the historical problem space: Whole-class text-based discussion in history class. *Teachers College Record, 117*(2), 1–44.

Reisman, A., Kavanagh, S. S., Monte-Sano, C., Fogo, B., McGrew, S. C., Cipparone, P., & Simmons, E. (2018). Facilitating whole-class discussions in history: A framework for preparing teacher candidates. *Journal of Teacher Education, 69*(3), 278–293.

Schleppegrell, M. J. (2004). *The language of schooling: A functional linguistics perspective.* Routledge.

Part III

EXPANDING TOWARD MORE EQUITABLE DISCUSSIONS

CHAPTER 9

Talking Politics Online
Educating for Online Civic and Political Dialogue

Erica Hodgin

I learned how to respectfully comment on other people's posts while dis-agreeing with them. I thought that was kind of cool—kind of a good thing to learn 'cause you can disagree with someone and bring up your points . . . without offending them.

—11th-grade student

This student had the opportunity to engage with other students from across the country via an online academic platform called Youth Voices. The student talked about how the most important thing she took from the experience was learning how to respectfully communicate with people with whom you may not agree. While reaching beyond the classroom walls and integrating an opportunity for dialogue across political differences may seem overwhelming to facilitate, a variety of online platforms enable youth to have more frequent opportunities to engage in civic and political dialogue, and doing so in the context of a classroom can lend needed support. In the past, youth typically only discussed civic and political issues in structured discussions or debates (like ones described in Part II of this volume) that took place in their classroom, school, or after-school activities that were facilitated or overseen by an adult, and with peers who were known to them (Kahne et al., 2016). Now, online dialogue can take place anytime, anywhere (Ito et al., 2013). While online dialogue can be riddled with conflict, engaging youth in productive civic and political dialogue in schools is increasingly critical as youth report relying on advice and support from adults—mainly parents and teachers or another adult at school—to help them navigate online conflict (Lenhart et al., 2011).

This chapter first outlines what we know about youth engagement in online civic and political dialogue and the role schools and teachers can and should play. The chapter also builds on traditional understandings of discussion to conceptualize five learning opportunities that can be integrated into the classroom as a means of building young people's capacity for civic dialogue and voice. Then, the chapter highlights four key challenges teachers face, as well as supports that are needed to integrate such learning opportunities in high-quality and equitable ways.[1]

ARE YOUTH ENGAGING IN ONLINE CIVIC AND POLITICAL DIALOGUE?

The affordances of digital media provide expanded opportunities to learn about issues, share one's points of view, be exposed to multiple perspectives, and push for change. These opportunities are particularly significant for youth, who have traditionally been limited in their ability to participate in institutional activities. Duggan and Smith (2016) found that 8 in 10 social media users reported that they feel social media platforms "help users get involved with issues that matter to them" and "[help] bring new voices into the political discussion." Similarly, a majority of teen respondents reported that they believe social media helps people their age diversify their networks, broaden their viewpoints, and get involved with issues they care about (Anderson & Jiang, 2018).

Although the digital age opens up expanded opportunities, online dialogue is also fraught with challenges, such as filter bubbles and echo chambers that limit one's exposure to varied information and diverse perspectives and individuals (Pariser, 2012; Sunstein, 2007). Youth and adults alike struggle to judge the credibility of online information driving a lack of evidence that can bolster political discourse (Breakstone et al., 2019; Kahne & Bowyer, 2017). In addition, increased anonymity can reduce interpersonal cues and fuel unproductive conflict (Min, 2007). From a nationally representative survey of youth ages 15–25, Middaugh et al. (2017) found that witnessing online conflict is common, especially for those most engaged with politics online. Furthermore, when asked to evaluate scenarios of conflictual online political dialogue, a significant number of respondents recommended withdrawing from the conversation rather than working toward productive dialogue. Therefore, engaging youth in productive online dialogue as well as teaching strategies to navigate disagreement and conflict are critical.

SHOULD STUDENTS ENGAGE IN CIVIC AND POLITICAL
DIALOGUE IN SCHOOL?

As discussed elsewhere in this volume, engaging young people in discussions of local, national, and international issues has long been regarded as a core component of civic education (Gibson & Levine, 2003). When youth engage in discussions of current events and decisionmaking, they report being more engaged in school as well as greater interest in politics, improved communication and critical thinking skills, increased civic knowledge, and a higher chance of participating in civic life as adults (Gould, 2011). In addition, it is key for youth to engage in discussion of controversial issues. However, research shows that not all youth have the same opportunities to engage in political discussion. In a study of over 2,000 California high school seniors, Kahne and Middaugh (2008) found a civic opportunity gap where higher academic standing, White, or higher income students had more civic learning opportunities, including discussions of social and political topics. In order to not replicate political inequality, all students need regular and meaningful opportunities to discuss civic and political issues.

SHOULD CIVIC AND POLITICAL DIALOGUE OCCUR IN POLITICALLY DIVISIVE TIMES?

Political polarization is growing worldwide, but it is particularly pronounced in the United States (Draca & Schwartz, 2020). We are more divided along ideological lines today than at any point in the last 2 decades, with a large majority of Americans reporting the tone and nature of political debate has become more negative in recent years as well as less respectful, less fact based, and less substantive (Doherty, 2017). For instance, a national survey found that social media users were more likely in 2020 than in 2016 to negatively describe political discourse in these online platforms, and 7 out of 10 found them "stressful and frustrating" (Anderson & Auxier, 2020). Contentious political discourse can also be found in schools and classrooms. In 2019, the Southern Poverty Law Center identified 821 school-based hate or bias incidents that were reported in the media. In addition, a 2017 study found that more than 20% of teachers reported heightened polarization on campus and incivility in their classrooms (Rogers et al., 2017). In this divisive context and with an increase of online communication, attending to the opportunities and challenges associated with online civic and political discussion in schools is more important than ever.

CAN AND SHOULD SCHOOLS PLAY A ROLE IN SUPPORTING ONLINE CIVIC AND POLITICAL DIALOGUE?

Fortunately, online publication and discussion has become more common in helping students build digital production skills and capacities. For example, blogging and other forms of online publication have drawn increasing interest from teachers because of the expanded focus on and interaction around writing (Schultz et al., 2015). However, instruction focused on online communication generally will not fully prepare youth for civic and political dialogue. For example, in a study of 15 young civic dialoguers, James (2016) found that participants noted a lack of (or "outdated") curriculum related to online civic participation. There is growing recognition that civic education must be redesigned for the digital age, and that media literacy education is needed to support youth participation in democracy and civic life (Kahne et al., 2016; Levine & Kawashima-Ginsberg, 2017). Therefore, educational efforts that combine media literacy development alongside civic learning are key to fully preparing youth for participation in the digital age (Hodgin, 2019). In addition, equity must be at the forefront of any effort in order to ensure that all students have access to such opportunities.

WHAT ARE EXAMPLES OF TEACHERS INTEGRATING ONLINE CIVIC AND POLITICAL DIALOGUE?

The next portion of this chapter draws on a study of six high school teachers' work implementing online civic dialogue in their classrooms and includes data from student interviews, classroom observations, teacher interviews, and teacher focus groups. The first phase of the study occurred in 2014 (Hodgin, 2016), and the second phase took place in 2020. Five of the six teachers taught in public high schools in the same city in northern California. The sixth teacher, who taught at a private high school in Utah, developed connections with the California teachers via an online platform called Youth Voices.

Five teachers utilized a school-based social network platform called Youth Voices that was developed by National Writing Project (NWP) teachers to bring students together online to share writing and engage in conversation. Around 30 middle schools and high schools across the United States participated in the site. Three teachers in the sample utilized other platforms in addition to or instead of Youth Voices such as Edublogs, Flipgrid, Instagram, and Twitter to support their students' engagement in online civic dialogue.

By interviewing teachers about their reasons for integrating online civic and political dialogue, I was able to identify three foundational learning goals that compelled teachers. In addition, I identified several learning opportunities that were key to developing students' capacities for online civic and political dialogue, as well as a range of obstacles teachers faced. These goals, opportunities, challenges, and supports highlight important considerations for educators and schools aiming to prepare students for civic voice and influence in the digital age (see Figure 9.1).

Student Learning Goals

Teachers in the study, who taught a range of English language arts (ELA) and history–social science courses at the high school level, shared four ways

Figure 9.1. Educating for Online Civic and Political Dialogue

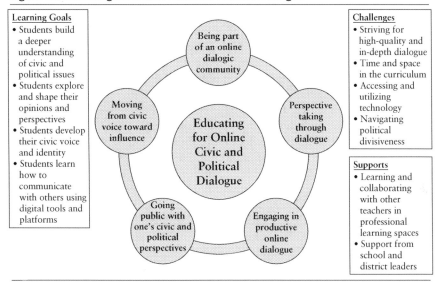

Learning Goals
• Students build a deeper understanding of civic and political issues
• Students explore and shape their opinions and perspectives
• Students develop their civic voice and identity
• Students learn how to communicate with others using digital tools and platforms

Challenges
• Striving for high-quality and in-depth dialogue
• Time and space in the curriculum
• Accessing and utilizing technology
• Navigating political divisiveness

Supports
• Learning and collaborating with other teachers in professional learning spaces
• Support from school and district leaders

Being part of an online dialogic community

Moving from civic voice toward influence

Educating for Online Civic and Political Dialogue

Perspective taking through dialogue

Going public with one's civic and political perspectives

Engaging in productive online dialogue

in which online civic and political dialogue supported their learning goals for students.

Building a Deeper Understanding of Civic and Political Issues. One learning goal was to help students build a deeper understanding of civic and political issues. Sam,[2] who taught ELA and media arts at a high school in Utah, explained that he hoped his students would develop the habit of carefully reading, thinking, and writing about societal issues. Through reading others' perspectives and crafting a written response, Sam encouraged his students to slow down and think about the various dimensions of and perspectives on each issue. The dynamic nature of dialogue can help bring to life the range of perspectives other people have on a particular topic, and by doing this online you have the potential to reach people with a diverse range of perspectives and lived experiences.

Exploring and Shaping Opinions and Perspectives. The second learning goal teachers described was the opportunity for students to gather ideas and perspectives from others as they explored and shaped their opinions and perspectives. Matt shared how he encouraged his students to have a growth mindset around their civic and political perspectives. He emphasized for students that "school is a place where you normalize growing in your thinking. And what you're thinking in January may or may not be what you're thinking in June. What you're thinking as a freshman will likely not be what you're thinking by the time you're a senior." Other teachers saw online dialogue as an opportunity for students to strengthen and refine the arguments they put forward even if their perspective didn't change.

Developing a Civic Voice and Identity. The third learning goal that teachers highlighted was for their students to develop their civic voice and identity. The study participants noted that adolescence is an important time when their students shape their identity, including its civic contours. Sam described how online dialogue can play a part in this process: "I want to encourage them to talk. And I definitely, never tell them how to think. But I tell them [to], 'Do some reading, form your opinions, look at different perspectives. Write about it, talk about it.'" Teachers noted they were careful not to shape what students think; however, they did seek to ensure students had information and evidence to draw on when forming and expressing their opinions.

Learning to Communicate Using Digital Tools and Platforms. The fourth learning goal teachers noted was for students to learn how to communicate with others using digital tools and platforms. These aims are clearly reflected in the Common Core State Standards (National Governors Association Center for Best Practices, Council of Chief State School Officers, 2010) and how they highlight the "use of technology, including the Internet, to produce and publish writing and to interact and collaborate with others." In addition, teachers noted the importance of understanding how to reach an audience and, in particular, how to engage with that audience when you don't agree with one another. Penny, who taught 9th-grade humanities in California, shared how online civic and political dialogue helps students build awareness of their audience, word choice, and tone as well as the mechanics of citing their sources.

Five Key Learning Opportunities for Online Civic and Political Dialogue

Five key learning opportunities surfaced that built on one another and helped students develop the various skills and capacities needed to engage in productive online civic dialogue. While there is no conventional way to move through these stages, teachers in this study generally implemented the experiences in the following scaffolded progression.

Becoming a Part of an Online Dialogic Community. One of the initial learning opportunities that teachers engaged students in was becoming a member of an online dialogic community. Teachers often asked students to first explore the online space in order to understand the community and its norms in addition to the technical features of the site. Teachers also encouraged students to draw on their own experiences to consider what they already know about the platform, or similar platforms, as well as what constitutes thoughtful and productive dialogue. For example, Penny used Youth Voices as well as more public-facing sites like Twitter and Instagram in her class-room. She talked about the importance of helping students see the differences between the platforms they were using and the affordances of each space. For example, Penny described how she worked with students to consider their identity and activity on various sites:

> With Youth Voices I . . . talk a lot about what it means to be published and what it means to have this academic identity because you could Google your article, right? . . . And then I think Instagram and social media is really powerful in terms of like 'message ready.' They see it themselves as an activist platform. So then I think it was more about, well, what does it mean to be you as the activist? And this is your footprint in that way. So what are you posting? How are you responding?

This requires students to develop a critical mindset to understand the affordances of various online spaces and the ways in which they aim to participate in that space. As platforms change and students' engagement shifts to other spaces, it will be important for them to utilize those discerning skills to navigate the digital world.

Another step in becoming a part of an online community that teachers facilitated was developing a profile and posting a brief biography. A student in Phoebe's classroom asked whether she should lie or tell the truth about herself in her biography. In response, Phoebe asked her what she would think if she read someone else's blog and later found out that it wasn't true. The class took up this dilemma in their discussion about whether to write about personal topics online. In the discussion, Phoebe encouraged students to write about topics that had meaning for them and make thoughtful choices about sharing their different identities, sometimes blending their personal, academic, and political selves.

When considering how to integrate this type of learning opportunity, teachers can reflect on the following:

- How can I introduce an online space to students and give them an opportunity to explore important norms, guidelines, features, as well as what constitutes thoughtful and productive dialogue on the site?
- How can students draw on their own experiences to consider what they already know about the platform or similar platforms?
- What are ways to help students consider aspects of their personal, academic and/or political identities they will share in the space and what they can accomplish on the site?

Perspective-Taking Through Dialogue. Next, teachers often encouraged students to explore and analyze other posts and discussions on an online platform to help expand their understanding of the topics about which they were learning. The opportunity to connect with students who were from different racial or ethnic backgrounds, from different geographic regions, or those who had different lived experiences was very compelling for the students. Phoebe described how "it's really inspiring to watch the dialogue back and forth, between people that would never talk to each other. I think outside of this blogging space, that if they pass each other on the street, I feel like all kinds of judgments would happen that would even prohibit eye contact sometimes."

Engaging in dialogue with a diverse group and navigating controversial topics like the minimum wage, economic inequality, or police brutality in an online setting could very easily lead to conflict or disrespectful disagreement. However, with positive and supportive norms in place on platforms like Youth Voices, teachers and students described the ways in which they were able to listen, develop empathy, and learn from one another. For example, students in Lin's 12th-grade economics class in California posted about economic inequality after interviewing community members who lived on the minimum wage. A student in Utah read these posts and was struck by the wage gap between CEOs and minimum wage workers, which she said isn't often discussed in her school or community. Another student in California shared how important Youth Voices was to her because it has made her rethink her perspective on racial justice issues:

> The last time I saw a post about . . . Black Lives Matter, I really learned a lot of things from the post. . . . We have talked about police brutality before, but this post was so different because I saw some of the comments that this post got, and some people were like, 'Oh, but police are good, and my cousin is a police [officer].' . . . And I didn't know that African American people have to go through a lot of things, and they're being really targeted by the police. Like you see a person walking. You don't know what's going in their lives, and it brings me to feel connected to their story.

These opportunities to connect with others across a number of differences and discuss pressing and controversial issues enabled students to learn about issues from different angles, as well as build empathy and humility as they consider other people's experiences. Thus, the following considerations will be important for teachers to reflect on:

- What positive and supportive norms need to be in place and what skills and capacities do students need in order to thoughtfully engage in online civic and political dialogue across differences?
- How can I support my students to reach beyond our classroom walls to listen to, learn from, and engage with people who are different from them and hold different beliefs?

Engaging in Productive Online Civic and Political Dialogue. Engaging in productive online dialogue by commenting on others' posts or responding to comments was another significant opportunity for students. Teachers talked about a range of strategies they used to support students to learn various conversational moves in an online setting to agree, disagree, or generally discuss someone's post while also backing up your opinion with reasons and evidence. Sam taught commenting as its own genre and framed it as an important contribution to the online community where students could share a resource, raise a question, and encourage someone to think more deeply about their topic. Several of the teachers set aside class time for students to engage in commenting on others' posts and would often assign students to comment on particular classmates first so that everyone received a comment. They encouraged students to slow down, think about the author's perspective or lived experience, and then write an indepth comment that was positive, constructive, and collaborative, which invites them to respond again. Penny shared a memorable example from her classroom:

> I will never forget this student, . . . who wrote a piece about gangs and a student from somewhere else, like basically wrote to her, 'I don't think that's true. Teenagers don't join gangs. That doesn't happen.'
>
> And she was so mad and she was like, 'What is going on? Like, how is this student saying this?'
>
> And I was like, 'Well, let's figure out how do we respond to not close the conversation down?'
>
> We went and looked up the school where they were from. . . . And we were like, well, this makes sense that this is our opinion, right? Like a 16-year-old there versus 16-year-old in our city have different lived experiences. So then that's when we were like, 'Well, what could we point that student to, to understand more?' Right? And then she really started to dig into how do I comment well?

Initially, when Penny started integrating blogging, she was focused on students posting their work, voicing their perspectives, and being published writers. However, after the 2016 presidential election when Donald Trump was elected, she realized that it was critical to help students build empathy for others and learn how to talk across political differences. She then began to set aside class time for commenting and supported students to practice the skills and mindset needed to engage in productive and respectful dialogue and handle disagreement. When someone received a particularly challenging comment, the class would often think together about what the person's perspective might be and how to respond thoughtfully and productively. Penny would often emphasize "How do we disagree without shutting the door? That was my big message to them."

In addition, Matt emphasized how important it is to begin with smaller or lower stakes topics that are still engaging for students in order to build up their analytical muscles and conversational moves to agree and disagree so that when students do engage in more controversial topics, they have a range of strategies to draw on. Drawing on these insights, teachers can consider the following when integrating opportunities for students to engage in productive online civic and political dialogue:

- How can I support students in learning and practicing online conversational moves?
- How can I support and guide students to comment or respond in a thoughtful, productive, and meaningful way?
- What can I do to support students to build empathy for others, learn how to talk across political differences, and disagree respectfully without ending the conversation?

Going Public With One's Civic and Political Perspectives. Going public, a core digital civic literacy, as outlined by Middaugh and Evans (2018), where students use digital tools and networks to share their perspectives on civic issues, was exciting for many students. Several students talked about how posting motivated them to reflect on their online persona, as well as improved their written communication so their audience would take them seriously. Phoebe said this was one of the reasons she used Youth Voices. "I really do enjoy seeing them step into a sort of more adult voice in some ways as they try to figure out how to navigate an online presence. And I think it's very different from how they're used to presenting themselves online and that that's super valuable . . . They want to be seen as thoughtful and smart individuals."

In these online spaces, students were able to craft an argument and publicly defend their perspective. This chance to express themselves politically seemed to contribute to students' sense of civic voice. Couldry (2010) defined voice as the capacity of people to "give an account of themselves and of their place in the world" (p. 1). For many youth whose voices, experiences, and perspectives are often neglected in mainstream dialogues, this was significant. Phoebe shared that "the public/private nature of blogging make it an ideal forum for the students [she] teach[es] who have a tremendous amount to say about the injustices of their world even while their voices as youth of color are often silenced or ignored by society." Students echoed this significance in describing a post they were proud of that focused on a range of topics from childhood obesity to Black power, to gay rights. One student described a post she wrote about young women being sexually assaulted when crossing the border into the United States:

> It was something meaningful to me because I come from a really poor country. I faced a lot of violence, and that's why I escaped my country, not because I just

wanted to come to the country because of money, because that's what some people think . . . but when you really have something in your heart, like you wanna just tell your story to other people. . . . I really love telling my story to other people so they can know what is happening in my life, so they can know what struggles I had to go through to get to where I am now. . . . I feel like nobody talks about my country. Nobody talks about my people . . . so I feel like I want people to know what these people are going through.

Students saw the opportunity to post their views in various online platforms as a way to express their political perspective and be heard by a new and different audience. To promote such experiences for students, teachers can consider the following:

- What types of student writing or media production are best suited for online publication and sharing with a broader audience?
- How can I support students to carefully prepare and build the confidence to publish or go public with their perspectives, reflections, and arguments?
- How can I help my students reflect on what to share publicly and their online footprint?

Moving From Civic Voice Toward Influence. The final learning opportunity that teachers integrated was moving students from voicing their perspectives to working toward influencing change (Allen & Light, 2015). Some students were able to use their voices to raise awareness about civic and political issues and push for change in a variety of ways using any media necessary (Jenkins et al., 2016). For example, Phoebe's students used Youth Voices to circulate and draw attention to their letters to the new superintendent of their school district. Students also used other social media tools, like Instagram, Twitter and Facebook, to further circulate content. One California student, for example, developed a Change.org petition compelling the state to provide more academic and mental health counselors for schools in high needs areas. Through her senior research project, she learned that her school had only one academic counselor and no mental health counselors supporting approximately 700 students, 30% of who were suffering from posttraumatic stress disorder. The student wrote a post on Youth Voices mobilizing others to sign the petition and collected 118 signatures in the end.

While the distinction between voice and influence may be subtle in many cases as young people begin to build a sense of civic agency through opportunities to amplify their voice, it is still important to take into account the knowledge and capacities that youth need to have a meaningful impact. In order to realize the full potential of digital media for civic engagement, all youth will need rich civic learning opportunities as well as media literacy education experiences that help them bridge voice to influence (Hodgin, 2019). To implement such learning experiences, teachers can reflect on the following considerations:

- What knowledge and capacities do my students need to work toward change and have a meaningful influence on issues that matter to them?
- How might digital tools and platforms support students in raising awareness, amplifying others' efforts, mobilizing others to get involved, and/or working toward change?

WHAT ARE THE CHALLENGES OF ENGAGING YOUTH IN ONLINE CIVIC AND POLITICAL DIALOGUE?

In order to facilitate such learning opportunities in frequent and effective ways, teachers highlighted four important barriers that educators may have to navigate. While the context of these classrooms is unique, the hurdles teachers faced raise important considerations for other educators.

Striving for High-Quality and In-Depth Dialogue

While teachers and students appreciated the opportunity to express themselves politically and engage in dialogue, the quality and depth of dialogue was a challenge at times. In a focus group with teachers, one teacher shared: "I'm still trying to get my students to write better comments beyond 'LOL, totally agree.'" Later in the year, while observing this teacher's 10th-grade English class, she asked her students to comment on a post: "I don't want you to just comment on the original post, but I want you to read through the comments so you get a full sense of the discussion. . . . Add to the discussion. Make it a real discussion." It was evident that teachers were refining and bolstering their approaches by modeling high-quality conversational strategies and encouraging students to go deeper in their dialogue with others. Clearly, drawing on topics and societal issues that matter to students and that are relevant to their lives also enables students to dive in more deeply.

Time and Space in the Curriculum

Teachers had to make complex decisions about how and when to fit online dialogue into their curriculum. Several teachers talked about the challenge of finding enough time to devote to students reading posts, engaging in dialogue, and preparing to go public with their writing. Taking students to a computer lab or getting a laptop cart also took a significant amount of time. One teacher in a focus group asked, "My big question [is] how do you make the time in your curriculum?" Another teacher responded by sharing that online publishing and engaging in online dialogue became a norm in her class, but that it took time to develop. Teachers not only need time and space in their curriculum, but they also need time and space to collaborate and learn from one another as well as engage in professional development.

Accessing and Utilizing Technology

Teachers and students raised challenges they faced with technology, ranging from spotty Internet access to limited computer labs or laptop carts, to broken computers. While access was becoming less of an issue in the second phase of the study, it was still a hurdle that complicated their ability to engage in online dialogue. Teachers also talked about having to take into account the technological skills students needed before they even began to blog, comment, or engage in online dialogue. Two of the teachers in the study taught 9th graders and talked about the foundational skills they helped students develop, such as remembering account information, drafting in Google documents prior to posting, and finding and posting images. Matt realized that he needed to find a familiar way to support students with the technical steps, so he created "how-to" videos outlining various steps in the process. Students could reference these videos when they ran into trouble or didn't remember the steps in the process. In short, support and resources for school infrastructure and media literacy learning opportunities overall will be critical for teachers and students.

Navigating Political Divisiveness

Political divisiveness alongside the increase in misinformation, disinformation, and even conspiracy theories that students would raise in the classroom were all challenges teachers noted. Sam talked about how the impact of filter bubbles and echo chambers in 2014 seemed minimal compared to 2020. As a result, he integrated more opportunities for students to judge the credibility of online information, to carefully analyze what they read, to make their thinking visible as they unpacked their logic and assumptions, and to practice perspective taking. The other teachers talked about creating space for students to talk through misinformation they came across, encouraging them to ask critical questions and emphasizing the need for factual evidence to back up their arguments.

At the same time, teachers also talked about the bravery their students demonstrated when they lifted up their voices, engaged in dialogue, and got involved in issues that mattered to them despite the polarized climate. Penny explained the changes she observed in her students and how going public with their perspectives was liberating for many of them:

> My population of students is like 92% Latinx. And so much of [Trump's] statements were just so egregious towards this population and many of them are immigrants or children of immigrants. . . . And now most of them have Twitter [accounts] and know about the news because of Trump. I think kids' larger social awareness grew and they saw other young people [on] YouTube as well right, other young people having platforms and speaking out and it made it okay for them to speak out. And say, 'I'm going to document it and this is my mom's story and you can't touch me and these are my rights and there's hundred thousand of us doing this on Instagram and following people from all over the country.'

The teachers I interviewed agreed that their students had become bolder and more willing to share online because they witnessed so many other young people using similar platforms in civic and political ways. They saw their peers at the lead of critical social movements raising their voices and pushing for change in very visible ways further amplified by digital tools and platforms.

WHAT ENABLING CONDITIONS CREATE A SUPPORTIVE ECOSYSTEM FOR TEACHERS?

Teachers indicated a few of the critical pieces they depended on or wished they had been able to draw on. The most important support teachers highlighted was being able to learn and collaborate with other teachers in a professional learning space or community. The teachers who used Youth Voices were able to connect with the community of other educators through the platform itself as well as through a virtual call that happened once a week facilitated by two veteran teachers who created the site. In addition, the teachers in California participated in a districtwide initiative focused on educating for democracy. As part of the initiative, teachers participated in small professional learning communities focused on particular components of civic learning. These spaces enabled teachers to experiment with new approaches, reflect together, share resources, and coordinate collaborative efforts where teachers could connect their students to engage in dialogue and comment on one another's work.

The second important condition that teachers noted was support from school and/or district administrators. Several teachers in this study mentioned that their principals supported their efforts to engage students in civic learning and political dialogue. They recognized that this may, in part, be due to the fact that they had been teaching for many years. Nevertheless, this made a difference. In addition, the California teachers highlighted the support they were able to draw on from one of the district leaders, which helped lend legitimacy to their efforts in the classroom. The district's recognition of civic learning helped to provide a foundation through which teachers were able to prioritize civic learning, engage with pressing and controversial issues, and also take risks to integrate innovative instructional approaches.

CONCLUSION

While democratic dialogue has always been key, new and expanded learning opportunities are needed for youth to successfully navigate civic and political dialogue in the digital age. If these opportunities are not provided, research suggests that youth may either minimize or withdraw their participation from online dialogue because of fears of negativity and conflict (Middaugh et al., 2017; Weinstein et al., 2015). And, if these opportunities are not provided equitably to all students, then political inequalities will be further replicated on- and offline. Therefore, schools are critical environments to engage youth in online civic and political dialogue because a majority of youth can be reached there and it is often more diverse than other settings in which youth spend time (Hess, 2009).

Teachers in this study facilitated five key learning opportunities that enabled students to learn different skills and strategies for productive and meaningful online civic and political dialogue. To get started, teachers might consider one or two experiences that can build or deepen students' capacity for online civic dialogue. In addition, teachers can seek out other colleagues in their school, district, community, or online networks they can collaborate with and learn alongside. Even by starting small and building over time, teachers can enable students to learn about civic and political issues, engage with diverse and multiple perspectives, participate in productive dialogue, go public with their viewpoints, and use their voices to influence change—all paving the way for meaningful and productive participation in democracy.

NOTES

1. This study began in 2014 and drew on four high school teachers' work with their students on a participatory academic platform called Youth Voices and included findings from teacher interviews, student focus groups, and analysis of students' online dialogue (Hodgin, 2016). From 2015–2018, the author facilitated a professional learning community with a small group of teachers in California focused on online civic dialogue. When offered the opportunity to write a chapter for this book, the author conducted a set of interviews with teachers from the original study (who were still teaching in the classroom), as well as teachers from the professional learning

community in order to learn about their experiences facilitating online civic and political dialogue in the context of increased technology use in schools and heightened political division in the United States. The original article has been updated and rewritten to draw on these new findings and reflect the current realities of educating youth for online civic and political dialogue.

2. All names are pseudonyms in order to provide confidentiality to the study participants.

REFERENCES

Allen, D., & Light, J. S. (Eds.). (2015). *From voice to influence: Understanding digital citizenship in the digital age.* University of Chicago Press.

Anderson, M., & Auxier, B. (2020, August). *55% of U.S. social media users say they are "worn out" by political posts and discussions.* Pew Research Center. https://www.pewresearch.org/fact-tank/2020/08/19/55-of-u-s-social-media-users-say-they-are-worn-out-by-political-posts-and-discussions/

Anderson, M., & Jiang, J. (2018, May). *Teens, social media and technology 2018.* Pew Research Center. https://www.pewresearch.org/internet/2018/05/31/teens-social-media-technology-2018/

Breakstone, J., Smith, M., Wineburg, S., Rapaport, A., Carle, J., Garland, M., & Saavedra, A. (2019). *Students' civic online reasoning: A national portrait.* Stanford History Education Group & Gibson Consulting. https://purl.stanford.edu/gf151tb4868

Couldry, N. (2010). *Why voice matters: Culture and politics after neoliberalism.* SAGE.

Doherty, C. (2017, October). *Key takeaways on Americans' growing partisan divide: 8 key findings.* Pew Research Center. https://www.pewresearch.org/fact-tank/2017/10/05/takeaways-on-americans-growing-partisan-divide-over-political-values/

Draca, M., & Schwarz, C. (2020). *How polarized are citizens? Measuring ideology from the ground-up.* Social Science Research Network. https://doi.org/10.2139/ssrn.3154431

Duggan, M., & Smith, A. (2016). The political environment on social media. *Pew Research Center.* http://www.pewinternet.org/2016/10/25/the-political-environment-on-social-media/

Gibson, C., & Levine, P. (Eds.). (2003). *The civic mission of schools.* The Carnegie Corporation of New York and the Center for Information and Research on Civic Learning.

Gould, J. (Ed.). (2011). *Guardian of democracy: Civic mission of schools.* Leonore Annenberg Institute for Civics of the Annenberg Public Policy Center at the University of Pennsylvania. http://civicmission.s3.amazonaws.com/118/f0/5/171/1/Guardian-of-Democracy-report.pdf

Hess, D. E. (2009). *Controversy in the classroom: The democratic power of discussion.* Routledge.

Hess, D., & McAvoy, P. (2015). *The political classroom: Evidence and ethics in democratic education.* Routledge.

Hodgin, E. (2016). Educating youth for online civic and political dialogue: A conceptual framework for the digital age. *Journal of Digital and Media Literacy,* 4(1–2).

Hodgin, E. (2019). Participatory politics and the civic dimensions of media literacy. In R. Hobbs & P. Mihailidis (Eds.), *International encyclopedia of media literacy.* Wiley. https:/doi.org/10.1002/9781118978238.ieml0179

Ito, M., Gutiérrez, K., Livingstone, S., Penuel, B., Rhodes, J., Salen, K., Schor, J., Sefton-Green, J., & Watkins, S. C. (2013). Connected learning: An agenda for research and design. *Digital Media and Learning Research Hub.* http://dmlhub.net/publications/connected-learning-agenda-for-research-and-design/

James, C. (2016). Getting into the fray: Civic youth, online dialogue, and implications for digital literacy education. *Journal of Digital and Media Literacy,* 4(1–2).

Jenkins, H., Shresthova, S., Gamber-Thompson, L., Kligler-Vilenchik, N., & Zimmerman, A. (2016). *By any media necessary: The new youth activism.* NYU Press.

Kahne, J., & Bowyer, B. (2017). Educating for democracy in a partisan age: Confronting the challenges of motivated reasoning and misinformation. *American Educational Research Journal, 54,* 3–34.

Kahne, J., Hodgin, E., & Eidman-Aadahl, E. (2016). Redesigning civic education for the digital age: Participatory politics and the pursuit of democratic engagement. *Theory and Research in Social Education, 44*(1), 1–35.

Kahne, J., & Middaugh, E. (2008). *Democracy for some: The civic opportunity gap in high school* [Working paper 59]. CIRCLE. http://www.civicyouth.org/PopUps/WorkingPapers/WP59Kahne.pdf

Lenhart, A., Madden, M., Smith, A., Purcell, K., Zickhur, K., & Rainie, L. (2011, November) *Teens, kindness and cruelty on social network sites: How American teens navigate the new world of digital citizenship.* Pew Research Center's Internet & American Life Project. https://www.pewresearch.org/internet/2011/11/09/teens-kindness-and-cruelty-on-social-network-sites/

Levine, P., & Kawashima-Ginsberg, K. (2017). *The republic is (still) at risk—and civics is part of the solution.* Jonathan M. Tisch College of Civic Life, Tufts University.

Middaugh, E., Bowyer, B., & Kahne, J. (2017). U Suk! Norms of online political discourse and the implications for youth civic development and engagement. *Youth & Society, 49*(7), 902–922.

Middaugh, E., & Evans, C. (2018). Did you know?! . . . Cultivating online public voice in youth. *Theory and Research in Social Education, 46*(4), 574–602.

Min, S-J. (2007). Online vs. face-to-face deliberation: Effects on civic engagement. *Journal of Computer-Mediated Communication, 12,* 1369–1387.

National Governors Association Center for Best Practices, Council of Chief State School Officers. (2010). *Common Core State Standards.* http://www.corestandards.org/ELA-Literacy/CCRA/W/

Pariser, E. (2012). *The filter bubble: How the new personalized web is changing what we read and how we think* (reprint ed.). Penguin.

Rogers, J., Franke, M., Yun, J.E., Ishimoto, M., Diera, C., Geller, R., Berryman, A., Brenes, T. (2017). *Teaching and learning in the age of Trump: Increasing stress and hostility in America's high schools*. UCLA's Institute for Democracy, Education, and Access. https://idea.gseis.ucla.edu/publications/teaching-and-learning-in-age-of-trump

Schultz, K., Hodgin, E., & Paraiso, J. (2015). Blogging as civic engagement: Developing a sense of authority and audience in an urban public school classroom. In E. Middaugh & B. Kirshner (Eds.), *#youthaction: Becoming political in the digital age* (pp. 147–168). Information Age.

Southern Poverty Law Center. (2019, April 16). *Hate at school report*. Learning for Justice. https://www.learningforjustice.org/magazine/publications/hate-at-school-report

Sunstein, C. R. (2007). *Republic.com 2.0*. Princeton University Press.

Weinstein, E., Rundle, M., & James, C. (2015). A hush falls over the crowd?: Diminished online civic expression among young civic actors. *International Journal of Communication*, 9, 84–105. http://ypp.dmlcentral.net/sites/default/files/publications/2901-13960-1-PB.pdf

CHAPTER 10

The Structures We Live In

Discussing Racialization of Neighborhoods to Transform the Null Curriculum

Jacob S. Bennett, H. Richard Milner IV, and Bryant O. Best

In this chapter, we describe how social studies teachers might broaden their discussion pedagogies by explicitly addressing the important intersections of race, racialization,[1] and neighborhood construction in their classroom curriculum. Using Nashville, Tennessee, as an example, we attempt to provide social studies teachers with powerful opportunities to interrogate, through discussion-based activities, issues of race and the social landscape by historicizing and analyzing their students' and their own community structures. This example has promise because students will have opportunities to discuss and apply connections between social engineering and neighborhood patterns to their own communities while also thinking about and discussing issues of racism. We conceptualize social engineering as the intentional planning of communities by state and federal governmental officials across the United States. Such programs became widespread after the Great Depression and enshrined racial segregation in communities across the country (Rothstein, 2017).

While discussions, in general, are extremely important within social studies classrooms, what is actually discussed is just as, if not more, important. By including curriculum that explicitly addresses contemporary outcomes of social engineering in social studies classrooms, teachers can close the gap between what has been called the "null curriculum" (Eisner, 1994) and students' understanding of racialization. Connections between the two are addressed in the next section. In what follows, we use Nashville as an example to present how social studies teachers may enact the sort of discussions around social engineering and race we recommend.

CURRICULUM

Curricula can be conceptualized as what students have the opportunity to learn both inside schools (Eisner, 1994; McCutcheon, 2002) and outside of schools (Gutiérrez et al., 1999). Students experience curriculum both through formal and informal aspects of learning (Milner, 2020). Eisner (1994) postulated several forms of the curriculum: explicit, implicit, and null. Explicit curriculum practices center student-learning opportunities overtly. This form of the curriculum is written down and draws from stated or printed documents, policies, and guidelines, such as course syllabi, the Common Core standards, or district and state websites. An implicit curriculum practice is intended or unintended but is not stated or written down; it is also known as the hidden curriculum. An example of this curriculum might be a teacher calling on only boys when asking questions regarding sports or asking only girls to discuss cooking. Such practices imply specific gender roles are understood in the classroom.

A third form of curriculum, the null curriculum, deals with what students do not have the opportunity to learn. Thus, knowledge(s) and learning opportunities that are not available or that are avoided are also forms of the curriculum because students are actually learning something based on what is not emphasized, covered, or taught (both implicitly and explicitly). What students do not experience in the curriculum become messages about what is and is not essential to know and understand. From Eisner's (1994) perspective, what is absent in curriculum practices is essentially present in student learning opportunities. When teachers avoid or are not able to hold conversations about race and racialization in regard to neighborhood construction, for instance, this teaches students such topics are meant to be avoided or do not require understanding.

RACE AND ITS NECESSITY

It is well accepted and understood that race is socially constructed and holds no place in the biological sciences (Bennett et al., 2019; Boutte & Jackson, 2014; Farinde-Wu, 2018; Gooden & O'Doherty, 2015; Laughter, 2018; Milner, 2015; Sealey-Ruiz, 2016; Skiba, 2012). The specific social constructions of race are phenotypically and physically constructed; people examine and interpret the physicality and outside markers of individuals (Fergus, 2017; McGee, 2016; Monroe, 2013; Singer, 2016). Race is also contextually, geographically place centered and spatially constructed (Alvarez, 2020; Green, 2015; Morris & Monroe, 2009; Pearman, 2020; Tate, 2008). For instance, race is conceptualized differently across continents, communities, and spaces. Race is also legally and historically constructed, as laws and policies influence what we know and do in society. At the same time, historical moments and movements such as slavery, eugenics, reconstruction, Jim Crow, redlining, desegregation, and busing have overtly influenced policy and practice (Alridge, 2003; Bell, 2004; Harris, 1993; Lynn & Dixson, 2013; Milner, 2014; Walker, 1996).

Race and Neighborhoods

Race and neighborhood analyses are important in social studies classrooms because they provide a tangible opportunity for teachers and students to examine their lives and hold discussions regarding race. For instance, researchers have described in great detail the ways federal governmental policies beginning after the Great Depression subsidized suburbia for white[2] families in the United States (Bennett & Cohen, 2019; Milner, 2013; Rothstein, 2017). Such subsidization was often wholly ignored by its beneficiaries while attempts to support populations of color (e.g., through affirmative action policies) were seen as "unearned" government handouts by the same white beneficiary groups (Gerstle & Fraser, 1989; Wilkinson, 2020). As historian Kevin Kruse (2013) explained, these policies had lasting effects on life in the United States, creating suburbs for white families that while in 1950 accounted for only one fourth of the population, by 1990 had expanded to more than one half. Moreover, these new suburban zones housed residents with both the political and social capital to understand zoning laws, leaving many metropolitan areas susceptible to developers who labeled such areas as industrial zones, resulting in "urban renewal" projects that saw whole communities leveled to the ground (Smith, 2017). Inclusion of discussion topics such as these within social studies curriculum are essential to develop deeper understanding of both student and teacher experiences inside and outside of school.

We believe this chapter serves as an important curricular exemplar to address the null curriculum, within discussion pedagogy, as it relates to neighborhood demographics, social engineering, and race. By discussing racialization and neighborhoods with students, the complete picture of how certain communities have come to look certain ways in regard to demographics could be realized. Such realization could then lead to better understanding of the ways structural policies have differentially influenced certain populations in the United States when it comes to economic well-being, or as Tate (2008) defined it, geography of opportunity. Nashville provides an example for how such analyses might be undertaken to reach this sort of understanding.

NASHVILLE AS A CURRICULAR EXEMPLAR

Because the public school a child attends is linked to the ZIP code where they live across the United States, racially subsidized suburban housing can also be connected to persistently racially segregated public schools. Lasting long after school integration was mandated throughout the United States, Orfield and Frankenberg (2014) showed schools in 2014 were more racially segregated than schools in the 1970s, with 57% of Black and 60% of Latin(x)

students attending schools with at least 75% "minority" student enrollment. How do these engineered demographics affect students' and teachers'
experiences both outside and inside of schools?

To begin interrogating racialized housing in their local community, social studies teachers should look for works (e.g., books, articles, essays)
already related to the topic to inform their curriculum designs. In relation to
Nashville, Erickson's (2016) detailed history of the city provides a thorough
description of ways policy makers used racialized social engineering in efforts
to ensure both prosperity and segregation for white citizens. The consolidation of Davidson County with the city of Nashville to become Metropolitan
Nashville-Davidson in 1962, as Erickson explained, "effectively meant vote
dilution, producing a county-wide government with half the proportion of
Black residents compared to the previously separated city" (p. 55). She went
on, "The multipart, state-sanctioned, and highly durable system of segregation built in these years proved resilient even as local civil rights attorneys
and activists struggled to apply *Brown v. Board of Education* to Nashville"
(p. 61). With consolidation, Metropolitan Nashville-Davidson became a
place where segregation was entrenched by weakening voter resistance to
segregation-centered policies. Even today, more than a half-century after
consolidation, Metropolitan Nashville-Davidson remains a largely segregated city, with school enrollments that reflect the segregated nature of the
community.

In the following section, we present data from the open-sourced website of the Metropolitan Nashville Public School (MNPS) district regarding
school demographics and enrollment to provide an example of how our
curriculum exemplar regarding analyses of racialized policies within communities could be applied across contexts. By undertaking similar activities,
social studies teachers across the country could use discussions to examine
community racialization as a way to reify the explicit curriculum on race. To
do so, using online platforms to connect schools and communities through
analyses of neighborhood demographics by ZIP codes can prove fruitful.

A Deeper Look: Structural Oppression by ZIP Codes

It is important for teachers to understand that "context-neutral mindsets" do
not allow educators to recognize deep-rooted and ingrained realities embedded in a particular place, such as a school in a particular community. Within
the communities that surround MNPS, students are affected by numerous
outside-of-school factors, the effects of which cannot be disconnected from
a history of racialized structural oppression. During the 2020–2021 school
year, MNPS (2020) reported a student population that was 40.24% Black,
29.10% Latin(x), 26.19% white, and 4.1% Asian. Demographics within
specific schools across MNPS, however, are not so "evenly" distributed by
race. For instance, of the 56 schools that have a majority Black student

Figure 10.1. Nashville ZIP Codes With Majority Black/Latin(x) Student Population Schools

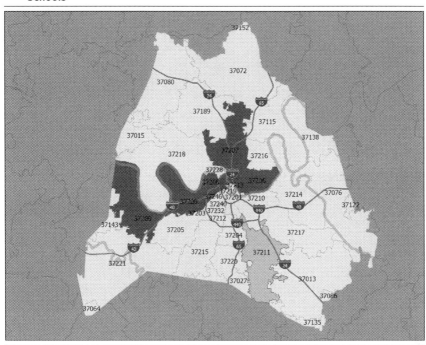

population (i.e., > 55%), 31 (55%) are located within four neighboring ZIP codes (37206; 37207, 37208; 37209). For the 16 schools with majority Latin(x) populations (i.e., > 55%), six are located within one ZIP code (37211) (see Figure 10.1).

If we dig deeper into the ZIP codes with majority Black student populations, all are located in the north section of Nashville. It is within these areas that the history of racialized segregation can be connected. For instance, Rothstein (2017) provided the Federal Housing Administration's (FHA) underwriting manual used to determine where FHA loans, which included recommendations that highways and natural barriers such as rivers be used to separate Black and white neighborhoods (Rothstein, 2017). Such a practice can be directly connected to Nashville.

In the 1960s after consolidation of the city, Mayor Beverly Briley, who served three terms (1963–1975) and was the first mayor after consolidation, admitted the construction of highway I-40 through the city formed a "barrier to the Fisk and Meharry area isolating it like a ghetto" (Erickson, 2016, p. 139). Both Fisk and Meharry Universities are historically Black institutions and located within the 37208 ZIP code. Today, the 37208 ZIP code has a population that is 86.2% Black (United States ZIP Codes, 2020a). The

Table 10.1. Metro Nashville Public Schools Student Population
by Race (2020-2021)

Race	%
Asian	4.10
Black	40.24
Latin(x)	29.10
White	26.19

Source: MNPS (2020)

majority of households earn an income less than $25,000, and owner-occupied home values are between $50,000 and $99,0000. Moreover, according to the Brookings Institute, 37208 has the highest incarceration rate in the United States, which in 2019 was 11% (Looney & Turner, 2018). In comparison, ZIP code 37204, which is located to the south of highway I-40 and was not "ghettoized" by the highway construction, has a population that is 77.7% white (United State ZIP Codes, 2020b). The majority of households earn an income between $60,000 and $99,000, and owner-occupied home values are between $200,000 and $399,999 (see Table 10.1).

When social studies teachers modify their curriculum to include discussions of the effects racialization and structural oppression have on neighborhoods today, explicit connections can be made between structural oppression and personal experience as each relate to racialization. By applying an analysis of racialized policies regarding school and community demographics as discussed to a classroom learning unit and/or lesson, social studies teachers can both engage students in historical analyses and become better informed regarding contemporary experiences in and around their school communities as they relate to racialization.

Next, we provide examples of grade-level specific applications and discussion questions for social studies teachers to support students in making connections between structural oppression and racialization. Before doing so, however, we provide the following caveat: Teachers should not engage in the types of discussions described and presented if they have not done the essential work of personal reflexivity (please see previous chapters' discussions on the importance of building trust and community). Without doing so, discussions can inevitably become more hurtful than helpful for students.

DISCUSSING STRUCTURAL OPPRESSION

Reflexivity

To understand the ways racialization has and does differentially affect communities of color and their white counterparts in the United States, teachers must first be willing to (re)engage their own identities and the ways their experiences affect their interpretations of structural oppression. Moreover, teachers must be aware of what Tuck (2012) described as "damage-centered approaches" to working with populations of color. As she explained, a damage-centered approach acknowledges historically resilient (Echo-Hawk, 2019) populations as more than mere products of oppression. As Chapters 11 and 12 in this volume attests, teachers must realize the power and agency of populations of color to move through and beyond oppressive structures such as racialized housing policies to find multiple and ongoing successes.

Along with self-awareness as well as an asset approach to teacher/student interactions and relationship development (Milner, 2007, 2012), the responsiveness of teachers must also be considered, as recommended by Wallace and Chhuon (2014). The ways teachers respond to and perceive the needs of their students has been shown to be influenced by the sort of conceptualizations they have about structural oppression (Bennett, 2019a, in-press). Moreover, such conceptualizations can be tied to the sort of practices teachers design within classrooms as they relate to both instructional and relational supports (Bennett, 2019b). It must be remembered that it is the learner, not the teacher, who is the active producer of knowledge (Freire, 2017). We urge social studies teachers (and others who happen to have found this chapter) to consider how their experiences with race and racialized oppression might affect the ways they respond to their students' needs to learn and create knowledge about racialization alongside them.

Application

After teachers have informed their curriculum by searching for analyses of their communities as they relate to racialized housing (or other) policies, either through finding works already completed or researching themselves, space can be provided for students to discuss the ways their lives outside of school affect their experiences within. To start, teachers can ask students to describe the communities where they live. Who are their neighbors? Do they share certain cultural and/or racial backgrounds? What sort of businesses and public spaces (e.g., parks, greenways) are close by? This activity will provide space for teachers to get to know their students, but also for students to better understand how their experiences outside of school are both connected to and dissimilar from that of their peers. Based on the grade level that social studies teachers are teaching, discussions might take different routes, as may the historical analyses of communities thereafter.

While we differentiate between grade levels in an attempt to provide more accessible reader comprehension, any and all of the activities/discussions described might be found useful to social studies teachers across all grade levels. The activities would be most effective if social studies departments provided space for teachers across grade levels to co-construct lesson designs, allowing multiple opportunities for students to discuss and interrogate racialization over multiple school years within multiple social studies classes (i.e., sequential co-planning). Moreover, based on the nature of the ways racialized policies have affected specific communities across the United States, all of the activities presented would need to be designed differently. Social studies teachers must consider the specific needs and relationships between themselves, their students, administrators, and parents within specific school contexts. What are the political and racial ideologies held by the community? Is structural oppression acknowledged by the school administration? Answers to questions such as these should guide teachers in decisions regarding how to present and discuss ways racialization has affected and still affects communities across the United States.

K-5: Elementary Grades. Within elementary classrooms, social studies teachers might ask students to draw places and people in their communities that mean something to them. Some questions teachers might ask students to reflect on with their drawings include the following: Who are the people that make you feel special in your life? Where are some places you like to go in your neighborhood/community? Teachers can design spaces within their classroom where students have the option of sharing the ways they interact within their communities (e.g., talk and turn, group sharing, full class presentations). As is everything in education, however, design and application of these strategies in a classroom must be tailored to the dynamics within their specific school and community. Considering this complexity, questions must be presented in a way that do not make students feel obligated to share, as some may live in complicated immigration or otherwise traumatic situations causing them to feel "outed" by teachers who may be asking information deemed sensitive by themselves and/or their parents.

In connecting communities to racialization, elementary social studies teachers might first engage students in an activity to lay the foundation for future critical reflections. The following activity is aimed at providing students the foundational knowledge to understand the concept of racialization by showing students that while all humans are "the same" in terms of biology, sometimes people are labeled and judged based on their appearance. To do so, teachers pass out pennies to every student in the class. The teacher then asks the students to look at their penny and notice how each has specific markings that make it unique. While all are the same (i.e., pennies), each is different because each has had a specific journey, spent time in different pockets, and found their path to the classroom in different ways. This way of thinking could then be analogized to the students in the room: Even though we are all the same, we are all unique with different experiences that have led us to the classroom.

Teachers could then begin to discuss how certain labels or ways of looking can make people think or interact differently with a person. Analogies could then be made to history, and how certain people, even though all the same, were labeled and treated differently based merely on the color of their skin. Teachers could then discuss how that makes students feel. How can we appreciate all of our individual experiences and still understand we are all the same? While elementary school students may not have the ability to conceptualize racialized oppression in ways that are fully developed, these early discussions could lay the foundation for future, more critical analyses when entering higher grades.

6-12: Middle and High School. Middle and high school students might be able to conceptualize racial oppression in ways their elementary school counterparts cannot. Therefore, the ways social studies teachers might design activities that address the effects of racialized oppression can be more systematic. For instance, the same beginning activity used in elementary contexts around drawing pictures of communities could again be undertaken; however, the activities used to connect neighborhoods and racialized oppression could be developed in more depth. Students might be guided in applying the concept of geography of opportunity (Tate, 2008) to their communities.

Informed by Briggs (2005), Tate (2008) explained that evaluation of the geography of opportunity "in metropolitan America includes the study of patterns of development where the fortunes of cities and suburbs are explored in tandem" (p. 397). Therefore, teachers could have students discuss the ways their community might look different than those from surrounding school districts/communities. What sort of differences do students see in suburban and city community designs? How do the public green spaces compare? What sort of business are represented in each? With these questions to think about, social studies teachers could then move students to historical analyses of federal lending and home ownership policies to make connections between geography and racialization.

Geography. Within geography classrooms (typically grade 9), teachers could use Tate's (2008) article in conjunction with excerpts from Rothstein's (2017) work regarding the FHA manual to analyze their community and list any possible physical barriers that seem to disconnect neighborhoods throughout their communities. Are these natural or engineered barriers? How might these barriers create "enclaves" within communities? Students could use websites such as "Mapping Inequality," an interactive database designed by the Digital Scholarship Lab at the University of Richmond, to research redlining practices in their local cities and those across the United States. Specific loan and home ownership policies could be researched using scholarship such as those presented by Rothstein (2017) to discuss how federal policies bolstered the development of suburbia across the United States.

Within civic/U.S. government classrooms (typically also grade 9), teachers could have students analyze the policies written during the New Deal and after that provided legislative power to enshrine segregation within communities across the United States. Teachers could also have students look at polices across the federal, state, and local levels to determine how laws were written, interpreted, and enacted within their communities. How were certain areas of the communities where students live zoned in the past and today (e.g., industrial or residential)? What effects do these labels have on the design within communities in relation to proximity to industrial parks, public spaces, and stores/shops?

World History. In world history classrooms (typically grade 10) social studies teachers have a unique opportunity to design activities for students to create international comparisons regarding racialized oppression. What sort of policies have been created across the world in relation to social engineering of neighborhoods? How do these policies and their outcomes as they relate to demographics and geography of opportunity (Tate, 2008) apply to neighborhoods and communities in the United States?

To better inform teacher practices regarding these connections, teachers could read and use excerpts from Anderson and Anderson's (2003) book *Eyes Off the Prize: The United Nations and the African American Struggle for Human Rights* to expose the ways the United States influenced the design of the United Nations. In short, under the direction of Eleanor Roosevelt, the U.S. delegation worked to make the international body less powerful in terms of enforcing human rights policies within sovereign nations because of African American disenfranchisement and other human rights abuses taking place in the United States (Anderson & Anderson, 2003). Some questions students might consider include the following: How did the United States affect the development of the United Nations? How did racialized oppression in the United States influence the power structure designed within the United Nations? Teachers could then have students discuss the organization and power of the contemporary United Nations and the ways the international body either does or does not influence polices/outcomes across the world.

U.S. History and Economics. In U.S. history (typically grade 11) and economics (typically grade 12, if offered) classes, social studies teachers have an opportunity to show how the history of policies discussed in grades 9 and 10 affect contemporary life in communities. In units/lessons that seek to address racialization in housing/community opportunity, teachers could share racial demographics of the communities surrounding their school and district. An essential question (i.e., one that should guide inquiry in the classroom and not have a single answer but create more questions) could be presented to the class: "Is contemporary racial segregation of our communities and neighborhoods throughout the United States a product of de jure (government sanctioned) or de facto (choice/chance) policies and decisions?" In what ways did/does race play a role in determining where individuals live within our community? Within economics classes specifically, teachers could design activities for students to connect the concept of geography of opportunity (Tate, 2008) with outcomes related to current levels and types of employment/unemployment (i.e., seasonal/cyclical, frictional, structural, institutional) in suburban and metropolitan areas across their local context.

The racial demographics of local communities could be discussed both anecdotally, with students discussing the makeup of their neighborhoods and schools, as well as statistically using online Census databases. Using websites such as "Mapping Inequality," teachers in U.S. history classes could have students analyze their school district and surrounding communities in relation to historic redlining. Then, using websites such as Zillow or Trulia, teachers could ask students to compare how contemporary home values in places labeled "risky" for loans during the redlining of the 1930s and 1940s compare to other parts of their district labeled "safe" during that time period. Are there more rentals in some areas compared to others? How might the amount of short- and long-term rentals in a community affect wealth accumulation compared to neighborhoods with more owner-occupied residences?

CONCLUSION

In this chapter, we provided a curriculum exemplar (of racialized housing in Nashville) to help students and teachers discuss and consider the connections between race and neighborhoods. Discussing examples such as this can help students learn about social engineering, neighborhood patterns, and the ways each can be connected to contemporary experiences of racialization. We argue that social studies teachers must be more explicit in adopting similar curriculum practices in their discussion pedagogies to help advance racial justice in society.

It is imperative that race be addressed and discussed in social studies classrooms across the country. The specific history of the United States in relation to race being used to categorize and organize populations demands it. Because of this history, while the reality of race being a social construction as described in the beginning of this chapter is indeed a fact, race has still played a very real role in affecting experiences and outcomes of individuals within the United States. It must be made clear, however, that it is not race itself that contributes to how a person survives and thrives in the United States. It is the history of how race has been used, as laid out in our curriculum exemplar, that has influenced outcomes (i.e., racialization). Making discussions of racialization even more important, emerging research shows how racialization connected to neighborhood construction can affect a person biologically.

A result of Black and Brown individuals being "ghettoized" by intentional social engineering policies throughout the history of the United States is that many families of color live in communities closer to industrial zones. These zones can be heavily polluted from chemical byproducts of industrial production in both air and water. Such proximity produces more susceptibility to chronic conditions such as asthma, which can lead to lifelong health problems that can affect a person's economic well-being (Harris, 2019).

Harris (2019) explained, "This structural place-based inequality creates a cycle of social and environmental injustice that over time both deepens individual and family disadvantage, and systematically perpetuates population-level disadvantage for our most vulnerable groups" (p. 91). As this chapter has shown, these "social and environmental injustices" are not products of chance, but intentional social engineering processes. It is conversations that address connections such as these (i.e., structural and biological injustice) that social studies teachers can and should address in their classrooms.

Without discussing racialization and its contemporary effects on neighborhood composition, students are taught that such issues do not matter, or are relegated to the past. Using the curricula practices presented in this chapter, social studies teachers can begin connecting our past to the present to make history applicable. In doing so, the null curricula can be closed as it relates to connections between race, space, and neighborhood construction.

NOTES

1. We use this term in connection with Leonardo's (2012) work, who explained racialization is different than "racial identities" in that racialization holds an element of power connected to our white supremacist history in the United States. Such a history places being "raced" at the whim of the white majority, who have the power and privilege to define and perpetuate stereotypes associated with certain races.

2. We intentionally leave this racial category uncapitalized to express our view that whiteness and white identity need not be represented as dominant.

REFERENCES

Alridge, D. P. (2003). The dilemmas, challenges, and duality of an African-American educational historian. *Educational Researcher, 32*(9), 25–34.

Alvarez, A. (2020). Seeing race in the research on youth trauma and education: A critical review. *Review of Educational Research, 90*(5), 583–626.

Bell, D. (2004). *Silent covenants:* Brown v. Board of Education *and the unfulfilled hopes for racial reform*. Oxford University Press.

Bennett, J. S. (2019a). Fostering relational trust to engage white teachers and researchers on reflections of race, power, and oppression. *Teaching and Teacher Education, 86,* 102896.

Bennett, J. S. (2019b). Removing race: How context and colorblindness influence conceptualizations of equity in a third-grade rural classroom. *Race and Pedagogy Journal, 4*(1) Article 2.

Bennett, J. S. (in-press). Important and unnecessary: The paradox of white preservice teacher perceptions of culturally relevant pedagogy. In G. Li (Ed.), *Superdiversity and teacher education: Supporting teachers in working with culturally, linguistically, and racially diverse students, families, and communities*. Routledge.

Bennett, J. S., & Cohen, B. (2019). What have you done for me lately? Educational research and urban schools. *Education and Urban Society, 51*(2), 175–194.

Bennett, J. S., Driver, M. K., & Trent, S. C. (2019). Real or ideal? A narrative literature review addressing white privilege in teacher education. *Urban Education, 54*(7), 891–918.

Boutte, G. S., & T. O. Jackson. (2014). Advice to White allies: Insights from faculty of color. *Race, Ethnicity, and Education, 17*(5), 623–642.

Briggs, X. (Ed.). (2005). *The geography of opportunity: Race and housing choice in metropolitan America*. Brookings Institution Press.

Echo-Hawk, A. [@echohawkd3]. (2019, September 7). *We are not a "historically" underserved population.* #indigenous [tweet]. Twitter. https://twitter.com /echohawkd3/status/1170371608894046208?lang=en

Eisner, E. W. (1994). *The educational imagination: On design and evaluation of school programs* (3rd. ed). Macmillan.

Erickson, A. T. (2016). *Making the unequal metropolis: School desegregation and its limits*. University of Chicago Press.

Farinde-Wu, A. (2018). #Blackwomenatwork: Teaching and retention in urban schools. *The Urban Review, 50*(2), 247–266.

Fergus, E. (2017). The integration project among white teachers and racial/ethnic minority youth: Understanding bias in school practice. *Theory into Practice, 56*(3), 169–177.

Freire, P. (2017). *Pedagogy of the oppressed*. Bloomsbury.

Gerstle, G., & Fraser, S. (1989). *The rise and fall of the New Deal order*. Princeton University Press.

Gooden, M. A., & O'Doherty, A. (2015). Do you see what I see? Fostering aspiring leaders' racial awareness. *Urban Education, 50*(2), 225–255.

Green, C. M. (2015). *Secret city: A history of race relations in the nation's capital*. Princeton University Press.

Gutiérrez, K. D., Baquedano-López, P., & Tejeda, C. (1999). Rethinking diversity: Hybridity and hybrid language practices in the third space. *Mind, culture, and activity, 6*(4), 286–303.

Harris, C. (1993). Whiteness as property. *Harvard Law Review, 106,* 1701–1791.

Harris, K. M. (2019). Mapping inequality: Childhood asthma and environmental injustice, a case study of St. Louis, Missouri. *Social Science & Medicine, 230,* 91–110.

Kruse, K. M. (2013). *White flight: Atlanta and the making of modern conservatism* (Vol. 89). Princeton University Press.

Laughter, J. (2018). Race in educational researcher: A technical comment on Li and Koedel (2017). *Educational Researcher, 47*(4), 259–261.

Leonardo, Z. (2012). The race for class: Reflections on a critical raceclass theory of education. *Educational Studies, 48*(5), 427–449.

Looney, A., & Turner, N. (2018). *Work and opportunity before and after incarceration.* Brookings Institution. https://www.brookings.edu/research/work-and-opportunity-before-and-after-incarceration/

Lynn, M., & Dixson, A. D. (Eds.). (2013). *Handbook of critical race theory in education.* Routledge.

McCutcheon, G. (2002). *Developing the curriculum: Solo and group deliberation.* Educators' Press International.

McGee, E. O. (2016). Devalued Black and Latino racial identities: A by-product of STEM college culture? *American Educational Research Journal, 53*(6), 1626–1662.

Metropolitan Nashville Public Schools. (2020, December). *Open data.* https://www.mnps.org/opendata

Milner, H. R., IV. (2007). Race, culture, and researcher positionality: Working through dangers seen, unseen, and unforeseen. *Educational researcher, 36*(7), 388–400.

Milner, H. R., IV. (2012). Beyond a test score: Explaining opportunity gaps in educational practice. *Journal of Black Studies, 43*(6), 693–718.

Milner, H. R., IV. (2013). Analyzing poverty, learning, and teaching through a critical race theory lens. *Review of Research in Education, 37*(1), 1–53.

Milner, H. R., IV. (2014). Culturally relevant, purpose-driven learning and teaching in a middle school social studies classroom. *Multicultural Education, 21*(2), 9–17.

Milner, H. R., IV. (2017). Race, talk, opportunity gaps, and curriculum shifts in (teacher) education. *Literacy Research: Theory, Method, and Practice, 66*(1), 73–94.

Milner, H. R., IV. (2020). *Start where you are, but don't stay there* (2nd ed.). Harvard Education Press.

Monroe, C. R. (2013). Discipline and diversity in the suburban US South. *Race Ethnicity and Education, 16*(2), 182–202.

Morris, J. E., & Monroe, C. R. (2009). Why study the US South? The nexus of race and place in investigating Black student achievement. *Educational Researcher, 38*(1), 21–36.

Orfield, G., & Frankenberg, E. (2014). Increasingly segregated and unequal schools as courts reverse policy. *Educational Administration Quarterly, 50*(5), 718–734.

Pearman, F. A. (2020). The moderating effect of neighborhood poverty on preschool effectiveness: Evidence from the Tennessee voluntary prekindergarten experiment. *American Educational Research Journal, 57*(3), 1323–1357.

Rothstein, R. (2017). *The color of law: A forgotten history of how our government segregated America.* Liveright.

Sealey-Ruiz, Y. (2016). Why Black girls' literacies matter: New literacies for a new era. *English Education, 48*(4), 290–298.

Singer, J. N. (2016). African American male college athletes' narratives on education and racism. *Urban Education, 51*(9), 1065–1095.

Skiba, R. (2012). "As nature has formed them": The history and current status of racial difference research. *Teachers College Record, 114*(5), 1–49.

Smith, L. (2017, August 15). *In 1965, the city of Charlottesville demolished a thriving black neighborhood: The razing of vinegar hill displaced familes and dissolved the community.* Timeline. https://timeline.com/charlottesville-vinegar-hill-demolished-ba27b6ea69e1

Tate, W. F., IV (2008). "Geography of opportunity": Poverty, place, and educational outcomes. *Educational Researcher, 37*(7), 397–411.

Tuck, E. (2009). Suspending damage: A letter to communities. *Harvard Educational Review, 79*(3), 409–428.

United States Zip Codes. (2020a, December). *ZIP code 37208.* https://www.unitedstateszipcodes.org/37208/#stats

United States Zip Codes. (2020b, December). *ZIP code 37204.* https://www.unitedstateszipcodes.org/37204/#stats

Walker, V. S. (1996). *Their highest potential: An African American school community in the segregated South.* University of North Carolina Press.

Wallace, T. L., & Chhuon, V. (2014). Proximal processes in urban classrooms: Engagement and disaffection in urban youth of color. *American Educational Research Journal, 51*(5), 937–973.

Wilkerson, I. (2020). *Caste: The origins of our discontents.* Random House.

Wilson, E. O. (1998). *Consilience: The unity of knowledge.* Knopf.

CHAPTER 11

Get Out of Your Own Way

Sharing Power to Engage Students of Color in Authentic Conversations of Social Inequity[1]

Dane Stickney, Elizabeth Milligan Cordova,
and Carlos P. Hipolito-Delgado

On a fall day in a western U.S. state, 18-year-old Devon[2] sat in a circle of his peers in his leadership class. The high school senior spoke about his extensive preparation for the SAT and his poor score on the test. He shared his realization of being stuck in a cycle as a Black kid going to a school earmarked by his state as inferior. He connected his life experience to a topic his class had been exploring: the school-to-prison pipeline, or the idea that school-based punishments lead students of color to a life in the U.S. carceral system. "It doesn't matter if it's a literal prison or not," he said. "We're in a mental prison right now. We're being set up for failure, and we know it."

This type of discussion—built on teachers sharing power with students to explore topics about race, social justice, and equity—is the crux of an approach called critical civic inquiry (CCI; Zion, 2020). CCI centers the voices of youth of color as they interrogate systemic oppression, identify a school-based problem, research it, craft a policy solution, and deliver it to real-world power players (Hipolito-Delgado & Zion, 2017; Kirshner et al., 2015). The work of CCI doesn't just happen; it's a process that takes time. As Devon's teacher, Joni—a White woman—later said in an interview, "Speaking your mind has to be a part of you."

Early on, it was not a part of Devon. He didn't speak or share much during his junior year, his first year in Joni's leadership class in which students engage in CCI. Devon slowly adopted leadership roles and began sharing his ideas in structured classroom discussions. Fortunately, he had older role models he could emulate, and Joni provided individualized support, helping him work through strong emotions tied to dynamics in his home. Devon took part in his class's final presentation (during his junior year), where students proposed antibias training for teachers in front of peers and leaders from the school district and community. During the presentation, Devon wore a placard declaring that a teacher once told him she felt nervous when he smiled. He later tore up the placard to affirm the idea that students are more than their labels. His class won the students' choice award at the competition.

Before his senior year, Devon was named one of three leaders for the leadership class. Early that year, students took part in an identity activity where they created masks as a reflection of their inner and outer selves. One by one, Devon's classmates shared deep and difficult truths and tensions. Most cried. Devon attempted to share but was choked by his own tears. He later described it as "ugly-face crying." He was able to choke out one phrase that Joni will never forget: "It's hard to be a Black man." His classmates—all of whom identified as Black, Asian American, or Latinx—showed empathy and support, vowing to check in on him more often.

These types of discussions are challenging emotionally, but struggling through them can inspire students' actions to transform systems (Diemer et al., 2010). That was certainly the case for Devon. A few months after the emotional sharing, Devon led a discussion about the school-to-prison pipeline with more poise and emotional control. The *mental prison* phrase became a slogan for the students as they crafted and proposed a new school rating system, one that de-emphasized standardized testing and acknowledged demographic factors like socioeconomic status and home language. Devon led much of this work.

Field notes and interviews with Devon and his teacher, Joni, revealed several instructional moves aimed at cultivating Devon's and the other students' leadership skills and agency, which in turn crafted a classroom community that empowered students to plan, lead, and debrief rich discussions about difficult topics. Among other things, in the elective leadership class that spans grades 9–12, Joni established a structure where older youth acted as exemplars for younger students; provided sheltered support for students, allowing them opportunities to discuss delicate and difficult topics in a critical yet safe space; and crafted with youth a participatory role in creating and revising agendas, facilitating parts of the discussion, and leading meaning-making debriefs and closure activities.

Although incubating a classroom for such rich and meaningful discussion isn't easy, it's worth noting that Joni's biggest asset was her mindset. She deliberately worked to decenter her voice while allowing the students to take the lead when they were ready. In that regard, we are not sharing a specific discussion strategy, per se, in this chapter. That is because CCI, as a pedagogical approach, is a way to build relationships and honor students' humanity as a sort of foundation on which deep and meaningful discussions can be built. This chapter melds our experience supporting classroom teachers in implementing CCI and our expertise as educators who have centered student voices. We aim to first describe the preconditions for an approach that empowers youth to speak about their own lived experiences. Then we advocate for teachers to do the difficult task of getting out of their own way by building relationships with students, centering student knowledge, sharing power by giving students a stake in discussion planning and facilitation, and creating avenues for students to engage in action.

CRITICAL CIVIC INQUIRY

CCI is a pedagogy designed to be implemented across academic disciplines in middle and high school contexts (Hipolito-Delgado & Zion, 2017). CCI draws influence from youth participatory action research, the learning sciences, critical pedagogies, and sociopolitical development (Zion et al., 2021). As part of CCI, students engage in the action civics cycle of identifying a problem of equity in their community, conducting original research, developing a policy to address said problem, and advocating for their policy solution with local policy makers and school leaders (Hipolito-Delgado & Zion, 2017). The ultimate goals of CCI are two-fold: first to foster the sociopolitical development (SPD) of youth so they come to see themselves as powerful civic actors who take actions to promote the liberation of marginalized communities; second to promote authentic student voice in school decisionmaking and educational reform.

Tenets of CCI

CCI is grounded in five main tenets: (1) sharing power with youth, (2) exploring critical questions, (3) participatory action research, (4) structured presentations to the public, and (5) ongoing youth adult partnerships (Zion et al., 2021). Though we will focus on the first, second, and fifth points as they most contribute to discussion, we believe that youth from marginalized communities will engage in school, in general, and class discussions in specific, when they view that classroom discussions are relevant to their lives, believe their opinions are taken seriously, and will have opportunity to enact positive change on issues that impact their lives (Thiessen & Cook-Sather, 2007). Therefore, efforts to engage youth who have faced trauma, struggled with poverty, endured discrimination, and overcame other life challenges in classroom discussions are likely to fail if topics are hypothetical and aims are merely academic.

When speaking of sharing power with youth, we consider this a relational approach to teaching, as educators are called to learn about the youth with which they are working and see the assets they bring into the educational space (Zion et al., 2021). Students also gain a stake in the classroom by providing feedback and helping to select and lead discussions. The educator aims to become an ally to youth, facilitating conversations, serving as a conduit to decisionmakers, providing critical feedback, and supporting student growth.

The second tenet of CCI entails adults and youth exploring critical questions. Such questions are fundamentally related to power and privilege, often viewed through the lens of race, gender, sexual orientation, or socio-economic status. The purpose of such conversations in CCI is to problema-tize what is viewed as normal and encourage thinking about what could be possible or more socially just (Zion et al., 2021). The ultimate goal of criti-cal questions is to inspire youth to select a problem of social justice in their local community that they would like to address through their research and policy solution. Espinoza and colleagues (2020) call this "social dreaming" or the act of putting "forth a claim on the future" (p. 20).

The last CCI tenet we would like to address in this chapter is ongoing youth and adult partnerships. CCI is not an academic assignment, rather a strategy for promoting youth voice in enacting social change. For this to be possible, there must exist a sustained partnership between youth and adults where adults respect youth voice and work with students to impact social change (Watts et al., 2011; Zion et al., 2021). Ultimately, the CCI theoreti-cal framework is successful in inspiring discussion with marginalized youth because it centers their experiences and creates opportunities for students to become leaders and agents of change (Zion et al., 2021).

Being an Adult Ally

Though the tenets of CCI speak to many educators, few are able to fully embrace their role as allies to youth. This is likely due to the fact that a commitment to student voice requires a rethinking of relationships in the classrooms and the goals of education (Zion et al., 2015, 2017). Note we consider these suggestions as the prework that happens before educators might implement the more specific strategies we will describe later. First, we encourage educators to commit to their own SPD; see the work of Watts et al. (2003) and Zion and her colleagues (2015, 2017) for a discussion of SPD in general and the importance of teacher SPD in supporting CCI. We also find it important that educators embrace the notion that education can be liberatory for marginalized communities (Kirshner et al., 2015). This makes the stakes of learning real, where the goal is not mere memorization of facts and figures but aiding marginalized youth in realizing liberation.

The final challenge is remaining vigilant against the schoolification of student voice so that it does not become another academic exercise and remains a viable outlet of social change (Hipolito-Delgado et al., 2021). This also requires teachers to break themselves of what Philip et al. (2019) called the "fetishization of methods" (p. 10). Approaches such as ambitious instruction (Thompson et al., 2013) and discourse patterns of initiation-response-evaluation (Barnes, 1992; Nystrand, 1997) place a strong emphasis on the teacher's discreet moves and role in affirming student responses and moving conversations forward. We see these approaches as short-sighted, limiting the role students can play in owning discussions themselves. Our approach focuses on de-emphasizing the control of the teacher while centering the voice and agency of youth. With such commitments in place, an educator might be more successful in the implementation of CCI and creating a space for marginalized youth's voice in the classroom.

PUTTING CCI INTO ACTION

The embodiment of CCI is an ongoing process that requires teachers and students alike to work together to shed prior definitions and identities of teaching and learning. Moreover, the premise of CCI is dependent on authentic dialogue. A teacher can state that they mean to share power with the students, but if this is done in a contrived way, it misses the point of CCI entirely. Thus, the implementation of CCI invites us to explore the ways in which students act on the invitation to share power, and what ultimately creates a space that respects their dialogue, knowledge, and power. In this section, we aim to move from a theoretical understanding to discussing tangible examples of CCI in action while acknowledging that there is no homogenous model. We will specifically provide suggestions for community building, centering student knowledge, sharing power, and taking action.

Community Building

In a traditional model of schooling, knowledge is viewed as stemming from the teacher, standards, and curriculum to be implanted into individual students; this is what Freire (1970) called the banking model. An important feature of this model is that transactions strictly occur from teacher to student. This is also consistent with the traditional discourse patterns of initiation-response-evaluation (Barnes, 1992; Nystrand, 1997), where a teacher asks a question, one student responds, and the teacher evaluates that response before starting the cycle over with another student. In this model of status-quo classrooms, the teacher acts as a hub in the middle of the wheel with spokes reaching each student. A CCI model, on the other hand, which centers student knowledge and power, is dependent on relationships of trust among peers. The hub has been removed with discussions pinging between peers as opposed to running through an adult intermediary. Sharing power with students by centering student voice and supporting students to plan and facilitate discussions relies on building a strong community.

Building community is not an engagement strategy, nor does it exist within team-building activities. Although there is a place for team building, the goal of CCI is to energize and connect collective action, drawing on the strengths of the group to establish collective knowledge and communal needs. The very tenets of the model, based in power sharing, partnership, and participatory research, are dependent on an authentic community where youth explore critical questions together, relying on one another's knowledge, talents, and thinking. This includes students helping each other revise, stretch, or interrupt incomplete or off-base thinking. This can bring youth closer to understanding their reality and social and political factors influencing their thinking. Building such an environment, though, takes time and deliberation because it cannot be accomplished until students feel safe enough to take risks.

Building Trust. On the first day of school in 2019, Emily gave her first high school civics class of the day an opening task of arranging themselves according to birthday, without further direction. Familiar with many of the students walking into her room, Emily felt confident that the many personalities in the class would have no problem leading their peers in this activity and hoped to forge low-stakes conversation as an entry point to more serious dialogue. The students remained mostly silent, walked reluctantly to various corners of the room, and leaned on the desks. One student, Elijah, began asking his peers about their birthdays, and while they answered, they did not follow his tentative direction. The uncomfortable silence was palpable; the activity at a standstill. Having committed to a classroom with shared power, Emily could not merely step in as the leader. She eventually directed students to find a seat, a notebook, and a pen. She asked reflection questions: What was that activity like for you? If you did try to lead, what compelled you to do so? If you did not try to lead, why?

The students, though reluctant to engage with one another in dialogue, easily articulated in writing that they did not know anyone in the class and, therefore, did not trust them. If the group would not share their birthdays, Emily feared, they would not share power in the classroom or ask critical questions central to their own identities. Emily apologized for asking the students to do something they were not yet comfortable with, acknowledging that the students who felt unsafe were not alone. She instead showed *The Power of Vulnerability* (Brown, 2010). The class, made up mostly of young Latinx and Black men, laughed at Brown's jokes and nodded when she spoke about the expectations society places on men to bury their vulnerability. The students had much to say about Brown's definitions of shame and vulnerability, and they said it through their writing, still not ready to share aloud, thus dictating their own methods of engagement.

The opening activity provided a window into the power dynamics of a classroom. Why, Emily asked the students, had they complied with her requests but not the requests of the few students who tried to organize them? Some wrote that they wanted more guidance from her: Were they supposed to arrange oldest to youngest, or January to December, and from which side of the room? This reaction among the students suggests that they have internalized the lessons of schooling: Adults know best, and you must comply with their requests but not those of your peers. Emily's students were trained to listen to her, but not to each other. The absence of compliance-based teaching also served as an important reminder that, in order to interact authentically with one another, students first must feel comfortable enough to take risks. Digging into critical questions requires a willingness to share one's own identity and truth; these are vulnerable things to ask students to share of themselves. Only when students feel safe and see a purpose for vulnerability can a classroom community do the personal work of CCI. By engaging with a video and using writing to communicate, Emily followed her students' lead and took the first step in building community.

Diving Deeper: Authentic Dialogic Problem Solving. One year later, Emily found herself navigating between stepping out of students' way and offering productive direction and guidance. The challenge of including all voices in the room, for example, provided a new dilemma for Emily (especially in the context of distance learning due to the COVID-19 pandemic). How might she offer protocols for students as they navigated sharing the space and hearing from everyone in the group? The students shared that they wanted others in breakout rooms to turn on their cameras; it would build trust, they said, knowing that their peers were fully present. They developed these norms and promptly broke them, all sharing reasons why they could not turn on their own cameras. What the students wanted from one another was something they could not deliver, so Emily worked to facilitate continual reflection on the ways that students were engaging with one another. She consulted the group on ways to make the breakout rooms less "awkward," providing, at their request, guidance on who should speak first, an ice-breaker question, and structuring the conversation. After each session, she asked them to rate the level of awkwardness and share ideas for improvement. Such shared negotiation engaged students as a community working to solve a collective problem. They began to look for progress, which in turn invited both individual and community reflections. Over time, the group bonded, albeit with their cameras off, around the challenge of this goal. Additionally, this open acknowledgement of the class's imperfections and desires to change laid the groundwork for working through challenges together through honest dialogue.

In a typical power structure, Emily might have used a rubric to build compliance; instead by naming the "awkwardness" and explicitly reflecting on it, the group worked to improve as a team. By building community in this way, teachers are relieved of the pressure of solving things on their own. Instead, teachers and students become equally invested in the classroom community, and we use this community to strengthen the team and move beyond teacher-centered structures.

Centering Student Voice

As seen from other chapters in this volume, when students draw knowledge from their experiences, it serves as far more than a tool of engagement. Centering students' voices is an acknowledgement that their knowledge is valid and valued; that it is important to our collective learning. When we build classrooms that affirm student experiences, this opens possibilities for dialogue and meaningful action.

Knowledge, students often are taught, exists in textbooks; they are often discouraged from using personal, ancestral, and/or communal knowledge as evidence in classes. Nahui Ollin (Cortés-Zamora et al., 2020) challenges this notion through the concept of "precious knowledge," or the expertise that emanates from one's lived experience. As this chapter and the following chapter shows, welcoming students' precious knowledge in class discussions conveys to students that their voice will be centered and their participation is valued.

Defining Knowledge. Alan was generally late to class, and though he was a brilliant thinker, he rarely finished an assignment in his high school social issues course. He was outspoken during class when discussing a policy that seemed unjust; otherwise, he was immersed in the world of his cell phone. On an October day in 2019, he engaged in class differently, sharing vulnerable stories of his own frightening experiences with police officers, as well as those he had witnessed online or heard about from friends. Alan captivated his peers as he spoke with eloquence and leadership. Afterward, Elijah spoke, reluctantly at first, his voice gaining power as he shared about the ways in which over-policing contributed to his older brother being in jail, for no reason other than his Blackness.

During the weeks prior, the class had a distinctively different feel from that pivotal October day: Students worked in teams of four on a topic they had selected, researching various news articles and resources related to subjects such as police brutality, climate change, housing discrimination, and immigration. The momentary energy they experienced when the classroom buzzed in conversations about the topics they would choose quickly waned as they navigated complicated self-selected news articles. Emily shallowly implemented the CCI tenets of student choice, believing she shared power by allowing students to make their own decisions about the project topic. In practice, however, students were flailing, wondering about the direction that they were "supposed" to go. Meanwhile, Emily wondered how to scaffold the process of selecting useful resources and articles for research.

Ultimately, while student choice had seemed to help check the box of student voice, the students' *knowledge* was not being centered in the classroom. The students were seeking what *others* wrote about problems they had identified, thus removing their own perspectives from the work. The knowledge of the students was not being invited nor harnessed, therefore resulting in the stagnant energy that teacher and students alike had come to feel about the project.

The shift from centering student choices to student knowledge opened Elijah and Alan's dialogue to their classmates—inviting them to share their precious knowledge. When the class chose to focus on police brutality as their topic, the students conducted research looking for evidence and statistics from academic sources because that is what we have trained students to view as knowledge. The distinction with Elijah and Alan's sharing was that students were asked to reflect on what they had experienced or observed in their own lives or been taught by their families, places of worship, and communities. As students shared their knowledge, listened to one another, and engaged in dialogue, they were able to build a new kind of communal learning. The fabric of students' lives therefore served as meaningful and rich *texts*.

Community Voices. While student knowledge and experiences serve as the center of the CCI classroom, community voices can enhance the dialogue. Though some students in the social issues class had important experiences to share, others had chosen the topic of police brutality in solidarity with friends and community members but did not feel they had much firsthand knowledge. A representative from a local community organization, led by people of color, visited the class to teach students about police brutality through historical counter-narrative. Weeks later, local police officers visited the students to engage in dialogue. Both the police officers and students approached a difficult conversation authentically, listening to and sharing with one another. Inviting in community members seemed to affirm the students' knowledge, expand their learning, and caused them to ask additional critical questions of their invited speaker and each other.

Later iterations of the social issues class would meet with elected officials and filmmakers. Emily helped students craft questions that felt important, such as "What is the attorney general's office doing to support the Black Lives Matter movement?" These dialogues aided students in problem selection and students would often, independently of Emily, reach out to guest speakers for further information or resources. Thus, involving community voice and student-centered knowledge not only engaged students of color in dialogue in the classroom, but engaged them in the broader community.

Sharing Power: Planning and Facilitating Discussions

If the goal is to engage students of color in discussions, the logical way is to include them in the planning and facilitation of said discussion. This often involves exposing students to a variety of conversation strategies and protocols, allowing them to choose a few they're interested in, and then trying it out. This certainly connects to the CCI pillar of sharing power with students, but it also provides an important avenue for youth leadership. Tasks as simple as leading a classroom discussion or being counted on to fulfill a part of a group project help develop students' leadership skills and in turn their sociopolitical efficacy—desire and belief in ability to impact social change (Hipolito-Delgado et al., 2021). Students of color often lack such avenues for agency in the classroom (Kirshner, 2015), which makes sharing the power of planning and executing discussions an intriguing lever.

As mentioned in the introduction of this chapter, Joni benefited from a strong tradition of community in her leadership class. During Devon's junior year, two confident and highly organized Latinas served as student leaders. Devon watched and participated as the leaders worked with Joni to coplan meeting agendas, lead discussions, and manage the student projects that focused on teacher implicit bias in the school. This experience provided Devon with an important exemplar of how students of color can exercise their agency, voice, and action to be heard and hopefully bring about change.

While Devon would certainly struggle at times with this leadership role, he perpetuated the cycle of acting as an important model for younger students, specifically two sisters who emigrated from the Congo and would eventually rise to lead the team the following year. Joni has essentially created a self-sustaining pedagogical approach: Share leadership power with students and they'll in turn help develop future leaders.

This approach shined during class discussions, as Joni carefully crafted an environment for these budding leaders to try out their skills and, often initially, struggle. Shortly after the presentation at the end of Devon's junior year, the senior leaders shared legacy resources that they hoped the team would use in following years. Essentially the seniors gave the underclassmen tools they thought they needed to succeed. Among them were ice-breakers and agenda-making strategies.

The following year, Joni engaged Devon and two other student leaders in the planning of the group's opening retreat. Though the students planned the agenda, they elected to allow district administrators to lead the discussion activity, which involved the ideas of masks and identity—described in our introduction. Although Devon's self-described "ugly-face crying" made it difficult for him to choke out his comment about life being hard for a Black man, this moment was a pivotal one for the group. Devon's emotional vulnerability empowered his classmates. Within weeks, Joni had taken a noticeable backseat in planning and facilitating meetings. Joni would often lead an opening before the student leaders would delegate tasks or lead discussions. Devon shared his "mental prison" comment during one of these student-planned and -led discussions. That comment crystalized the students' hard-to-articulate thinking and set them on a clearer path for their civics research and policy development. One Latina student crafted a powerful poem about the perils of standardized testing based on Devon's *mental prison* theme, 2 and another developed a piece of artwork depicting the idea. Devon's agency in planning and facilitating the discussion sparked his peers into action. Although this process took more than a year, Joni crafted an environment that provided Devon support from older students and then authentic opportunities to show leadership himself. She did so, specifically, by positioning older students as exemplars, who left legacy resources when they graduated for younger members. Those underclassmen then stepped up to be leaders but were given room to fail and grow. Once they showed comfort in the role, Joni gave them more agency to plan and facilitate activities. This resulted in Devon, quite literally, finding his voice.

Students Taking Action

As any teacher might tell you, the end of a semester, unit, or project is a blur. Teachers are trying to cram all of the learning activities into too few remaining days. The first thing that usually gets cut is the authentic application of the learning. The writing teacher who intended to publish student stories, the civics teacher who intended to mail those persuasive letters to elected officials, the science teacher who just couldn't pull the public presentation of learning together. All three of the authors have been there; we're not judging. But we implore teachers to do everything they can to hold sacred time at the end of each unit for students to share what they have learned with folks who need to hear it. This final application, this final *action*, provides an exclamation point to the learning that makes it pop, makes it echo.

This final presentation of learning is a key tenant of CCI. Through our partnership with a major school district in the western United States, students from close to 30 high schools gather on a spring day and share their policy presentations with their peers and leaders from the district and community. (This is the event where Devon and his classmates wore the placards and proposed implicit bias training for their teachers.) The event is a day-long tribute to student voice, and the products are staggering. At that event, in addition to the issues of policing and youth of color covered in this chapter, other students successfully proposed and negotiated comprehensive health classes in high schools that didn't have them before. They've worked with the board of education to reunify high schools that we previously separated via school reform initiatives. They recommended the school board remove police officers from all schools in the district, and the board members agreed. But the wins don't have to be so large to still have an impact. We urge teachers to provide their students a platform to take action—be it a splashy presentation or something like circulating a petition, engaging in a letter writing campaign, or using social media platforms to amplify youth voice. We very much see this as a form of *discussion*: students engaging in authentic, civic discourse. What is more, it gives a reason for engaging in discussion of social equity issues in the classroom. It moves from consideration of social issues to attempting to impact social systems.

Having won the in-person competition in 2019, Devon and his class were eager to repeat, and the 2020 competition date in April provided an important motivator. Joni constantly reminded students that they would have to present in front of adults at the end of the year. This added a weight to every class meeting and, especially, every discussion. By engaging in conversations like the one where Devon referenced the "mental prison," students were essentially pulling double duty. They were building their critical thinking and presentation skills by engaging in deep and difficult discussions, but they were also partaking in important formative learning experiences that would inform their final presentation at the end of the year. In preparation, Joni and the students scheduled their own mini-presentation at the end of the first semester. Devon and his classmates (as well as students from other civics classes within the school) shared policy proposals in front of their principal, a school board member, and several other community members. Devon helped lead a presentation about how much stress the SAT places on students, ultimately asking for the exam's impact to be reduced on school performance ratings. Afterward, they fielded specific, rigorous questions from the audience. Their principal asked for clarification on what exactly the school-to-prison pipeline was, and Devon elaborated. Many of the same phrases and ideas from in-class discussions popped up in Devon's answer. He talked about the struggles of being a student of color. He recited his "mental prison" rallying call. The principal, with a satisfied look on his face, nodded and smiled at Devon's answer. This moment may have seemed small, but it signified a summative win for Devon, evolving from a student who rarely shared to one who used his own lived experience to succinctly explain a difficult construct, the school-to-prison pipeline. Younger students, future Devons, nodded and snapped their fingers in agreement and support.

NAVIGATING CHALLENGES AND TENSIONS

The kind of pedagogical shift for which we are advocating is not easy. For a teacher, freeing oneself from a stodgy adult-centered approach and moving toward a socially reconstructed classroom where students feel safe to lead the way presents a host of issues. Barriers can take the form of prescribed instructional practices and adapting to online learning.

In the spirit of this chapter, which is more about sharing insight than providing a checklist of steps, we want to relay a few cautionary tales to make sure teachers are prepared with the tensions that come with this work. Dane, the first author, was nearly fired for utilizing a CCI-based approach in a high-support charter middle school writing classroom a decade ago. The principal chided him for leading classrooms that didn't incorporate the school's preferred method of management, specifically when it came to discussions. The school required students to sit in SLANT (sit up straight, lean forward in attention, ask and answer questions, nod in understanding, and track the speaker). In Dane's class, students were often seated in circles and shared without raising their hands. The disapproving principal ultimately changed her tone when the students produced incredibly high test scores. While the scores certainly weren't the goal, they were fortunate results that showed students had mastered the standards, which allowed for students to learn with Dane about topics such as undocumented student rights, gun control initiatives, and gentrification. Elizabeth, the second author and a high school teacher, struggled adapting the CCI approach initially, recognizing how much of her previous approach to teaching, despite offering student choice, remained instructor centered. Elizabeth has found the challenge to provide adult partnership while ensuring student voice and experience is centered in the classwork to be iterative; it is a process that provides new challenges with each new group of students and global context. In addition to her own learning and unlearning, Elizabeth is challenging herself to develop tools that invite students to engage in a similar process of critically analyzing what, from their schooling experiences, they must shed and what they can embrace to embody student-centered practices.

These challenges are real. We know this. But they should not be barriers to editing out status quo pedagogical practices and replacing them with approaches that better engage, serve, and empower students of color. We're asking you to make the move despite the personal discomfort, administrative pushback, and suboptimal teaching supports.

We make this specific ask while wrestling with our own tensions. Each of the three students mentioned in this chapter—Devon, Elijah, and Alan—are young men of color. That wasn't intended, and we want to avoid stereotyping. In discussing this chapter, however, the authors discussed the idea of certain students serving as classroom barometers. In other words, when planning something like a discussion, we often did so with a specific student in mind. If we could get that one student hooked, chances are the other students would be engaged as well. In the examples, all three of those barometers were young men of color. We've heard the narrative, both in schools in which we have worked and in articles we have read, about young men of color: disengaged, at risk, and dangerous. We don't see the students as the problem; it's the approach that needs changing. We hope this chapter highlights this last point, as the shift to CCI helped to better engage these three young men.

FINAL THOUGHTS

We see the CCI approach as one way to break down traditional discussion approaches and rebuild a classroom that empowers students to drive the dialogue themselves. The first step is building a classroom community conducive to this work. If students don't trust that the space will be safe, inviting, and affirming, they likely will not share. They will engage more deeply when the discussion connects to problems in their own lives that peers can help illuminate and mediate in new ways. Second, shift the academic spotlight to students' lived experiences, providing a space for their precious knowledge. Focus not only on "academic material" but also on what students already know. Consider engaging members from the surrounding community or neighborhood in discussions that center and stretch preexisting knowledge. Third, share power with students by allowing them to plan and facilitate discussions. In other words, get out of your own way. If teachers want students to talk, allow youth the agency to develop and control the way that discussion happens. Finally, make action sacred. Leave plenty of time for students to authentically share what they've learned in a real-world setting or with a practical output. What action could students take to make their learning visible, public, and powerful? Public presentations, sit-ins, walkouts, petitions, and social media campaigns are all successful ways we've seen this happen.

Our goal in this work is to provide means to a more just end, specifically building a trusting classroom community, centering student lived experience and voice, allowing students to lead in the classroom, and saving space for action to create an environment where students of color deeply participate in discussions. We hear this in the words of Alan, who emerged from the sidelines of his civics class to take center stage and share powerful experiences that pushed his classmates' thinking. We see this in the actions of Elijah, a budding leader who only needed a space where he could be seen and allowed to flourish. We feel it in Devon's evolution from a quiet follower to a powerful exemplar. In each case, teachers made the conscious decision to remake their classrooms in ways that empowered students of color to make their voices heard.

NOTES

1. This work was supported by the William and Flora Hewlett Foundation under grant 3248; and by the Student-Centered Learning Research Collaborative under grant 1557569.
2. This and all following youth, educator, and school names are pseudonyms, per IRB.

REFERENCES

Barnes, D. (1992). *From communication to curriculum* (2nd ed.). Heinemann.
Brown, B. (2014, March 4). *The power of vulnerability* [Video]. TED. https://www
.ted.com/talks/brene_brown_the_power_of_vulnerability?language=en

Cortés-Zamora, M., Charupe-García, E., Nuñez-Gonzalez, N. (2020). Building intellectual warriors: Engaging students in a culturally relevant learning environment. In R. A. Cordova & W. M. Reynolds (Eds.), *Educating for social justice: Field notes from rural communities* (pp. 107–139). Brill.

Diemer, M. A., Wang, Q., Moore, T., Gregory, S. R., Hatcher, K. M., & Voight, A. M. (2010). Sociopolitical development, work salience, and vocational expectations among low socioeconomic status African American, Latin American, and Asian American youth. *Developmental Psychology, 46*(3), 619–635. https://doi.org/10.1037/a0017049

Espinoza, M. L., Vossoughi, S., Rose, M., & Poza, L. E. (2020). Matters of participation: Notes on the study of dignity and learning. *Mind, Culture, and Activity, 27*(4). 325–347. https://doi.org/10.1080/10749039.2020.1779304

Freire, P. (1970). *Pedagogy of the oppressed.* Seabury Press.

Kirshner, B. (2015). *Youth activism in an era of education inequality.* NYU Press.

Kirshner, B., Hipolito-Delgado, C. P., & Zion, S. (2015). Sociopolitical development in educational systems: From margins to center. *Urban Review, 47*, 803–808. https://doi.org/10.1007/s11256-015-0335-8

Hipolito-Delgado, C. P., Stickney, D., Kirshner, B., & Donovan, C. (in review). *Fostering youth sociopolitical action: The roles of critical reflection, sociopolitical efficacy, and transformative student voice.*

Hipolito-Delgado, C. P., Stickney, D., Kirshner, B., & Maul, A. (2021). Beyond the trifold in civics presentations: The measure of youth policy arguments. *Journal of Youth Development, 16*(4), 149–165. https://doi.org/10.5195/jyd.2021.1011

Hipolito-Delgado, C. P. & Zion, S. (2017). Igniting the fire within marginalized youth: The role of critical civic inquiry in fostering ethnic identity and civic self-efficacy. *Urban Education, 52*, 699–717. https://doi.org/10.1177/0042085915574524

Nystrand, M. (1997). *Opening dialogue: Understanding the dynamics of language and learning in the English classroom.* Teachers College Press.

Philip, T. M., Souto-Manning, M., Anderson, L., Horn, I., Carter Andrews, D. J., Stillman, J., & Varghese, M. (2019). Making justice peripheral by constructing practice as "core": How the increasing prominence of core practices challenges teacher education. *Journal of Teacher Education, 70*(3), 251–264. https://doi.org/10.1177/0022487118798324

Thiessen, D., & Cook-Sather, A. (2007). *International handbook of student experience in elementary and secondary school.* Springer.

Thompson, J., Windschitl, M., & Braaten, M. (2013). Developing a theory of ambitious early-career teacher practice. *American Educational Research Journal, 50*(3), 574–615. https://doi.org/10.3102/0002831213476334

Watts, R. J., Diemer, M. A., & Voight, A. M. (2011). Critical consciousness: Current status and future directions. *New Directions for Child and Adolescent Development, 2011*(134), 43–57. https://doi.org/10.1002/cd.310

Watts, R. J., Williams, N. C., & Jagers, R. J. (2003). Sociopolitical development. *American Journal of Community Psychology, 31*(1), 185–194. https://doi.org/10.1023/A:1023091024140

Zion, S. (2020). Transformative student voice: Extending the role of youth in addressing systemic marginalization in U.S. schools. *Multiple Voices: Disability, Race, and Language Intersections in Special Education, 20*(1), 1–12.

Zion, S., Allen, C. D., Jean, C. (2015). Enacting a critical pedagogy, influencing teachers' sociopolitical development. *Urban Review, 47*(5), 914–933. https://doi.org/10.1007/s11256-015-0340-y

Zion, S., Kirshner, B., Sung, K., & Ventura, J. (2021). Urban schooling and the transformative possibilities of participatory action research: The role of youth in struggles for urban education justice. In H. R. Milner IV & L. Lomotey (Eds.), *Handbook of urban education* (2nd ed.; pp. 507–522). Routledge.

Zion, S., York, A., & Stickney, D. (2017). Bound together: White teachers/Latinx students revising resistance. In R. M. Elmensky, C. C. Yeakey, & O. Marcucci (Eds.), *The power of resistance: Advances in education in diverse communities* (Vol. 12, pp. 429–458). Emerald. https://doi.org/10.1108/S1479-358X20140000012020

Supporting Youth to Engage in Authentic Civic Dialogue in Our "Actually Existing" Democracy

Nicole Mirra and Antero Garcia

Take a moment to imagine an exemplary model of civic dialogue, one in which the participants embody all of the dispositions you consider most crucial to social harmony and progress. What do you see?

Perhaps you envision a group of individuals listening to one another in a spirit of respect and compassion about compelling issues of the day. Participants voice their opinions as equals, supported by relevant and persuasive evidence, and come to consensus about next steps that may not fully satisfy everyone but that all agree seek to address the common good.

If this vision resonates with you, it is no coincidence. This deliberative paradigm is foundational to how discussion is conceptualized and taught in U.S. civics curricula; indeed, it is often situated by politicians and educators alike as the ideal model of Western democratic discourse (Gutmann, 2004). As further evidence of the weight given to this type of discourse, many chapters in the first portion of this volume thoughtfully model and facilitate myriad versions of this dialogue for students in the classroom.

Yet, as political theorist Nancy Fraser (1990) reminded us over 30 years ago, we do not live in an ideal democracy; as she argued, "There is still a great deal to object to in our 'actually existing democracy'" (p. 56). That reminder is as prescient as ever today as we consider the existential threats our society faces, from pandemic and economic collapse to systemic racism and climate disaster, all developing amidst rancorous political and media divides. To further problematize this vision, patterns of residential and school segregation (see Chapter 10 in this volume for more on this topic), which often map onto these divides, often make it difficult to get to know (let alone engage in vulnerable dialogue with) those who share diverse ideological perspectives (Kahlenberg, 2012).

Such a context necessarily exposes fault lines in the deliberative dialogue frame. Within a systemically inequitable society along the lines of race, class, gender, and other social constructs, can we ever deliberate as equals? If our civic experiences are shaped by those constructs, how common is our perception of the "good"? To what extent are current governmental structures sufficient to meet our multiple needs?

Much like the authors in the previous chapter, we suggest that focusing only on exemplary forms of dialogue is not enough. Educators who teach only toward the ideal vision of democracy do students a great disservice in terms of preparing them to navigate the very real civic challenges of our time. Instead of education that serves as abstraction, we advocate for approaches to civic teaching and learning that wade into the messy realities of "actually existing democracy" and encourage renewed consideration of the purpose and practice of classroom dialogue that is humanizing, generative, and oriented toward equity and justice.

In this chapter, we offer emerging principles and strategies for designing such dialogue based on our experiences facilitating the Digital Democratic Dialogue (3D) project, an initiative that brought together six geographically and ideologically diverse classroom communities from across the United States to explore the roots of civic community, foster productive discussion across difference, and dream of potential social futures. Much like CCI described in Chapter 11, our experiences learning with the teachers and students of the 3D project have led us to articulate three commitments that we consider core to the project of centering equity in civic discussions. We argue that classroom discussion should (1) start with students rather than topics; (2) center storytelling rather than sources; and (3) privilege dreaming for the future over settling for the present.

We begin by teasing out the ways in which mainstream approaches to civic education often foreground the structures and procedural norms of classroom discussion rather than the identity experiences of the students involved. We then outline recent trends in civics research and practice that support a more critical and sociocultural paradigm and describe how these informed the development and implementation of the 3D project. Finally, we delve into the findings that emerged and use them as the basis for further analysis of the commitments undergirding equitable classroom civic discussions.

STUDENTS OVER STRUCTURES:
FLIPPING THE EMPHASIS IN CIVIC LEARNING

As in previous times of public turmoil, the challenges of the current moment have led to renewed calls for explicit instruction in civics, the rationale being that understanding of democratic structures, practices, and values will contribute to increased social and political tolerance, the fostering of a collective national identity, and commitments to leverage public institutions for common problem solving (Warren, 2019). And as this volume demonstrates, the learning opportunities considered best practices within the mainstream conceptualization of civics are often oriented toward socializing young people into democracy as it currently functions, including explicit instruction in government, simulations of political processes, and classroom discussions (Gould, 2011).

Many of the strategies that social studies teachers are encouraged to utilize in order to foster classroom discussion involve mimicking the procedures of various policy and legislative bodies (e.g., Model UN, mock trials, youth government programs). Take debate (as seen in Chapter 6), for instance; this discussion model encourages students to take opposing stances on civic topics and then give speeches and engage in pointed cross-examination, often as if they are proposing actions by the federal government or other actors. Appointed "judges" consider the quality of evidence and persuasiveness of arguments presented in order to declare a "winner." The logic behind these models of discussion holds objectivity as a prized value and privileges credentialed sources as sources to be trusted over individual or group experiences, raising questions about who benefits from them and what role they play in maintaining power in an inequitable society (Mirra & Debate Liberation League, 2020).

Such discussion protocols—and indeed, the socialization that they represent writ large—are predicated on faith in democratic institutions as a source of steady social progress. Yet, as discussed earlier and in Chapter 11, this drive to integrate students into existing civic and political structures creates cognitive dissonance for young people, particularly youth from minoritized communities, whose experiences have continually revealed gaping contradictions in the meritocratic narrative of the American Dream (Watts & Flanagan, 2007). Despite these contradictions, students are much more likely to be taught a narrative of American life that skirts the realities and shortcomings of a diverse democracy (Banks, 2017). The National Assessment of Educational Progress (NAEP, 2014) civics framework suggests that while students should be made aware of past challenges, they should conclude that ultimately "Americans have joined forces to work toward the achievement of their shared ideals" (p. 19).

In response to this problematic framing, a growing body of civic education scholarship, dubbed by education journalists as the "new civics" (Korbey, 2019), has undertaken a reconsideration of the narrow and single-minded push to assimilate students into existing political structures by attending to students' identities and how they matter in public life. Instead of inscribing narratives of ignorance, failure, or disengagement upon young people from minoritized communities when they do not participate civically in traditionally sanctioned ways, researchers have sought to identify how school instructional practices act to perpetuate socioeconomic opportunity gaps in civic engagement (Kahne & Sporte, 2008; Levinson, 2012).

Furthermore, the emergence of the participatory politics framework has sought to expand what counts as civic participation in the digital age and to foreground the innovative uses of civic voice among youth previously dubbed disengaged to foster political friendship and action (Clay & Rubin, 2020; Kahne et al., 2014). These shifts are aimed at making the daily experiences of young people the catalyst for formal civic education, or what Cohen, Kahne, and Marshall (2018) describe as a "lived civics approach" (p. 3). This approach is the basis for action civics programs that seek to transform rote memorization of factual knowledge about the branches of government into participatory inquiry in which students pursue remedies to self-identified community issues (Blevins et al., 2016; Levine, 2015).

Discussion continues to play a large role in these programs, but with shifts from a focus on institutional structures to the lived experiences of young people, and from abstract simulations to real-life dialogue (e.g., see CCI in Chapter 11 as an example). Literacy is key to these shifts; the acts of storytelling and narrative creation that are central to communication across difference in a democratic society (particularly amidst the proliferation of new media tools) are the first steps in the design of new social futures (New London Group, 1996). In order to learn more about the possibilities of leveraging the affordances of digital media to connect young people from far-flung classrooms in authentic civic dialogue, we developed the 3D project.

PROJECT CONTEXT

Because we were interested in privileging the civic voices, ideas, and experiences of young people and their teachers rather than working within existing civic educational approaches or structures, we conceptualized the 3D project as a social design-based experiment (Bang & Vossoughi, 2016). Social design-based experiments represent a powerful way for researchers and teachers to work together to transform what is possible within classrooms and schools because they encourage focused inquiry and play to embrace new perspectives and try new approaches grounded in equity (Gutiérrez & Jurow, 2016).

We worked in partnership with six classroom communities from across the United States during the 2018–2019 school year to coconstruct what we deemed a hybrid digital "school/non-school" learning environment that encouraged young people to define their civic communities, which civic issues they wanted to talk about with peers from different parts of the country, and how they chose to imagine and represent their civic futures. We defined civic futures expansively, encouraging young people to dream about how they would like to live in community with others even (and especially) if their imaginations took them beyond the bounds of our "actually existing" democratic experiment.

The 3D project was also a form of participatory action research because it involved teachers and students as collaborators in the creation and implementation of the study's curriculum (Mirra et al., 2015). The research questions we explored together were "How are young people remixing the civic present and future through digital storytelling and dialogue with their peers? What are the implications for the (re)imagination of democratic education?"

Our Community Members

The 3D project grew out of the authors' longstanding involvement in the National Writing Project (NWP), a nationwide network of educators that "envisions a future where every person is an accomplished writer, engaged learner, and active participant in a digital, interconnected world." Through its Educator Innovator hub, the NWP has created multiple opportunities for students and teachers to utilize digital platforms to write about social issues they care about and share that writing with public audiences in an effort to write their civic futures (Garcia et al., 2019). We recruited teachers from the NWP network who had demonstrated interest in connecting literacy and democratic engagement in their classrooms and were interested in collaborating on the design of a cross-country digital learning community.

We recruited six high school English language arts (ELA) teachers from across the United States to participate in the 3D project, representing communities from the states of Alaska, California, Colorado, Michigan, Pennsylvania, and Texas. We consciously sought out ELA teachers because of our specific interest in literacy practice as a pathway for civic storytelling and discourse and to counter the trend for mainstream civic education to be siloed in social studies classes alone. Indeed, one of the beliefs undergirding our work is that civic learning can (and should) be cultivated creatively across all subject areas. While we did not seek representativeness in our sample, our group possessed generative levels of geographic, demographic, and political diversity.[1] The six teachers each chose one or more of their classes to participate in the study (ranging from AP courses to required ELA courses to electives) and worked to integrate the project into their existing day-to-day curriculum. While the number of students fluctuated during the year as some students moved into or out of their schools, this paper reports on the activities of a core group of 228 students.

Our Curriculum

During the summer of 2018, the 3D project team (the two of us researchers and the six teachers) gathered for a multiday planning retreat to discuss our goals for critical democratic education in the literacy classroom and develop design cycles that the teachers would adapt to their individual school contexts during the 2018–2019 school year. The team created three iterative design cycles aimed at encouraging students to move through a developmental progression of defining themselves as civic actors, engaging with fellow young citizens from across the United States, and imagining their collective civic futures.

Design cycle 1 (September–December 2018) asked students to consider the following questions: Who are we as individuals and how are we connected as a community? What possibilities and tensions do I experience in my communities? How are they shaping who I am in the world? Students chose how they wanted to express their responses (e.g., photo essays, text, video) and shared their stories on a semi-public digital youth publishing platform sponsored by public radio station KQED to invite comment and dialogue from students at the partner schools.

Design cycle 2 (January–April 2019) asked students to choose a civic topic that emerged from design cycle 1 about which they wanted to engage in further conversation with a small group of peers from across the partner schools. Online conversation groups were set up using the Edmodo website, and students were encouraged to engage in free and open discourse in whatever directions that took them. They then chose a medium to reflect on the benefits and challenges of engaging in online civic discourse about controversial social issues.

Design cycle 3 (May–June 2019) gave students free rein to imagine potential civic futures and represent their imaginings in any expressive format they chose. Students were asked "What kind of future do you see? Is it a drama? A tragedy? A comedy?" Students created projects from civic superheroes to *teatro* tableaus to communicate their stories.

As the design cycles progressed, teachers wrote weekly reflection memos and participated in monthly online team meetings to discuss what students were producing. Nicole visited each class community for a 2–3-day period during the school year, during which time she conducted interviews with the teachers and selected students to discuss themes emerging from the project. During the summer of 2019, our group reconvened for another retreat to analyze data together and analyze the lessons learned that can inform civics instruction more broadly.

LESSONS TO INFORM INSTRUCTION

Since the 3D project was an initiative inspired by civic storytelling, we share some of our stories here to highlight three lessons that we believe can inspire teachers to reimagine their approach to civic discussions.

Lesson 1: Encourage Students to Excavate Their Civic Pasts as a Catalyst for Analyzing Their Civic Present

The 3D project sought to provide students with opportunities to talk about themselves and the issues that mattered to them on their own terms. In keeping

Figure 12.1. Student-Identified Communities

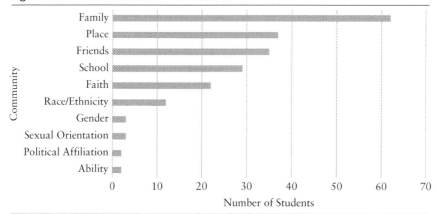

with our commitment to honoring students before structures, we made the choice to organize our design cycles to cultivate talk about identity before issues. Design cycle 1 encouraged students to define the communities that mattered in their lives and excavate some of the civic experiences in their pasts so that later discussions would be grounded in a certain level of relational trust.

The multimodal stories that students composed to share the communities that mattered in their lives reflected the immediate contexts of their lives and revealed how the relationships commonly associated with adolescence were experienced in similar and unique ways across the sites. Nearly all of the students highlighted one or more interest-based communities in their responses, ranging from art to gaming to sports and beyond; while the great majority of these interests intrinsically involved multiple communities (friends, school, etc.), the way students constructed the stories made it clear that their personal interests predominated as primary sources of meaning for the 3D project students. Figure 12.1 summarizes the remaining communities that students explicitly named in their responses.

In planning meetings, adults on the 3D project team noted the ways that sociopolitical constructs showed up in these communities, particularly how each student who chose to discuss race/ethnicity, gender, sexual orientation, and ability identified with a group characterized as nondominant in U.S. society: non-white, women, LGBTQ+, or (dis)abled. They also noted the substantive role that place played in many students' self-identifications. Knowing this, and watching students comment on each others' posts and start to build relationships, helped the teachers have conversations with their own classes about what it would mean to have conversations about controversial civic issues that were based in care and that were aware of perspective and power.

Only after this foundation had been laid did the project introduce issue-oriented dialogue. In groups that met asynchronously across the four different time zones, students utilized the school-friendly social platform Edmodo to facilitate talk that crossed geographic, socioeconomic, and ideological boundaries. The most popular topic that students chose to discuss on Edmodo was guns, which was not surprising considering the prevalence of gun incidents occurring nationally and in each of the local communities during the course of the study. Students also chose to discuss issues as wide ranging as health/health care, drug abuse, gender, immigration, race, and technology.

After much deliberation and consultation with their classes, the teachers decided that instead of asking students to research and debate multiple "sides" of their chosen issue or construct directed public awareness campaigns, they would simply encourage students to talk to each other to see what emerged organically. Alaska teacher Lacy acknowledged afterward how "scary" it felt to "let students loose" into dialogue without carefully planned structures; as she mused, "We know what they are seeing all around them in politics, on cable news—how would they treat each other? What is our responsibility?" The group did agree to ask students to consider the grounding themes of the 3D project—personal/community connections, points of commonality/difference, and the ease/difficulty of talking to each other—but otherwise attempted to engage in what Pennsylvania teacher Isabel called "a little de-schooling" by letting students take the lead.

This step back was a manifestation of the 3D project's commitment to craft civic learning opportunities with young people at the center rather than immediately orienting them to think about issues in ways (e.g., debates, campaigns) dictated by existing civic practices or structures. Yet, as noted in our previous finding, attempting to "de-school" an activity taking place within the context of "school"—particularly a civic learning activity—was inherently contradictory and produced tension for students as they started to dialogue in Edmodo. On top of logistical concerns about time zones and Internet access, we noticed that students seemed a bit confused about how to proceed in their discussions without a formal assignment to complete.

Yet, after some initial awkwardness, students began sharing. Teachers also worked to find times when groups of students could video chat in real time—activities that students across the schools deemed to be the most meaningful experience of the entire project. As Pat, a student from Texas, explained, "It's kind of surreal because it's kind of like, 'Hey, there are people out there outside of you and there are people that exist, and have lives, and have experiences that aren't you.'" Just as students were intrigued by the similarities they saw across their contexts, they were equally interested in the differences. As California student, Aidan, shared:

> It's really interesting how people who live in different parts of the country can have completely different perspectives on something. . . .
> And I think that actually connecting to teenagers who are going through

that, because when you're a teenager you're kind of going through a very developmental stage, and you're kind of figuring out what it is that you believe, and you're starting to distance yourself a little bit from what your parents believe versus what you personally believe.

Lesson 2: Lean Into the Possibilities (and Discomforts) of Perspective Taking and Real Talk

When Texas teacher Connie reflected on the school year, she was most struck by the ways that the cross-school dialogues helped her students to "step outside of their own perspectives." She was particularly struck by the experience of Daniel, a student who had begun the school year "using the word 'gay' as an insult" and refusing to consider arguments for gun control because of his comfort with guns in his own household. After engaging in a video chat with a student from Philadelphia who had lost a close friend to gun violence, he told his teacher that he "could understand why people with that experience would feel so differently." As Daniel explained afterward in a reflection, "I just realized that nothing is going to happen unless we start to listen to each other's stories." In this moment, Daniel was decentering his own experiences and allowing himself to be moved (at least temporarily) by the stories of others.

We find it important to note that these processes of decentering and imagining did not come easily to all youth (or adults) and that tensions emerged as political ideologies clashed. The experience of Cory, one of the students from Alaska, serves as one illustration of this tension; instead of taking up the invitation to broaden civic perspectives, Cory took the 3D project as an opportunity to advocate for his deeply held beliefs. He embraced the combative spirit that dominates in today's political discourse when in one of his reflections he declared, "I personally love debate and politics, and so it was enjoyable to have discussions with people who disagree with me." He chose to join a discussion group about gender issues and quickly staked a claim for what he believed were the appropriate biological and social divides among "women" and "men."

Each time one of his female peers sought to share a personal story about an experience they interpreted as gender discrimination, he immediately leapt past the storyteller's perspective and discounted those individual experiences by appealing to data that he found on far-right conservative websites (e.g., Prager U) that supported his perspective. He then returned to his own absolute generalizations and challenged his peers to argue with him; for instance, on the issue of LGBTQ rights, he insisted, "There are only two genders." He followed this up with an invitation to his peers: "I can rebuttal some of your other points if you would like."

Cory's rhetoric forced the entire group of 3D adults, and particularly his teacher, Lacy, to confront fundamental and delicate challenges that classroom educators in public schools must continuously negotiate between respecting individual students' freedom of speech while maintaining a safe and nondiscriminatory learning environment for the collective student body. During a monthly team meeting, Lacy expressed worry to her colleagues about the possibility that Cory was offending their students and wondered aloud if more structures should be put in place to lead students away from sharing potentially explosive opinions and toward safer and more removed academic analysis. "Should I tell him that he needs to prove the validity of his sources?" she asked the group. She struggled with how to add nuance or even challenge his views in the politically conservative community in which she taught, saying "I've been censoring myself as a teacher . . . because we can't talk about all these issues [the administration] labels too controversial." Lacy's concerns echo those of teachers across the United States who choose to forego discussions of controversial issues rather than risk potential fallout (Hess & McAvoy, 2016). Yet her 3D project colleagues continued to push each other to lean in despite this discomfort; as Philip responded, "These are opinions that students are going to hear out in the real world. They have to figure out how to manage that!" The group insisted that the conflict opened an authentic space for students to sharpen their civic literacy skills and brainstorm how to proceed with dialogue amidst conflict and polarization.

And so the dialogue continued (while adults kept a watchful eye on the sidelines). In Texas, Connie held a debriefing session with several of her female students who were in Cory's discussion group. She first listened as they vented their frustration; one student, Laura, fumed, "One girl shared her story about being discriminated against in a basketball game and Cory was like, 'I see no problem with this.' And she gave evidence and tried to be civil. And he said the same thing!" The group of students threw their hands in the air and groaned. Yet the group soon turned to possible responses. One student, Amy, suggested trying to get past the data to personal storytelling: "I try to ask probing questions like, why do you think that? What have you experienced? What do you know?" Connie also encouraged them to think about what it means to respectfully challenge a dialogue partner instead of shutting down; indeed, Laura tried posting a response to one of Cory's provocations online:

> I am not trying to be disrespectful but I think that you saying that women don't face real issues and that they are just using the 'victim card' is extremely one sided. Many of the girls on this chat have already sent non-biased resources on the different obstacles women are facing, so I don't feel the need to. But by your statement I can't help but think that you did not read any of them.

This dialogue did not change Cory's perspective or approach to conversation; however, we did notice fleeting moments when he, and other students, seemed to be working through contradictions in their own beliefs. In the same presentation in which he laid out his preferred civic future, Cory also acknowledged, "We must find a way to see through our differences and respect each other as human beings." Our group continues to ponder how to foster and extend these moments of potential civic "seeing" as we simultaneously wonder what it means to move forward as a civic body when individuals have such different views on issues that are fundamental to the safety, identity, and humanity of some. Cory's interactions with his group offer a crucial reminder that dialogue and youth voice in and of themselves are not always liberatory—particularly in classroom contexts; indeed, they often replicate deeply entrenched ideologies of a normative and historically violent instantiation of civic life that we argue the speculative imagination must deliberately speak against. Yet at the same time, hopeful moments also emerged in which students, however briefly, experienced flashes of perspective taking, openness, and empathy.

Lesson 3: Instead of Being Hemmed in by What Exists, Envision Civic Futures

In the final design cycle of the 3D project, students put storytelling to use when offered the opportunity to wildly imagine possible civic futures. They developed origin stories for their own civic superheroes and described how these heroes addressed issues that they identified as most pressing, often complete with accompanying illustrations. Simone created Home Girl, who "got her power to create homes for the homeless by once being homeless herself" (see Figure 12.2). Anthony wrote that his superhero, Anahita, is "able to give close minded people a temporary experience of the life of a minority." Ana's Immigration Reform Girl "makes sure people aren't being treated unfairly, just for wanting to start a new life in America."

The students' construction of superheroes, as well as their cross-school dialogues, engaged with a speculative view of civic life as young people gave themselves permission to imagine what could be accomplished in society if the intractability of structural inequities magically fell away and a radical empathy guided public decisionmaking.

This push and pull hung over the entire project. Even as the students demonstrated curiosity and creativity in their imaginings about possible civic futures, they ended the school year with a substantial amount of doubt about the willingness of the public writ large to engage in the same practice as they surveyed the behaviors of their parents' generation in public life. When teachers asked all of the students in the project to quantify their feelings about the possibility of people in the United States being able to dialogue productively about controversial social issues in their lifetimes, with 1 being extremely pessimistic and 4 being extremely optimistic, the great majority of students (186 out of 228) found themselves in the 2–3 range. Their

Figure 12.2. Student Civic Superhero

Origin-
Home Girl has the power to create homes and take families off of the streets - also people who are on the verge of getting put out. She got her power to create homes for the homeless by once being homeless herself. She slept in abandoned buses and homes. One night after sleeping in an abandoned bus she woke up in the middle of the night. She saw a bright green object glowing. Home Girl got up and walked towards it. She picked up the glowing ball of who knows what. It exploded all over her! The next morning she woke. But she woke up in a nice home. How weird that was, she wondered. Home Girl knew she had something special.

One Day Home Girl was driving under a popular bridge called H Town Bridge. There were multiple homeless people. Women, men and even children. So she went to talk to them all. She gathered them up and told them to close their eyes. Home Girl then transported them to an open field. She explained that homes would be built for them and they would not have to worry about a thing. They were all full of joy! Home Girl then created their homes for them. Everyone was amazed but more than anything grateful. Home Girl was able to take multiple families off of the streets. Home Girl also provides utilities for each home she builds so they don't have to be worried about anything but finding work or bettering themselves.

accompanying open responses indicated their uneasiness about the tenor of today's public dialogue and the extent to which individuals are willing to truly empathize across lines of difference. Heather from California wrote, "I don't believe people in this day and age are mature enough to handle talking about things they disagree about without fighting or arguing as is often shown in our political system." Sixty-eight percent of open responses referenced dialogue as devolving into arguments or name-calling.

Yet, in a reflection of the pull between futurist and pessimist perspectives, students also offered tentative gestures of hope. Ana from Texas reflected, "I think our generation is growing to have better conversations." The act of "future-making" (Montfort, 2017, p. 4) is not work that necessarily has clear, measurable and standards-aligned goals. The speculative optimism and pessimism that students voiced throughout this project bring to light that youth leading requires pedagogic support in classrooms and will require constant reflection, reevaluation, and revision. As Tara from Michigan wrote, "I'd like to be optimistic and think people will evolve." Twenty-two percent of the responses demonstrated the mixture of hope and resignation exemplified in the musing of Monica from Pennsylvania: "I hesitate but I do have hope."

TOWARD THE "ACTUALLY EXISTING" TOMORROW

Considering the lessons learned through the 3D project by students, by teachers, and by us as researchers, we want to reemphasize three key strategies illustrated in our findings. As we consider the steep climb that is supporting youth civic imagination today, educators might find purchase in their journey through (1) focusing on topics that students are interested in, (2) centering opportunities for students to imagine new stories about the world around them, and (3) casting dialogue and thought toward future making.

Throughout the experiences we documented in this chapter, the tensions we noticed across school sites spoke to the generative spirit of dialogue. By basing conversations in the topics that students cared about, even students that agitated other group members, like Cory, were able to "find a way to see through our differences." Notably, these affinity groups were intentionally focused on *dialogue* (as the project's name implies), and students were not positioned to debate or to convince others of their perspectives. By providing young people with the space for exploring, questioning, and collectively *wondering* about topics they are passionate about, civic foundations for action and advocacy were developed.

At the same time, the writing practices that this project documented also spoke to moving beyond the norms of deliberation and persuasion. By telling stories, students wielded the power of their imaginations for wondering how things *could be* rather than reformatting the documented present in a slightly revised format. This does not mean that work lacked rigor. Instead, storytelling means building on tacit knowledge, on the facts and concepts that might be covered in various classroom activities, and on sustaining structures of creative writing and multimodal production that emphasize communicating civic thought for myriad audiences. It is a heavy lift and requires repositioning civic learning as a set of creative tasks for wondering, playing, and dreaming.

Finally, hand in hand with the practices of storytelling and centering student-chosen topics, providing a space for taking seriously the civic dreaming of young people in schools is imperative. Too often, civic concepts in classrooms are positioned as purely practical. You vote. You donate. You encourage others to act on behalf of your best interests. Emphasizing passive forms of democracy and the seemingly limited set of tools at the hands of minors in today's civic society takes away the potent bite of young people hungry for a future that ascends higher than their present state. We must fold in ongoing spaces for students' dreams to be articulated, examined, and celebrated.

While this chapter zooms in on these three different strategies as discrete aspects of what civic learning in classrooms can look like, they are also intertwined and complementary. The superheroes that students created—Anthony's hero that blasts apart the ideas of "close minded people" and Ana's Immigration Reform Girl—hew closely to the topics these students hold onto dearly. Too, they tell new stories about what young people believe about themselves, about their community members, and about the world that may eye them with skepticism or distrust. Finally, these superheroes, while living in the imaginative power of stories spun from the minds of young people seeking something new, offer new directions for the civic worlds these students are inhabiting for tomorrow. While Immigration Reform Girl may be a response to the present and moral atrocities of the past, she represents Ana's unwillingness to settle for the status quo of the present day.

Reflecting on his approach to writing, science fiction novelist Samuel Delany (2020) describes how "mundane" (e.g., nonscience fiction) characters "succeed or fail against the background of the real world so that their successes are always some form of adjusting to the real world. Their failures are always a matter of being defeated by the real world." One powerful component of telling stories about the democracy that students are weaving for tomorrow is that they are not patching over the holes and rips of the tattered present. Rather, they are advocating around the topics that matter *now* while rejecting expectations that they must respond to the turmoil that surrounds us; the pragmatics can be set aside if we are looking to tomorrow. While this approach may not leave students with all of the actionable answers for achieving particular civic goals, it allows them to imagine directions, participatory footholds, and previously obscured pathways that may have never seemed accessible in the "actually existing" every day.

We encourage teachers to keep in mind both the ease and the complexity of constructing a digital civic discussion network as they consider potential opportunities to transform their own practice. Considering the proliferation of technology tools that can forge connections across time and space (hello, Zoom!), linking students across schools, cities, or even countries can be facilitated relatively easily if built on existing colleague networks or professional organizations like the NWP. Yet this ease of technical connection belies the much tougher work of building the kinds of productive, empathetic, and trusting relationships that made the 3D project meaningful. The teachers in our group spent dozens of hours planning with each other and with their students to ensure that the project integrated into the curricular mandates of their own schools and that dialogue across schools was undertaken with cultural sensitivity and open-mindedness. We encourage teachers who want to provide opportunities for their students to engage in authentic dialogue with peers to start small and start carefully; for instance, a pilot experiment with a subset of students could offer lessons about the best strategies for courageous conversations in particular contexts. These small moves can build over time into radical acts of connection.

At the same time, however, we are not naïve to the fact that the present moment demands more than what may seem feasible for the young people in our classrooms today. In some ways, the heft of white supremacist legacies, the fallout of climate disaster, and the tenuous nature of a democracy that has been literally and violently challenged require immediate action from students entering this civic system. And yet, the past generations illustrate how the incremental changes and forms of passive acceptance of democratic norms that are taught in classrooms do too little for too many of our students. By centering our pedagogies in stories of the future that are anchored to the needs of the present, young people transform the "actual existing," arching it toward freedom and liberation.

NOTE

1. For more information regarding the methodology of the study, please see Mirra and Garcia (2020).

REFERENCES

Bang, M., & Vossoughi, S. (2016). Participatory design research and educational justice: Studying learning and relations within social change making. *Cognition & Instruction, 34*(3), 173–193.

Banks, J. (2017). Failed citizenship and transformative civic education. *Educational Researcher, 46*(7), 366–377.

Blevins, B., LeCompte, K., & Wells, S. (2016). Innovations in civic education: Developing civic agency through action civics. *Theory & Research in Social Education, 44*(3), 344–384.

Clay, K., & Rubin, B. (2020). "I look deep into this stuff because it's a part of me": Toward a critically relevant civics education. *Theory & Research in Social Education, 48*(2), 161–181.

Cohen, C., Kahne, J., & Marshall, J. (2018). *Let's go there: Race, ethnicity and a lived civics approach to civics education.* Civic Engagement Research Group. https://www.civicsurvey.org/publications/lets-go-there

Delaney, S. (2020). Why I write. *The Yale Review.* https://yalereview.yale.edu/why-i-write

Fraser, N. (1990). Rethinking the public sphere: A contribution to the critique of actually existing democracy. *Social Text, 25/26,* 56–80.

Garcia, A., Levinson, A., & Gargroetzi, E. (2019). "Dear future president of the United States": Analyzing youth civic writing within the 2016 Letters to the Next President project. *American Educational Research Journal, 57*(3), 1159–1202.

Gould, J. (2011). *Guardian of democracy: The civic mission of schools.* Leonore Annenberg Institute for Civics of the Annenberg Public Policy Center at the University of Pennsylvania. https://www.carnegie.org/publications/guardian-of -democracy-the-civic-mission-of-schools/

Gutiérrez, K. D., & Jurow, A. S. (2016). Social design experiments: Toward equity by design. *Journal of the Learning Sciences, 25*(4), 565–598.

Gutmann, A. (2004). *Why deliberative democracy?* Princeton University Press.

Kahlenberg, R. D. (Ed.) (2012). *The future of school integration: Socioeconomic diversity as an education reform strategy.* Century Foundation Press.

Kahne, J., Middaugh, E., & Allen, D. (2014). Youth, new media, and the rise of participatory politics. In D. Allen & J. S. Light (Eds.), *From voice to influence: Understanding digital citizenship in a digital age* (pp. 35–55). University of Chicago Press.

Kahne, J., & Sporte, S. (2008). Developing citizens: The impact of civic learning opportunities on students' commitment to civic participation. *American Educational Research Journal, 45*(3), 738–766.

Korbey, H. (2019). *Building better citizens: A new civics education for all.* Rowman & Littlefield.

Levine, P. (2015). *We are the ones we have been waiting for: The promise of civic renewal in America.* Oxford University Press.

Levinson, M. (2012). *No citizen left behind.* Harvard University Press.

Mirra, N., & Debate Liberation League (2020). Without borders: Youth debaters reimagining the nature and purpose of public dialogue. *English Teaching: Practice & Critique, 19*(3), 253–267.

Mirra, N., & Garcia, A. (2021). In search of the meaning and purpose of 21st-century literacy learning: A critical review of research and practice. *Reading Research Quarterly, 56*(3), 463–496. https://doi.org/10.1002/rrq.313

Mirra, N., Garcia, A., & Morrell, E. (2015). *Doing youth participatory action research: Transforming inquiry with researchers, educators, and students.* Routledge.

National Assessment of Educational Progress Civics Project. (2014). *Civics framework for the 2014 National Assessment of Educational Progress.* National Assessment Governing Board. https://www.nagb.gov/naep-frameworks/civics /2014-civics-framework.html

New London Group. (1996). A pedagogy of multiliteracies: Designing social futures. *Harvard Educational Review, 66*, 60–92.

Warren, S. (2019). *Generation citizen: The power of youth in our politics.* Counterpoint.

Watts, R., & Flanagan, C. (2007). Pushing the envelope on civic engagement: A developmental and liberation psychology perspective. *Journal of Community Psychology, 35*(6), 779–792.

Concluding Thoughts

Jane C. Lo

Hans-Georg Gadamer (2006), the well-known hermeneutician, suggests that "the true reality of human communication is such that a conversation does not simply carry one person's opinion through against another's, or even simply add one opinion to another. Conversation transforms the viewpoint of both" (p. 17). This means that our understanding of the world is mediated through language, especially conversations and dialogue with others. This book is an exercise in written communication (a book) as a way to facilitate broader communications (discussions)—so that social studies classrooms might promote better understandings of ourselves, one another, and the world. While Gadamer (2006) may argue that all conversations help lead us to broader understanding, the chapters in this volume show that making meaningful and productive discussions work in a classroom is challenging but worthwhile work. In what follows, I summarize some lessons and themes that span across all of the chapters in this volume. Whatever the social studies discipline or school subject, whether in high school, middle school, or elementary school, for well-resourced schools or not, these are things teachers can learn and adapt from chapters in this book about how to make discussions work.

QUALITY DISCUSSIONS ARE CHALLENGING

It is no coincidence that all of the chapters in this volume begin with the challenges of facilitating quality discussions in the classroom. As the introductory chapter in this book suggests, most teachers would like to include more quality discussions in their classrooms but may not fully understand what it looks like or how to go about it. There is no way around the fact that discussions, as can be seen from every method and technique mentioned in this volume, do not come naturally. Discussion is not something that teachers can leave to chance or wish will spontaneously occur. Even though conversation and discussion are a part of everyday life, the type of quality discussion we hope to facilitate in our classrooms requires more than just

"getting students talking." That said, teachers should not shy away from
including more discussions in their classroom, and I hope this is where the
following lessons learned from these preceding chapters can be a guide.

DISCUSSIONS NEED BUY-IN

Perhaps the first hurdle to quality discussions is teacher's belief that all students have the ability to conduct productive discussions in the classroom.
As all of the proceeding chapters suggest, both students and teachers need
to believe that everyone in the classroom is capable of engaging in quality discussion. Chapter 8 in particular discusses the importance of including students of all abilities in these structured conversational activities. Not
only is representation of different voices paramount for quality discussions,
but *all* students have the opportunity to learn through quality discussions.
Since discussion is about knowledge construction, all students should be
involved in building knowledge for themselves. Since a foundational basis
for learning and schooling is about gaining and constructing knowledge of
the world, it would be unconscionable to not include all students in discussions. It is important to remember that discussion isn't just for certain kinds
of students or particular kinds of classes. Quality discussion can and should
occur everywhere—for everyone—so that all will have the opportunity to
broaden their understandings through structured conversations.

DISCUSSIONS NEED PLANNING

Since meaningful discussions often require structuring, to facilitate quality discussions necessitates good planning. When it comes to structures of
a discussion, the planning can be initiated and prepared by the teacher or
students, but detailed planning of the structure of discussion must occur. As
all of the chapters suggest, discussion can be structured or planned around
a text (SAC), source (inquiry), or reasoned arguments (authentic civic dialogue). Readers might recall that while feelings and emotions of students
play important roles in the discussion (see Part III for the importance of including more diverse perspectives), quality and meaningful discussions never
rely on feelings alone. A discussion could have emotive beginnings (e.g., issues that bother students or are in the forefront of their minds), but quality
discussions always include structures to help facilitate those emotions and
feelings. It is good to remember that discussion is not talk therapy—while
quality discussions could be therapeutic, the goal of quality discussion is
the co-construction of knowledge and understanding. This is why planning
and structure is important, so participants can be guided toward this goal
of broader understanding. Even student-centered discussions are not a free

for all of he said she said; instead a tenet of quality discussion is providing reason and evidence to support emotive and controversial issues.

DISCUSSIONS REQUIRE COMMUNITY BUILDING

Since emotions may be high when discussions of controversial issues occur, simply structuring a discussion with general guidelines is not enough. Quality discussions also require a healthy amount of trust and respect in the classroom. It requires courage of the teacher to plan and facilitate the discussion, but it also requires courage of the students to participate and share honestly. All of these can only occur if there is trust and respect between everyone within the classroom—teachers and students alike. This is why all of the preceding chapters describe a need to build a strong sense of community and rapport as a precursor to quality discussions in the classroom. It is impossible to have genuine, productive, and quality discussions without first building a sense of community in the classroom. In the most basic sense, from the various chapters that discuss cooperative learning, this means that the classroom environment must be conducive to cooperative learning so that students can learn together. In a more profound sense, as seen in later chapters on youth agency, this means facilitating a classroom community where students play important roles in creating the kind of classroom that they want to be a part of.

THE NEED FOR SOCIAL EMOTIONAL LEARNING (SEL)

To create such a trusting community means that teachers and administrators must be mindful of social emotional learning. For quality discussions to occur, the classroom cannot just be about learning more content or reaching particular objectives and goals. Based on studies presented in various chapters (especially Chapters 2, 11, and 12), quality discussion can only occur in environments where students feel like their social and emotional well-being are taken care of. As an extension of the ideas presented on community building, a classroom focus on SEL can help support successful community building and yield more fruitful discussions in the classroom. In other words, quality discussion depends on thoughtful community building, which in turn requires a focus on SEL.

EMPOWER STUDENTS TO CO-CONSTRUCT KNOWLEDGE

Once the classroom environment is conducive for discussions and structures for discussions have been planned, an important tenet for all of the examples presented in this book is a need to empower students as co-constructors of knowledge. Since quality discussion is ultimately about expanding our understandings of the world, students need to be empowered to be creators of knowledge. Rather than rote memorization or recitation of past information, discussion is all about the co-construction of knowledge together via dialogue. This means putting students at the center of their own learning. As can be seen from all of the chapters in this book, quality discussion occurs when students can draw on both their prior knowledge and experiences as well as new information and evidence. It is the open interplay between newly discovered information and prior understanding that helps everyone see new thinking and discoveries at work. The true power of quality discussion is this process of thinking aloud about new information in the open that benefits both the listeners and the speakers. Therefore, it is imperative for students to not only feel safe but empowered to share their ideas and thoughts.

WORKING THROUGH THE DISCOMFORT

At the same time, thinking aloud in the open (or voicing something new for the first time) about something new can be extremely uncomfortable for both teachers and students. However, it is important for both teachers and students to recognize, accept, and embrace this discomfort as a part of the power of discussions. This is why building a community centered around SEL is so important to the process. Nevertheless, to successfully co-construct knowledge together through dialogue means that a natural sharing of power must occur. Teachers may have to give up some traditional notions of the power that comes from being the knowledge giver (i.e., sage on the stage) and instead take on a co-constructor role that helps facilitate the process. This is not to suggest that teachers and students are somehow equal—they are not. Recall that the teacher generally sets up the structure and facilitates the discussion, but this is not because they know more or are controlling the situation (e.g., playing God in the classroom); rather, it is because they have had more practice, experience, and hopefully more wisdom and forbearance to model for students how good discussers interact in quality discussions. This may be a tall order, but to facilitate quality discussions requires teachers to also be seasoned discussers, hence the lessons learned about helping to support teachers in Chapter 2. Beyond modeling good discussion techniques for students, these types of discussions give teachers an opportunity to model democratic values and healthy relationships among equals.

DISCUSSIONS TAKE PRACTICE

Lastly, quality discussions take a good amount of practice. As can be seen from the kind of community and relationship building that goes into this work, high-quality discussions are not things that can simply be done once in a while or relegated to one project, assignment, or unit. Quality discussions are a result of relationship building and a steady practice of listening and talking. As mentioned in Chapters 1 and 3, early discussions ought to be more structured, with classroom norms and rules that can help students (and the teacher) get used to what deep dialogue feels and looks like. As teachers take time to build a student-centered community in the classroom, students should have opportunities to build myriad skills required for quality discussion: listening, talking, reasoning, perspective taking, warranted arguments, and humanizing others. These are all skills that require practice over time, but with practice students will become seasoned discussers who can handle challenging topics and issues.

MOVING FORWARD

In the end, even though quality discussions are challenging, they are worth the effort, because they both help students learn and do democracy in the classroom. Recent political events suggest that productive engagement with varying perspectives in the public sphere is in decline. It is more important now than ever to help young people take up these skills in earnest. A recent National Academy of Education (NAEd, 2021) report suggests that civic reasoning and discourse help us grapple with questions like "How should we live" and "What should we do?" The chapters in this book provide ways for teachers to help students wrestle productively with those questions, especially when different answers to them exist amongst a pluralistic polity.

But even as the methods and examples provided in this book help support quality discussion in the classroom, the landscape of our democratic public sphere is shifting. As Chapters 9 and 12 point out, the digitalization of dialogue and the onslaught of social media on dialogic norms is changing how we, especially young people, engage in civic discourse and reasoning. What does discussion look like in a sphere that is not truly public or truly private, but blended between these nodes (Papacharissi, 2010)? How might students transfer the skills they learn through quality discussions to digital spaces where discussers might be anonymous, the community does not feel safe, or not everyone abides by the same rules? These are all broader questions and challenges that we will tackle in years to come. While this book may not address these challenges head-on, it provides a foundation upon which new ideas and practices around quality discussions can be built. As the old adage suggests, things that are worth doing are not always easy, but I hope this book provides readers with support and encouragement on this worthwhile journey toward more quality discussions in the classroom.

REFERENCES

Gadamer, H.-G. (2006). Language and understanding (1970). *Theory, Culture & Society*, *23*(1), 13–27. https://doi.org/10.1177/0263276406063226

National Academy of Education. (2021). *Educating for civic reasoning and discourse*. https://doi.org/10.31094/2021/2

Papacharissi, Z. (2010). *A private sphere: Democracy in a digital age*. Polity.

Pledge of Allegiance Mini Unit

Persistent issue: What role should schools play in molding patriotic citizens?

Central question: Should students be required to say the Pledge of Allegiance?

Class 1 90 min	Activity 1 45 min	Grabber: Short discussion on whether students should be required to recite the pledge in schools?
	Activity 2 45 min	Pledge of Allegiance ticket: Completed individually, given to teacher to read over in preparation for next class's Socratic seminar
Class 2 90 min	Activity 1 70 min	Socratic seminar: Remind class of norms, conduct seminar
	Activity 2 20 min	Debrief seminar (oral and written)
Class 3 90 min	Response groups 30 min	Students in groups of five work through two Supreme Court Cases: *Gobitis* (1940) and *Barnette* (1943).
	Culminating activity 60 min	Students work in Supreme Court groups to study and decide *Frazier v. Winn*. Groups report decisions, teacher leads class in final discussion of the arguments and their individual choices. Examine the fundamental constitutional and ethical values: liberty, general welfare, national security, human dignity, freedom of conscience, free speech.

Ticket to Pledge Seminar

Name: _____

Directions: Please complete this as a ticket to participate in a class seminar.

I <u>Pledge</u> <u>allegiance</u> to the <u>flag</u> of the United States of America, and to the <u>republic</u> for which it stands: one <u>nation</u> <u>under God</u>, <u>indivisible</u>, with <u>liberty</u> and <u>justice</u> for <u>all</u>.

What do you think about when you say these words in the pledge? Describe your thoughts and/or emotions for each term in your *own* words. Elaborate on the word's meaning to you. It is okay to describe these in terms of symbolism.

Pledge:
Allegiance:
Flag:
Republic:
Nation:
Under God:
Indivisible:
Liberty:
Justice:
All:

BRIEF HISTORY OF THE PLEDGE OF ALLEGIANCE

The Pledge of Allegiance was written during "the flag movement" of the 1880s and was authored by Francis Bellamy in 1892. Following the Civil War, loyalty oaths to the Constitution and the Union along with displaying the American flag became quite common. Mr. Bellamy was a Christian socialist and former Baptist minister who was an author for a popular children's magazine known as *Youth's Companion*. The magazine knew the

400th anniversary of Columbus's arrival would provide great potential to sell magazines. This was also a time of heightened anti-immigrant sentiment. Bellamy wrote of his concern that continued Confederate celebrations, capitalism, and "every alien immigrant of inferior race" was eroding society and felt children saying a pledge in public schools would ensure "that the distinctive principles of true Americanism will not perish as long as free, public education endures."

The original pledge was "I Pledge allegiance to my flag and the republic for which it stands, one nation, indivisible, with liberty and justice for all." Bellamy wanted to include the word "equality" along with liberty and justice but removed it because he felt it would be too divisive. He also resisted language referring to God, again feeling it was too divisive. In 1923, Congress edited it to read, "I Pledge allegiance to the flag of the United States of America." The phrase "under God" was added in 1954 when Congress, under pressure from religious groups and supported by President Eisenhower, added it to distinguish the United States from communism during the Cold War.

For more information on the history of the pledge of allegiance, see the following websites:

https://www.smithsonianmag.com/history/Pledge-allegiance-pr-gimmick
    -patriotic-vow-180956332/
http://bostonreview.net/politics/jack-david-eller-Pledge-allegiance
https://www.history.com/news/who-created-the-Pledge-of-allegiance
https://www.ushistory.org/documents/Pledge.htm

Pledge Discussion Guide

WHEN YOU SAY THE PLEDGE OF ALLEGIANCE, TO WHAT ARE YOU PLEDGING?

What is allegiance?

- How do you define allegiance? (loyalty, pride, sacrifice, feeling, devotion)
- Does allegiance mean giving up protesting?

Flag?

- What does the flag symbolize?
- Why do we have flags?

Nation?

- What is a "nation"? What is it not?
- Is it the physical borders or something else?
- What is unity? Is unity required in a nation? Is it desirable (pros/cons)? High school analogy: Can you be part of the school and not be totally on board with everything your peers or the school does? Would we want everyone to agree?

Republic?

- What is a republic?
- What is central to our republic? How is our republic different than other republics (e.g., People's Republic of China)?
- What values are central to a republic? (justice, equality, freedom, rule of law, minority rights versus majority rule—representatives supposed to represent both those who voted for them as well as those who did not; does the president only represent those who voted for him?)
- When they say the pledge, are they thinking of historical events, time periods, modern-day American Revolution and Founding Fathers or today's republic?

Summarizing question: Flag, nation, republic

- What is the text saying we're pledging?
- Commas—what does the grammar indicate?
- What would a totalitarian or dictatorship encourage people to pledge to?

Under God?

- What does this mean?
- Should this be included or excluded?
- Does it imply the Christian God?
- What if we used a lower case "g"?
- Why was this phrase added after the Cold War?
- Blending of theism and patriotism; is this good/bad?
- Does this mean God especially blesses the United States and not other countries?
- Could other countries see it that way?
- Does history influence your thinking about this phrase?
- Refer to students' definitions of under God.

Indivisible?

- Does this imply unity? Does unity imply conformity?
- Majority rule versus minority rights?
- Can you have differences without division?
- Refer to students' definitions of indivisible

Liberty

- Refer to its definition.
- How does liberty differ from freedom?
    - » Freedom is the broad idea that while liberty is specific acts that are allowed or limited by law, we have freedom of religion, but there are limits on the liberties in which we can express our faiths.
- What aspects of liberty do you feel have not been achieved?
- Why is liberty important to governing? What role should the government play in protecting liberties? Restricting liberties?
- Do limits on liberties negate the Pledge?

Justice

- Refer to its definition. Is justice punishment? Rule of law? Revenge? Rights of accused?

- What kinds of justice are important for a republic?
- What aspects of justice do you feel have not been achieved?

For all?

- Are these ideals or reality?
- Are there any groups of people in the United States today who might feel we are not achieving this? Who might they be, and why might they feel this way?
- What is the role of the citizen—protect or achieve democracy? Is it only the job of the government, or do citizens have a role to play?

School

- Why is it required? (Does this increase or diminish interest in the pledge?)
- Every day versus special occasions—which would make it more meaningful?
- Brainwashing? Do they know what they're saying?

What is patriotism?

- How patriotic is saying the pledge?
- Is it patriotic to refuse to say the pledge?
- Can patriotism be divisive or cause international conflicts?
- Nationalism versus patriotism?

Text

- How do the commas impact the "pledging"?
- Are we pledging allegiance to everything preceding a comma?
- What are those ideas following "republic"? How do they fit with the pledge?
- Does indivisible mean you have to agree with "under God"?
- Does saying "under God" create more divisiveness?
- Why does the pledge use the word "stands"? (as opposed to "is")

What might be missing in the text?

- Originally Bellamy wanted the pledge to say "liberty, equality, and justice for all." Should we add equality?
- What other values would you add?

Final question: Pledging allegiance—to what are you pledging?

The Pledge of Allegiance Supreme Court Cases

Minersville School District v. Gobitis (1940)

Lillian and William Gobitis were expelled from the public schools of Minersville, Pennsylvania, for refusing to salute the flag as part of a daily school exercise. The Gobitis children were Jehovah's Witnesses; they believed that such a gesture of respect for the flag was forbidden by biblical commands.

In an 8-to-1 decision, the Court declined to make itself "the school board for the country" and upheld the mandatory flag salute. The Court held that the state's interest in "national cohesion" was "inferior to none in the hierarchy of legal values" and that national unity was "the basis of national security." The flag, the Court found, was an important symbol of national unity and could be a part of legislative initiatives designed "to promote in the minds of children who attend the common schools an attachment to the institutions of their country."

1. According to the Court, does the government have the right to require someone to salute the flag? Why or why not?
2. What reasons does the Court give for its decision?

West Virginia State Board of Education v. Barnette (1943)

The West Virginia Board of Education required that the flag salute be part of the program of activities in all public schools. All teachers and pupils were required to honor the flag; refusal to salute was treated as "insubordination" and was punishable by expulsion and charges of delinquency.

In a 6-to-3 decision, the Court overruled its decision in *Minersville School District v. Gobitis* and held that compelling public schoolchildren to salute the flag was unconstitutional. The Court found that such a salute was a form of utterance and was a means of communicating ideas. "Compulsory unification of opinion," the Court held, was doomed to failure and was antithetical to First Amendment values. Writing for the majority, Justice

Jackson argued that "[i]f there is any fixed star in our constitutional constellation, it is that no official, high or petty, can prescribe what shall be orthodox in politics, nationalism, religion, or other matters of opinion or force citizens to confess by word or act their faith therein."

1. What does the reversal of the decision say about the historical context in 1943?
2. Why did the Court change its mind and decide schools could not compel students to say the pledge?

You Be the Judge: *Frazier v. Winn*

Directions

Read through the facts of the case and then the arguments of the two sides. Answer the questions to consider in order to better understand each side. Once you have fully developed an understanding of each side, as a group, become the Supreme Court.

Facts of the Case

A teacher, Mrs. Alexandre, questioned an 11th grader, Charles Frazier, why he was not standing to recite the Pledge of Allegiance. The teacher ordered him to stand and say the pledge, which is required by state law. The Florida law, passed in 1943, mandates that

> the pledge of allegiance to the flag . . . shall be rendered by students standing with the right hand over the heart. The pledge of allegiance to the flag shall be recited at the beginning of the day in each public elementary, middle, and high school in the state. Each student shall be informed by posting a notice in a conspicuous place that the student has the right not to participate in reciting the pledge. Upon written request by his or her parent, the student must be excused from reciting the pledge. When the pledge is given, civilians must show full respect to the flag by standing at attention, men removing the headdress, except when such headdress is worn for religious purposes.

Frazier was removed from the classroom by the principal. Frazier sued the teacher and won in the 11th Circuit Court of Appeals that he did not have to stand for the pledge if he had parental permission. Frazier then sued because he felt he should not have to have parental permission to state his political views in school. This case focuses on the question "Should students be required to have parental permission when refusing to say the pledge?"

Argument on Behalf of *Frazier*

To be denied the freedom of speech requires a compelling state reason in the least burdensome manner. Frazier believes the state does not have a compelling reason (a very good reason) to limit his freedom of speech (right to refuse to say the pledge). He argues that the law is a blatant violation of the Supreme Court's decision in *West Virginia v. Barnette*. To make a student seek permission to object from saying the pledge is equal to stating that one can only exercise free speech with permission. Another argument Frazier makes is that through asking parental permission, the state is asking parents to do what it cannot do: require students to say the pledge. This argument portrays parents as a tool of the state; they are the means of suppressing free speech, not the state (which cannot do so).

Questions to Consider

- Are students capable of determining whether they should stand for the pledge? In other words, can they make a reasoned decision to either stand or not stand without parental approval?
- At what age do you think students become aware of and know how to exercise their freedom of speech?
- Why might students like Frazier argue that parents should have less control over their behavior, ideas, and values learned and expressed in school? Why would Frazier argue parental permission violates the purpose of education?

Argument on Behalf of Winn (and the State of Florida)

Parents have a fundamental right to determine how their children are raised. To allow a student to choose for themself what they will and will not participate in violates the recognized right of parents to direct the upbringing and education of their children. Most notably, the Court has recognized that parents, not schools, should direct what civic values their children will embrace. The parent's right to direct the education of their children outweighs the child's free speech rights. In several past school cases, the Supreme Court has acknowledged that student rights do not automatically equal the rights of adults. The Court has found this particularly true in schools, where the mission of schools must be protected (meaning students must be kept safe and education must not be disrupted). The Florida law has the purpose of instilling respect and patriotism in its students; the law also outlines proper procedures for how individuals are to stand during the National Anthem. To overturn a law based on its violation of freedom of speech requires strong evidence. In addition, the law is not an absolute denial of speech to students; the ability to have a parent sign a permission form provides a reasonable outlet from saying the pledge.

Questions to Consider:

- What other ways do parents have legal decisionmaking ability for students?
- Why would parents want to decide whether their children should say the pledge, or direct other aspects of their child's behavior and decisions in school?
- If the Court were to rule in favor of the student in this case, why could that pose problems for parents making decisions about other aspects of their children's education?
- Which right do you believe has more importance: freedom of speech of students or rights of parents? Why?

HOW WOULD YOU RULE?

Step 1: Discuss the merits (arguments) of the different sides. List two to three strong arguments for each side in a t-chart.

Frazier	*Winn* (State of Florida/School)
☐	☐
☐	☐
☐	☐

Step 2: Take a vote in your group and check the box of the side that wins (majority rules).

☐ *Frazier*   ☐ *Winn* (State of Florida/School)

List the three primary arguments that helped your group reach its decision.

1.

2.

3.

Step 3: How do you personally feel? Do you agree with the majority of your group or do you dissent?

List the three primary arguments that support your personal decision.

1.

2.

3.

About the Editor and Contributors

Jane C. Lo is an assistant professor of teacher education at Michigan State University. She is interested in the political engagement of youth, how social studies curriculum and instruction influence them, as well as the impact of inequitable civic experiences on our polity. Her methodological expertise includes mixed-methods designs and design-based implementation research. Before becoming a teacher educator, Lo was a high school government and economics teacher in Austin, Texas.

Terence A. Beck is distinguished professor in the School of Education at the University of Puget Sound in Tacoma, Washington. His research interests focus on the nuances of fostering civic discussions in K–12 classrooms. He teaches courses in social studies and literacy methods at the undergraduate and graduate levels.

Jacob S. Bennett taught high school social studies, mainly economics and U.S. history, in Atlanta, Georgia, and Nashville, Tennessee. Central to his teaching philosophy was that learning best occurs when teachers and students share in trusting and meaningful relationships. He earned a PhD in curriculum and instruction from the University of Virginia and currently works as a postdoctoral research fellow at Peabody College, Vanderbilt University.

Bryant O. Best is a doctoral student and Russell G. Hamilton scholar in the Department of Teaching and Learning at Peabody College, Vanderbilt University. Bryant is pursuing his PhD in justice and diversity in education with areas of research interests in urban education, education policy, and culturally responsive teaching and leadership. His research aims to better understand policies and practices that contribute to the school-to-prison pipeline so that he can help disrupt and dismantle it.

Mary Ellen Daneels is a national board-certified teacher who facilitated the nationally recognized legislative simulation (Campaign for the Civic Mission of Schools, 2010) at West Chicago Community High School. For the past 4 years, she has served as the lead teacher mentor and instructional specialist for the Robert R. McCormick Foundation.

Antero Garcia is an assistant professor in the Graduate School of Education at Stanford University. His work explores how technology and gaming shape both youth and adult learning, literacy practices, and civic identities. He previously taught high school English language arts in Los Angeles, California.

Noorya Hayat is the Center for Information and Research on Civic Learning and Engagement's (CIRCLE) senior researcher who joined CIRCLE in 2016 and has led the evaluation partnerships in Illinois and Massachusetts around the passage of state civic education policy and its implementation. Her background is in international economic and educational development, particularly around cross-sectoral work in poverty alleviation, public health, and human rights education.

Carlos P. Hipolito-Delgado is a professor of counseling in the School of Education and Human Development at the University of Colorado-Denver. His research interests include the sociopolitical development of youth, fostering cultural competence of counseling professionals, and the ethnic identity development of Latinx and Chicanx youth. He is also a coprincipal investigator in the Critical Civic Inquiry Research Group.

Erica Hodgin is the codirector of the Civic Engagement Research Group based out of the Graduate School of Education at the University of California, Riverside. Hodgin's current research focuses on the distribution, quality, and influence of youth civic learning and digital civic learning opportunities. Previously, Hodgin taught English and social studies and served as an instructional coach at the middle school and high school level.

Amanda Jennings is a research investigator at University of Michigan. She supports the Teaching Reasoning and Inquiry Project in Social Studies in the design, implementation, and evaluation of professional development. Her scholarship focuses on understanding children's naive economics theories in an effort to better design social studies curricula. Prior to working at University of Michigan, Jennings taught middle and high school and earned her PhD at University of Delaware where she worked as a researcher.

Jeff Kabat is a Read.Inquire.Write. collaborating teacher who supports the project with curriculum development and testing. He holds a BA in history from the University of Michigan and currently teaches 6th- and 7th-grade social studies in Michigan. Previously, he worked in schools in Korea for nearly 15 years. His hobbies include reading, spending time with his family, and traveling.

Kei Kawashima-Ginsberg is a civic education researcher who often partners with practitioners, such as nonprofit organizations and coalitions of practice groups, to understand and support civic learning for diverse students and communities. Kei directs the Center for Information and Research on Civic Learning and Engagement (CIRCLE), a nonpartisan research institute that has been involved in the civic education community for 20 years.

Jada Kohlmeier is a professor and program coordinator of secondary social sciences education at Auburn University. She teaches preservice and inservice teachers, focusing on authentic pedagogy, specifically substantive classroom discussions of complex social issues. She researches teacher learning in professional development and secondary students' historical, legal, and ethical reasoning.

Bruce E. Larson is a professor of social studies and secondary education at Western Washington University. His research examines the use of classroom discussion to explore controversial public issues and the use of discussion to develop content knowledge and civic participation skill. Larson has written numerous articles and two books about teaching strategies and instructional design.

Arine Lowery is a doctoral candidate in the Department of Teacher Education and Learning Science at North Carolina State University. Her research interests include youth political activism and classroom discussions of political issues. Lowery has worked as a classroom teacher, district social studies program coordinator, and teacher educator.

Paula McAvoy is an associate professor of social studies education at North Carolina State University. Her research focuses on ethical and empirical questions concerning the relationship between schools and democratic society, with a particular focus on engaging students in political discussions. She is the coauthor of *The Political Classroom: Evidence and Ethics in Democratic Education* (Routledge, 2015).

Elizabeth Milligan Cordova is a social studies instructor and instructional coach at Northeast Early College in Denver, Colorado. She coaches student civic leaders as part of Denver's Student Board of Education program and serves as the president of the Colorado Council for Social Studies. Elizabeth received her Master of Arts in Social Studies Education at Columbia University Teacher's College and is a James Madison fellow.

H. Richard Milner IV (also known as Rich) is Cornelius Vanderbilt distinguished professor of education and professor of education in the Department of Teaching and Learning at Peabody College of Vanderbilt University. His research, teaching, and policy interests concern urban education, teacher education, African American literature, and the social context of education.

He is an elected member of the National Academy of Education and a fellow of the American Educational Research Association.

Nicole Mirra is an assistant professor of urban teacher education at Rutgers, the State University of New Jersey. Her work explores the intersections of critical literacy and civic engagement with youth and teachers across classroom, community, and digital learning environments. She previously taught high school English language arts in Brooklyn, New York, and Los Angeles, California.

Chauncey Monte-Sano is a professor of educational studies at the University of Michigan. Her scholarship centers on how adolescents learn to reason and write with sources about historical and social issues, how teachers learn to teach these practices through inquiry, and how such instruction can challenge inequities in students' literacy outcomes. She leads the Teaching Reasoning and Inquiry Project in Social Studies (TRIPSS) lab at the University of Michigan, which designs and studies curriculum and professional development to advance social studies inquiry and argument writing with sources. Prior to her work at U-M, she taught high school in California, earned national board certification, completed a PhD at Stanford University, and worked at the University of Maryland.

Walter C. Parker is professor emeritus of social studies education at the University of Washington, Seattle. His books include *Educating the Democratic Mind* (State University of New York Press, 1996), *Teaching Democracy* (Teachers College Press, 2003), *Social Studies Today* (Routledge, 2015), and *Social Studies in Elementary Education* (Pearson, 2017). He is a member of the National Academy of Education, a fellow of the American Educational Research Association, and recipient of the Distinguished Career Research award from the National Council for the Social Studies.

María del Mar Estrada Rebull supports research, curriculum development, and professional development at the Teaching Reasoning and Inquiry Project in Social Studies (TRIPSS) lab at the University of Michigan. As a doctoral candidate at U-M, she also teaches social studies methods, and she works with teachers from Mexico to develop inquiry-based and literacy-infused history and social education for adolescents. María del Mar is from Mexico, where she has participated in Indigenous and rural educational projects, researched educational policy, and taught at various grade levels.

Abby Reisman is an associate professor of at the University of Pennsylvania's Graduate School of Education. Reisman's research centers on the challenges of teaching document-based historical inquiry. Her scholarship investigates the design and implementation of curriculum materials, assessments of student learning, teacher education, and professional development experiences that support document-based analysis and classroom discourse.

Dane Stickney is a senior instructor, education researcher, curriculum designer, and doctoral candidate at the University of Colorado-Denver, where he focuses on student voice pedagogies, youth participatory action research, and sociopolitical development. Stickney worked as a newspaper reporter for a decade before teaching middle school writing and social studies. He has been part of the Critical Civic Inquiry Research Group for the past decade.

Index